W9-BGP-977

WHERE I STOPPED

The following is a true account of what happened, according to my memory. The names of some people, and in some cases their identifying characteristics, have been changed for their protection.

G. P. Putnam's Sons
New York

WHERE I STOPPED

Remembering Rape at Thirteen

MARTHA RAMSEY

G. P. PUTNAM'S SONS
Publishers Since 1838
200 Madison Avenue
New York, NY 10016

The poem "Testimony" originally appeared in New Letters *in 1988. It is reprinted here with the permission of* New Letters *and the curators of The University of Missouri-Kansas City.*

Published simultaneously in Canada

Book design by Gretchen Achilles

Library of Congress Cataloging-in-Publication Data

Ramsey, Martha, date.
Where I stopped : remembering rape at thirteen / by Martha Ramsey.
p. cm.
ISBN 0-399-14107-3
1. Ramsey, Martha. 2. Rape victims—United States—Biography. 3. Rape—United States—Case studies. I. Title.
HV6561.R34 1996
362.88'3'092—dc20 95-17415 CIP
[B]

Printed in the United States of America
10 9 8 7 6 5 4 3 2 1

This book is printed on acid-free paper. ♾

TO ERIC

ACKNOWLEDGMENTS

Many people freely offered and generously gave time, encouragement, and means so that this book could become a reality.

Arthur Rosenthal, Patricia Williams, Emma Rothschild, Zeke Berman, Laura Lein and Benjamin Kuipers, and the Vogelstein Foundation gave significant early support that made it possible for me to begin and keep on.

I am deeply grateful to the MacDowell Colony, the Fine Arts Work Center in Provincetown, and Ann Stokes for providing environments where parts of the book were written.

The people who gave interviews did so simply out of goodwill and the desire to help others. I am deeply grateful to all of them.

Whitney Wolff, Martha Cooley, Richard Hoffman, Ann Stokes, Michael Korie, Suzanne Keen, Sarah Smith, E. J. Graff, Sarah Jackson, Bill O'Donnell, Don Hannah, Paul Lisicky, Matthew Klam, and Joan Larkin gave insightful criticism and invaluable guidance in the writing process.

My husband, Eric Beutner, gave a chunk of his life.

The skill, intelligence, and sensitivity exercised by my agent, Kim Witherspoon, were extraordinary.

My editor, Laura Yorke, showed me how to make this book what I dreamed it could be.

My gratitude is beyond words.

CONTENTS

The day it happened I was wearing a red dress. It was a simple dress. My mother had made it, with her hands that were dry and rough from hours of gardening. She had sewn the bright cotton into a sleeveless shift with a round neck and two darts and hemmed it where I said I wanted it, more than halfway up my thigh. Rows of white dots made a diagonal crisscross pattern; tiny yellow flowers bloomed inside every other square.

This perfect dress, maybe the best dress I'd ever had, fit just right. It didn't sag in the bust, where I wasn't full enough, and it didn't bind my shoulders, which were already very broad. The short skirt gave me freedom to swing one leg up over the back wheel of my bike when I mounted it, to circle my legs around fast when I pedaled down a hill, to rise from the seat and pump the pedals hard, going up.

The dress was sexy. When riding my bicycle I let the skirt hang over the back of the seat. I liked having just my underpants against the seat, perched inside the shadow of the dress, close to the world but curtained; covered but close to being uncovered, flirting with the danger of being a woman, of having something between my legs that meant something. I wasn't sure exactly what.

When I rode down a long hill, gripping the seat with my thighs, my lean legs hanging limp in blissful inaction, toes lifted just off the road, my dress clung to me loyally. The wind marked my curves, plastering the dress against my small breasts, my stomach, my hips. I hoped someone would see me fly by, slender and desirable. They would be overcome with awe. They would wonder, who *was* that fleeting beauty?

One evening earlier that summer wearing this dress I had sailed down Green Hill Road, a mile-long coast through woods down to the river. Two older boys whistled at me over a hedge as I slipped by their house in the dusk. I did not see them, just heard their loud calling. Their voices thrilled me. Someone was cheering my passing. If I felt any twinge of uncertainty about why exactly they called and whistled, I kept it a secret from myself.

Wearing this new dress I could go anywhere, into unknown little towns where I might stop and walk into a general store to buy a soda, past houses and barns where people might watch me flash by, away from anyone or any place that knew me, because it was a great dress. It was the red flag of my independence. It was the right line, the right color, the right length.

There was no way it could be wrong.

I was never sure if what happened had meant anything at all. The red dress, the rape—I outgrew them both. They passed into history. My clothes became pieces of evidence, tagged and stored in a closet in the county courthouse. I never thought to ask how long they would lie there, when or if they would be thrown out. The transcript of the trial, microfilmed, lay in the archives of the state of New Jersey. I did not think about that either. Rape seemed to have taken place in a gap in time, an episode out of connection with my other memories of adolescence. The memory was stored somewhere in me. I did know it was there.

At sixteen I began to mention it to others as a piece of my history. It became something I confessed to nearly every lover: "I was raped when I was thirteen." Yet whenever I said it—lying naked and nervous in a man's arms, or gazing across a restaurant table at a new friend—the words echoed strangely in my own ears. A robotic shadow-Martha had walked on for a moment, said them, and vanished, refusing notice. It was almost as if I had told a lie, as if it had never really happened; except that I remembered it so clearly.

Surely I had come through it very well, undamaged. It was as if it were really nothing.

Or perhaps it was a great deal: a whale I thought I might have seen for a moment, that might really be lolling, huge and mysterious, under the surface of the blank waters.

Or it might just be a figment of my imagination, floating in the sea of my imaginary life.

At thirty-four, I set out to learn what rape had meant.

I began by writing what I remembered.

MEMORY

I could not have said which I loved more, my new dress or my bicycle. The bicycle was not new; my father had unearthed it from our cellar and proudly oiled it until it worked smoothly again. My older brother, Loch, had used it for a few years, but this year he had turned seventeen and got a new Dunelt. Alida, eleven, had got my old blue girl's Schwinn, and now this one was mine. It was a British "touring bicycle," my father said. He had ridden it in the countryside in France when he was twenty-one. Its elegant, thin wheels ticked whenever they moved, lending it and me an air of class.

Underneath my calico dress I wore a bra, lime green with white polka dots. With its broad white elastic band that hugged my ribs, comfortable and snug, it was the best bra I'd owned so far, my third. I'd found it for myself on the rack at a discount store and talked my mother into buying it. The slight padding made my breasts more prominent but also protected them.

Most sexy and fashionable of all were my prescription sunglasses, which had tortoiseshell frames with deep green bifocal lenses. Somehow I had convinced my mother that I must have these sunglasses, and somehow she had found the money to pay for them. I had worn regular glasses since I was four and knew that I was ugly in them. They hid my eyes and made my face look pinched.

That summer I was beginning to think I might be beautiful. In the mirror I could see someone who might have stepped out of a photo in *Seventeen:* high forehead framed by neat brown hair, a straight nose, mouth round and full; a long neck, slender legs, and the beginnings of curves. With my eyes remote behind their shades I was mysterious, sophisticated, alluring.

I wore sunglasses over my eyes and my feet were bare. What was the point of wearing shoes? They were hot. Or sandals? They slid around on your bike pedals and made your feet slip. My feet were still walking in the grass, the dirt, and the hot tar. By August every summer they had thick calluses.

So there I was, walking up the road with my boy's bike, my young girl's dress, my woman's glasses, and a child's feet. Who knew who I was? It must have showed touchingly in all these things, while all my dreams of myself were held within.

My bike ride that day was a special one, my first long expedition. The night before I had called up Betsy Retivov, my English teacher, and asked if I could ride my bike to visit her. My mother had given me permission to make the trip. I plotted my route along the back roads, using the Geological Survey map, and I set my alarm for seven. Early morning was the best time for riding, before the sun heated the asphalt like a grill.

No one was up when I ate my breakfast that morning. The kitchen was cool and shadowy. Sun and leaf shadows mottled the two screen doors at either end of the long room. The birds were singing and the trees and grass were sparkling in the dew. I slipped out of the house, careful not to let the screen door slam.

Betsy lived near my school in Bucks County, Pennsylvania, and to get there I had to cross the Delaware River. A dirt road, Quarry Road, led off from our road directly to a footbridge we could cross on our bikes to get to Lumberville, just across the river. We often rode the mile and a half down to the general store there to get soda and ice cream.

That morning a thousand cobwebs hung in the fanned silver cables of the footbridge, each strand strung with drops of dew. The bridge cop, who lived in an old stone house at the Pennsylvania end, for once did not come out to stop me with his arms spread and scold me for riding on the bridge. Who could resist the swoop across the level pavement of the bridge, out in space over the slow, green river spread far below?

The air in the valley, freshened by the night-cooled river, sped me across. The sun warmed my back, first sign of the blinding August heat to come. No tourist in a car could cross here; only a bicycle could travel the route I'd mapped. Leaving the river, I plunged back into shade. My new, secret road followed a creek through woods, winding gently uphill through trees that hung leggy and black in the riotous green of the swampy creek valley. The name of the road, and the creek, was Fleecydale.

My visit with Betsy was not exciting. Her new baby took most of her attention, and another teacher visited, and they talked about matters I did not fully understand. We sat around in her yard. It was very hot, too hot even to talk much. We made hamburgers and brought them outside for lunch. I had thought of Betsy as my friend but being with her this way was awkward. I would rather talk as we did in English class than sit around like a child with ordinary adults. But I didn't mind. Riding there and then home again on the back roads was what really mattered. After a while I decided I might as well leave. My mother had said I must be home by dinner.

Coming home, I pedaled as hard as I could up the slope at the bottom of Quarry Road, the steepest of the whole trip, and when my breath began to labor I quit and started to walk. I was in no mood to push myself.

At the crest of that first hill we usually stopped and climbed up between the trees on a bank alongside the road to look down into the quarry. The dark pool lay far below, half screened by trees, its depth unfathomable. We talked about jumping, or falling, from our perch by the road. It would be fatal. We threw in a stone or two. A hand-sized rock shrank to pebble smallness as it fell, then hit the water with a distant, powerful splash. Today, alone, I did not stop there.

Walking up a second steep but shorter hill, I passed the old lane to the quarry, a rutted track overgrown with grass that led off into the woods. My brother had followed this track to its end; I had never dared. Our parents told us the quarry was very dangerous, and I respected this warning. I'd heard stories of people skinny-dipping there and getting caught by the police. Loch said some boys liked to jump in from a lower cliff. Maybe someday I'd be brave enough to do that.

After the quarry track the road curved sharply, twice, with gentler slopes. I could start pedaling slowly around the curves if I wanted to make time or get my feet up out of the hot dust. On this day it was too hot. I just kept walking slowly on up the road, hugging its edge, where a couple of trees cast small circles of shade. I would get home long before dinnertime.

It was around three-thirty in the afternoon.

It was a great adventure to be out on the road, away from home. At that age, though, I still liked nothing so much as the return. Home—where Mom was, my all; making my dinner and my life; the creator, out of an acre and a half of woods, of an entire universe. Our house, which she and my father had built, with many big windows and unfinished walls, was hung with my grandfather's early abstract paintings, crammed with books, echoing with music, and fragrant with the smell of a kitchen run by a housewife with a serious culinary gift. The house was held in nature, in the excitement of birds, fluttering down to scratch for our seeds in the crisp snow etched with the black shapes of trees, or singing all day long, a quiet rain of notes in a well of green.

My mother sewed for me the bright, skimpy dresses I wanted but she wore old clothes, mostly men's clothes, and in the summer, dresses from thrift shops. She was brave and unadorned, determined not to conform in any small or large way she could refuse. She surged through the house, the outdoors, and the garden, dressed in old galoshes and a man's shirt. In the morning, she sang. She practiced the piano, ragtime usually, sometimes

Bach or Brahms, and her music wove us together; father, children, garden, woods, snow and rain.

On small, sloping lawns and in the woods that surrounded us she made flower gardens: irises along a stream, a currant bush in a small clearing, a round bed of periwinkle under a dogwood. She had made a terrace outside the kitchen door, lugging her stones in from the old fence-rows that crisscrossed the woods. She transplanted delicate flowers from the woods to her wildflower garden. In spring white narcissi and daffodils nodded here and there where she had sprinkled them in the woods.

Her flower gardens and terraces were her work toward a vision of the place she never realized. A tiny pond Loch had dug out for her below a spring, where we had played with the frogs in the mud, was someday going to be lined with cement and surrounded with plantings. She said, "I don't have time to do the flower gardening." The sadness of this remark seemed to encompass the whole of her burden—the burden of us.

She was a free spirit, and she loved the free spirits in us. She sometimes grew angry, though, in grim, held-in storms that terrified me. Her spirit needed alcohol. Under its influence, as the years passed her spirit was becoming more manic, her anger more grim, and her exhaustion, more and more, an oppression.

She was the pivot, the magnet, the fulcrum of our universe, but not a grounding center of balance, rather a heavily leaning, off-balance axis around which we all revolved in a fascinated turning. Her beauty, her apparent energy, and her inspired touch in ordering our daily rhythms and surroundings kept us all enthralled; and as bitter as she grew over her daily life, she fed on our enthrallment with her. It was her daily bread.

Near the end of her life, lying in bed sick with advanced cancer, she said to a friend, "I think I don't know what love means. When my sister was here, she said to me, 'I love you.' And I realized that I didn't love her."

Yet she did love us, her children. Maybe only us.

There was something stiff and paralyzed in the center of her, something of rock or of iron in her even when she was giving me a hug. Gradually, as I grew out of childhood and outgrew her delight in children, I worried more and more that she did not love me.

My father in his study, every day, what was he doing? He was chain-smoking, that we could tell from his wastebasket.

He did more than one thing in his field. He photographed and interviewed musicians, mainly unrecognized African-American musicians, and recorded their music, and wrote books, articles, and liner notes about it. He was furious about the continual theft of important music from its African-American inventors and the stereotyping and patronizing that went with the selling of that music to obtuse white audiences.

He was an accomplished and uncompromising man, who dedicated his life to serving the music and the musicians he loved in whatever way he could. When I was twelve he made a TV documentary on Mississippi and then was offered a steady job in television at a salary of twenty-six thousand dollars a year, an astronomical sum to our family. He thought about it hard and turned it down: television work disgusted him. It was an honorable decision. We stayed poor.

He drank, but not so you'd notice it—at lunch, at dinner and into the night until he "fell asleep"—passed out quietly in his chair. My mother stood by him, ready to fulfill her part of the bargain, to care for him and his children, to feed and clothe us every day as long as was needed. Perhaps that drove him further and further away from us, our needs more than he could bear.

He was gifted, a good writer, and instilled some of his own gift in me even as a child. But whatever he was doing in his study all those years, he wasn't writing a substantial work, and it shamed him. As his child I was an important matter in this failure, having come into his life by my mother's choice, not his. Much as I delighted him, sometimes, when he least expected it, and made him proud, he never could quite make up his mind to invite me in.

Later I understood that his whiskey made us inessential to him. No matter how brightly I could call him to admire me, he would always sink back into the murk of his withdrawal.

How can I tell about home, without falling into its dark charm? Our home atmosphere was lit brilliantly with such flashes of energy, laughter, and warmth that we didn't really *see* how dark things were. Our passions toward each other were both dramatic and repressed.

In the summer the gardening gripped my mother in a fever, and the path between the earth and our house was wide and open. The vegetable garden was down the lane toward the road, in a large area that she, my father, and Loch cleared more of every year. Every day we carried baskets of tender young lettuce, new carrots, fat warm tomatoes, and long fine green beans down the lane, past the herb garden by the front door, and through that door into her great, long kitchen. At dinnertime we would gather like bees to honey, waiting. My father sat in his chair by the china cabinet, making old-fashioneds or gin and tonics for himself and her, watching her cook, sometimes cutting her vegetables.

I set the table, my job since I was five, laying knife, fork, and spoon in their proper position at each place. Napkins perfectly folded, stemmed wineglasses for them, milk glasses for us. It helped me inside to get these things straight. I loved making rooms neat, tidying objects and dusting them, as if every table and countertop were an altar.

My passion for order mimicked hers. By pleasing her this way I hoped to keep her with us, to make an order in which she could continue to manage, to be in a good mood, to take care of us. I sensed that she was close to the edge and that it was important to try to keep her on my side of it. I counted the squares in the tablecloth to make it even on every side, and centered her plate exactly, and my father's plate opposite, rectifying great uncertainties, counteracting the wobbling of my world.

When dinner was ready, she would call *"à table,"* as the French do, and we would take our seats, she and my father facing each other across the round table, Loch between them. I fought covertly with Alida for the chair next to our mother. Sitting next to Fred, as our father had wanted to be called ever since we were small, disgusted and scared us. He was big, and his middle-aged belly, which we knew was swelled by beer, was monstrous. His hands were defiled by his constant smoking, and the smell of drink on him made us strangely uneasy. If you sat next to Mom you were in her magic circle, special and safe.

When Fred stood up to carve or serve us our meat, he was sure to blow up at us all, sooner or later. In a dangerous, thrilling game we teased and goaded him. "I don't want that piece, Fred, can I have that one please?" we called out just after he had filled our plates. We yelled for more pan juice as he tried to spoon it out with absolute equality.

Step by step each night we sabotaged his outmoded politeness until he came apart in a tantrum. Then we derided him for being so sensitive to what we said was "only kidding." When he tried to say *he* was only kidding, we said, "No you're not Fred, don't try to get out of it that way."

We knew she would laugh with us, laughing at him because he just couldn't figure out how to handle us. We did not celebrate each other but we celebrated ourselves, with a too-tight togetherness. We ate delicious garden food together every night, we laughed as we teased and quarreled. We enjoyed and were proud of ourselves as a family.

Underneath, something was wrong. Was it the way the wine sank in the bottle my father guarded on the bureau at his elbow? How old were we when we began to notice it? When did we first notice that it upset our mother? When did we begin to wonder about it, then worry about it? When did we begin to watch it in obsessed silence? When did we begin to complain of it? How drunk was he, in the years before we noticed?

Years later, dying, my mother told her friend, "I used to have three drinks at dinnertime, just to get through it."

Which came first, his drinking, her first breakdown? Her drinking, his drinking? Who drank more, who drank more compulsively, who was really in trouble?

I grow soft for Fred when I remember how he tried to get it right for us. But then I remember her cause. To make dinner she worked herself up to a creative excitement, and then we kids routinely demolished it, he drank as many glasses of wine as he could sneak in, and we all went for each other, round after round. Wasn't it true that he wasn't holding up his end of things? He wasn't working at a conventional job, nor was he trying hard enough to get writing jobs. Wasn't it true that he wanted to live like a fourth child to her, avoiding all care of children and home? Wasn't it true that his goaded rage toward us was out of proportion, frightened us even as we giggled? Wasn't it true that he wished we hadn't been born?

Was it she we were fighting over, herself colluding in that contest, all of us fighting the fear that she might be in trouble?

They were in trouble together. They kept suffering and they kept clinging to their dream of a free life apart from a constricted society, and they leaned on the cooperation, loyalty, and affection of their children.

My nostalgia conflicts with my sense of pain, which is common when remembering one's childhood, but I wonder how common it is to have nostalgia while it is happening. Very early on I began to think of myself as a child in a story. We were all in a story, about an extraordinary family that had no money but knew that books and music, love and the arts were the real riches of life. This family wore clothes they got from the thrift shop or made themselves, lived out of their garden, and didn't have to do anything the way most people did. They were free.

Living within this myth that was my parents' life project, I escaped into other stories. Almost any story at all would do. It began when we were small and our mother read *Mary Poppins* to us. She was a perfect Mary Poppins, stern and unbending during the children's day, mysterious and elusive during their adventures in the night. She closed the book; we begged for more. She said firmly, but with a faint, satisfied smile, "No, that's all for tonight."

As soon as I could read I was reading all the time. My appetite for stories drove me to odd expedients. In school I often had the reading book open on my lap, hidden below my desk. The stories were thin, the people in them simplistic, but they kept me going some days.

Eventually I discovered that my father had stored, in the cellar, piles of old *St. Nicholas* magazines saved by his mother. Reading my way through them, I lived in the imaginary world of children of the 1890s. The black-and-white engravings, the girls in white dresses and boys in black knickers drawn with care and charm, drew me in more than anything I saw in new magazines or on TV. They were perfect, they were old-fashioned, and they were still.

As a young child I had also liked the orderliness of school. Black letters spelled out "Delaware Township School" clearly on the orange bus. We drove through Rosemont, a tiny hamlet, where a row of small white houses with neat, green lawns beckoned me to a coloring-book life with clear outlines. The teacher wrote her name on the blackboard on the first day of school and she told you in each hour what to do. When it was lunchtime you got in a line and walked, quietly, down the hall. The teacher was in charge, and things were definite.

At the beginning of my first year of school my parents had an important talk with me. They told me that my nursery school and kindergarden teachers both thought that I had been so far ahead in my reading at nursery school, I should skip kindergarten and go right into first grade. They told me I could stay in kindergarten if I wanted to and that would be fine. I thought it was a great idea to skip, though. Being smart clearly meant that I was better in some way and more grown up.

I loved learning. It was another kind of ordering, as when I set the dinner table. It was crucially important that the house be cleaned, the clothes washed and hung out on the line even in winter or summer, the dinner cooked—these rituals guaranteed the continuance of our home. A similar anxiety drove my learning, my hopeful and commanding seizing of knowledge, my bringing it home every day to my parents: my daily offering to my uncertain gods.

Arithmetic, Social Studies, Language, and Reading were all easy. I ate them up like candy. They were boring, too, sometimes, but that calmed me. At home I was full of what my mother called nervous energy—thin, eating huge amounts, and shooting up fast. I burned up what I ate with astonishing rapidity, talked, and jumped from foot to foot. In the classroom I contained myself, except when I was proud of what I'd learned and waved my hand in the air to be called on, to proclaim the answer.

Every morning that I was allowed to in first grade I stood proudly in front of the class, reading aloud the psalm for the day. But from the first day I was struggling to catch up with the older ones, who had mastered the rules that could not be written down or found in any book, the rules you just had to know, about who talked to whom, who was popular and why, who was cute and who was ugly.

Riding the school bus I watched the world closely through the windows, trying not to be distracted by the kids yelling, teasing, and jumping in and out of the seats in a chaotic togetherness that perplexed and scared me.

As soon as I was old enough I began to explore a widening territory around our house. Gradually I made private routes along deer paths and streams through the woods to my favorite places: a nearby creek, the Lockitong; the wooded ridge above it; an abandoned farmhouse set back from its banks in an overgrown orchard.

As I walked through the rustling leaves along the ridge, or stepped through myriads of small flowers in the shade in spring, or sat in a hollow under a beech tree by a stream, someone seemed to appear. As I walked through an overgrown meadow, someone was near me. The field was a blaze of sun thick in pale grass and brilliant flowers, black-eyed Susans, daisies, asters. I was in a movie. My friend walked with me, an eager watcher of my life who admired my exploring walks and saw that I was beautiful.

In seventh grade I began attending Solebury School, a small, progressive, private school across the Delaware in Bucks County, Pennsylvania. I loved my new school. Right away I started learning great things there. At the end of seventh grade my English teacher declared to the faculty that eighth grade English would bore me and I should skip eighth grade, along with a boy in my class who was also very smart. My parents were not sure it was a good idea, but neither he nor I could choose not to be prodigies.

That year I wrote my first real "papers" and began to learn Latin, spending the evenings studying in my room where no one could disturb me, my kingdom. The sheets and blankets on my bed hung down evenly on both sides, and the diagonal lines of small blue pompoms that decorated the white bedspread met exactly at the bed's edge. Doing my homework at my elegant oak desk I felt more and more grown up, like an adult in a study.

By the end of ninth grade I seemed to have managed the leap to an older self. That spring I sat in the gym and took my first real "final exams." The Latin exam was going to be hard; Wilson was proud of us and wanted to see what we could do. As I waited, my heart pounding, he gave me my exam with one hand and with his other hand quietly gripped my shoulder. "Don't worry, Martha," he said. "Just do your best. I'm sure you will get at least a B." His quiet affection astonished me.

I felt even happier about Betsy Retivov, my English teacher, who was as proud and excited about my writing as if she were my parent. She had opened for me the door to the world of literature: besides the Bible and the *Inferno,* we had read the Greek myths and some haiku. I thought I might learn to read them all in the original. Like Virgil who guided Dante's journey, she was by my side as I walked forward in this new realm of literature, awed. I loved her intensely, with a childish conviction of total reciprocity. I wanted to be exactly like her, when I grew up. She was about twenty-three, and I thought of her as my best friend.

When summer came and I began to explore the back roads more and more, and wanted to try a long challenging trip on my bicycle, Betsy, with her new baby in her new home next door to Solebury, was the perfect destination, eight miles away.

I don't remember exactly what I was dreaming on the road just before it happened, but I remember that more and more often my imaginary companion was becoming like a man. He was a hero or a god or a woods dweller like Robin Hood. Watching me from a distance he stalked and admired me. One day he would quietly appear, stepping out from behind a tree, but not so you'd call it stepping. He'd simply coalesce out of the leaf shadows, so adept was he at concealment. He would kiss me and hold me in his arms. Then when I was ready he would carry me down a magic path to his home, an ancient woods hidden deep within this simple New Jersey woods. In that fairy, secret place I would stay as long as I liked and be greatly admired.

Something, probably a slight sound, prompted me to turn and look back.

I saw a man coming out of the woods and running slowly toward me.

The shape of his head was strange. He looked like a costumed figure, a character in a circus. Startled, I stopped, wondering what the joke was. His body was solid and lunkish, and he was loping toward me at a clumsy trot. Then I saw that his head was rounded by a nylon stocking that also covered his face and I was afraid.

His right hand hung straight down, apelike, clasping a large rock; his fingers spread around it. I stood still, watching him, frozen by the sight of him, but not really seeing him, my mind fogging over. He ran up to me and stopped, his face close to mine.

He mumbled something in my ear. Then I understood: "Don't drop your bike." My hands were glued to it. Awkwardly he pulled at it, loosening my grip, and helped me to lay it down on the side of the road.

Staying close to me, he put his arm around me and began to pull me across the road and toward the woods on the other side. "Hey!" My strangled yelp. "What are you doing?"

He put his hand over my mouth. He was breathing hard. He said slowly and clearly, "Don't scream. If you scream, I will choke you."

If I struggled I would be a matchstick in his hands. I did not struggle. I could not move as fast as he wanted and he dragged me like a stiff-limbed doll, both of us stumbling, into the woods.

This piece of land had been cleared and farmed within the last generation. The trees around us were first growth, mostly cedars, with some open, grassy spaces still among them.

He drew me along as if he knew exactly where he was going, as if to a prearranged meeting place. I was thinking maybe one or two other men were waiting back there, maybe to kidnap me.

But when he stopped there was nothing there. Just a cleared spot.

My body was acting slow, clumsy, far away, as if I were no longer located in it. Fright had made me a frozen animal, slowed everything in me to near paralysis. I had turned into something brittle and transparent like glass. I had no solidity, no color. Yet my body, so far away, could still be felt, shaky, as if the glass could tremble like gelatin.

"If you scream, I'll choke you."

He tied a blindfold, a red bandana, around my eyes. He told me to take off my clothes.

I understood now that he was going to rape me.

Strangely, it didn't matter. Afterward, he would kill me. I thought only of that.

He unzipped my dress. I stepped out of it. I took off my bra and panties. He tied my wrists behind my back with what felt like a piece of canvas.

Part of my mind was left. That part was far away, at a preternatural distance. Whatever I said to him came out of this place, my mind grasping for ways to talk, ways to act, that might get him not to rape me or just not kill me.

"I'm not going to hurt you," he said.

He told me to lie down.

"Are you a virgin? Ever fooled around with anybody before?"

"No, I've never even had a boyfriend."

I almost whimpered it, as if I were angry at him, because it wasn't fair for him to do this to me when I didn't even have a boyfriend yet, the boyfriend I wanted so badly.

My voice with its thirteen-year-old whine was partly fake. I was trying to turn my fear into the sound of a child too young for him to take an interest in. But I must not sound too angry, as if I were going to resist.

Lying on my back, blindfolded, I felt his lips at my nipple. Then at the other one. A brief, wet touching.

I made up a lie.

"I'm not really a virgin." Maybe he only wanted a virgin, and would change his mind.

My own voice sounded like a twig scraping a window on a cold day.

"Oh yeah? When did this happen?"

Silence as I tried to elaborate the lie.

"Last . . . last summer."

My voice came from where my mind was, somewhere above and behind my head. Faint, strange.

I was lying naked on the ground. Underneath the flattened grass the ground was hard with small stones. My arms and hands, tied under me, hurt. They were tied very loosely, and I was able to slide them out from underneath my back.

"I'm moving my hands," I said. "But I'm not going to do anything."

"If you scream, I'll have to gag you."

"I'm not gonna scream."

I knew I had to open my legs, but I could not do it. He opened them. They were reluctant, sluggish.

He felt into my crotch with his fingers . . . his fingers felt in my vagina.

Could he tell that I was really a virgin?

Would he kill me now because I had lied to him?

His hand drew out of me; it had been a quick probe, as if just to find out something.

When something blunt and knifelike pushed into my crotch it hurt.

I was afraid I might cry out.

"It hurts," I said. "I might have to scream."

"If you scream I'll have to gag you."

"I'm not gonna scream."

His penis sawed in and out of me a few times, hurting me as though I were being stabbed there.

I don't remember feeling him lying on my body. I don't remember his smell or the feel of his skin or his breath on me. I remember only this disembodied piercing.

I lay quietly. Inside the quiet containment of my body, something writhed in revulsion and refusal.

I had grown more numb and gelatinlike, my voice and mind more distant.

"That—feels—good," I said.

Somehow I could tell he wanted to believe that what he was doing was not hurting me, maybe even was good for me. If I told him it felt good maybe he would not get angry and kill me.

Shortly he withdrew and stood up. I could hear him moving about in the grass as I lay blindfolded. In a lurid flash I saw my own naked body, lying in a ditch, my father and my brother finding it.

"I promise I won't tell anybody," my distant, faint voice said. It sounded strangely quiet and composed.

"Please don't kill me."

I tried to sound calm, as if I were asking a small, reasonable favor.

"Please don't kill me." I tried to hypnotize him with my calm voice, to remind him gently that he had the choice not to kill me, in case he was planning to, at the same time trying not to arouse his thought of killing me.

"I promise I won't tell anyone," I repeated, for good measure.

I was lying. If I got out of there, I was going to go home and tell it right away. But I thought I might fool him. I tried to sound convincing.

I heard a jingling noise.

"What's that noise?" I said. I thought it might be the gun or some other weapon he was going to kill me with.

"It's the keys to my house," he said.

Another silence.

"What are you doing?" I said.

"I'm putting on my shoes."

Then he said, "Turn over, lie face down, and count backwards from a hundred."

I turned over. Now he would do it.

I began counting. "One hundred, ninety-nine, ninety-eight, ninety-seven . . ."

He untied the blindfold and took it off. I kept my eyes shut tight. I did not want him to see me look at him.

I heard him walk away through the high grass, swishing sounds. I heard a car start up somewhere nearby and drive away.

I stopped counting. Silence. He was gone.

He had not killed me.

I was still here.

I opened my eyes and got to my feet. I was shaking. I looked down at the flattened grass. Out of my crotch came a stream of blood mixed with a white fluid. It fell onto grass bright in the sun. I stared at it in the curious, detached way we stare at our own blood. It showed me what had happened to me.

I looked around. My clothes were gone.

No matter.

I made my way through the trees back to the road.

There was my bicycle. It lay crookedly by the roadside looking just as it always did when I stopped somewhere and put it down. Still packed in its basket was a big red sweater I'd worn in the early morning. I put it on. It reached as far as my hips. Pulling its hem down, I pinned it between my legs with the large safety pin I used to gather the hood around my neck when I was chilly.

I walked home, blindly bringing my hurt home to my mother. I walked in a trance, holding on to my bicycle with both hands.

As I walked up our driveway I thought I might find my parents working in the garden, but the garden was empty. When I came to the house I walked down under the porch first to put my bicycle away out of the rain, as I had been told many times. I found my father there, standing at his work bench doing some carpentry.

"Where's Mom?"

He did not stop his planing long enough to look at me closely. I did not want him to.

"She's inside taking her nap," he said.

With grim purpose I parked my bike in its usual place and walked back up the hill and into the kitchen door, through the kitchen, through the library, to open the door to my parents' rooms, a door we were forbidden to open during her afternoon nap. Walking into the sacred room of her sleep, I went to stand by her bed.

I leaned over and touched her shoulder.

"Mom—wake up."

"Mom."

She sat up, startled and groggy, and then saw me, standing deranged and naked except for the red sweater pinned under my crotch.

The shock registered in her face while she was swimming awake.

"Mom—I was raped."

She opened her arms to me.

"Oh, honey."

I began to cry, and sank down to be held in the circle of her arms.

But the crying felt strange and far away, and I felt awkward there.

After a moment I stopped my crying. My tears dried up. With my entire will I struggled to regain control of myself, not to lose control any further.

I pulled myself out of her embrace.

"We have to call the police, Mom. So they can catch him. We have to stop him so he can't do it to anyone else. I have to tell you and Fred everything right away, before I forget anything."

She went to tell my father.

The next thing I remember I am still in their bedroom, sitting on the bed or still standing, rigid, on the rug. I am telling my father exactly what happened and everything I can remember about the man, and my father is writing it all down. Then he is calling the police.

Loch was about to ride his bike down to Lumberville to work the night at his summer dishwashing job at a restaurant on the river.

Probably Fred, in his distraught state, told him what had happened. Loch crashed out of the house, threw himself on his bike, and rode as fast as he could down to Quarry Road. I remember only the sound of it. I heard, distantly, his mad scramble for his bicycle, the scrape of the wheels as he rammed them hard over the gravel of our lane.

We had to go to the hospital. Before we left my father mixed drinks for the three of us.

"Would you like a drink?" he said to me, trying to sound concerned but calm, as if he were speaking to a woman, not a child, and wanted to be careful not to offer her the wrong kind of comfort.

"It might help you calm down," he said.

But he was moving in jerks as if he didn't know how to stir the ice. I felt calmer than he.

He gave me the glass with deliberate simplicity. Now was not the time to display the old-world courtesy he'd learned from his father, the painter who had once lived in France. But the habit, the gesture of the host, faintly showed itself. Surely this ritual, and this sacred liquor, would make me feel better.

He was trying to take care of me.

I remember the tall glass, the ice cubes, the three of us standing awkwardly on the bare quarry tiles of our kitchen floor. I gulped the drink. It seemed to have no effect on me. My mind still separated from the scene, I stood like a numb doll on the tiles, speaking with I knew not what voice to these two people, mother and father. I must trust them absolutely to know what to do.

They did not know what to do.

My mother helped me put on some clothes so that we could go to the hospital.

My crotch hurt badly.

"I think he might have—torn something," I said.

It was hard to get the words out. I tried to sound confident. I thought that maybe my vagina was not ready for intercourse and that he had done damage, had prematurely forced it open.

My mother said she thought probably he had not.

"I don't think he—ejaculated," I said. "I didn't feel anything like that."

I knew the word. We had had a sex education class after school one day in the spring.

At the hospital we sat and waited on plastic chairs in a hall with people coming and going. Then a nurse led us to an area with a doctor's table in the middle of it and a curtain drawn all the way around. I had never been given this kind of exam. My mother stayed near me the way she always used to in the office of our family doctor, Dr. Rosenfeld, when I was younger and scared of him. She and the nurses helped me onto the table and helped my feet find their way into the stirrups.

The doctor seemed like a nice man even though his tallness made him remote from me. He explained that he was just going to examine me, there was nothing to be afraid of. The nurse reassured me. My mother was there in case I needed her.

I was not all there. I understood that the exam was necessary for my own good. The cold metal instrument against my inner flesh felt strange, but not as strange as the raw pain I already felt in my crotch that remained bleary and wounded.

The doctor reported his findings to us, and I found out I was wrong about what had happened inside me.

He said there was some bleeding of tissues in my vagina but no serious damage. It would heal itself and be fine.

He had found semen. That meant that I could become pregnant. There was no way to absolutely prevent it, but there was an experimental pill informally called a "morning-after" pill. A massive dose of estrogen, it would prevent pregnancy in most cases when taken soon after intercourse. It was not thought safe for general use but he thought in this situation it was warranted. It might make me feel sick but that was better than the alternative.

When I heard that the doctor had found sperm I was shaken. I hadn't thought of it: I could be pregnant. I had seen semen mixed with blood fall to the grass, but my mind had not registered what it was. Even now, hearing the doctor's findings, I refused to think again of the moment that fluid had begun to make its way so far inside me.

The doctor, the nurse, my mother, my father—they all knew and believed that I could be pregnant. This man had spat something into my body that could take root there and grow. They could not draw it back out of my body. It was too late.

I could not be cleansed. The rape was not now only a memory but an actual presence. I held *him* in my belly.

My mother gave me the pill after we got home and I swallowed it willingly.

The police came that afternoon, before or after our trip to the hospital, but I have no memory of my first encounter with them.

That night my mother was in my room, staying near me for reassurance and preparing to sleep next to me in my bed. I didn't mind. She thought it was a good idea. I could not tell what was a good idea. Probably better for her to stay with me.

I stood facing the open door of my closet, getting undressed. She had turned down the covers of the bed and was sitting on it watching me. Getting my clothes off and hanging them up on the closet hooks seemed to call for great effort. But I had to do it myself.

Her voice came, faint but clear, to my ears.

"How are you feeling?" she said.

I did not turn, but paused.

I looked down into the bottom of the closet, down under my school clothes on their hangers to where my shoes lay in the dark. Her words dragged memory to the surface. I remembered the moment of rape, the feel of his penis stabbing me.

It had felt like his penis was made of shit.

I had not known it had felt like that until now.

I could feel, down inside my crotch, the loosened place, the hurting place where the sharp pain had happened. Where my hymen had been was now a strange gap as after losing a tooth.

How could I tell her what it felt like?

I felt a terminal weariness, an intimation of death. Something had ridden over me, finished with me, and left a haunting. I imagined this was how an old woman must feel who has seen it all and no longer has a reason left to live.

"I feel . . . very old," I said.

How could she possibly know what I meant? But I could not manage to say any more. I had gone beyond being able to be comforted like a child by my mother being near. I knew what this was like and she did not. I climbed into my bed and lay next to her, cut off in the darkness that surrounded us.

I tried not to touch her. Her body did not belong in my bed with me. Her flesh was aging. She smelled like cigarette smoke and held a darkness of her own.

Soon I was violently sick from the morning-after pill. I lay over the edge of the bed and vomited into a saucepan from the kitchen. She helped me, holding my hair back, mopping my face. The pain and wracking of the vomiting surprised me. I hadn't thought I could feel any worse.

I fell back into a dead sleep.

I always wondered why I stopped crying right after I said, "Mom, I was raped."

Seeing her face fill with concern had brought on my tears in a familiar way, just as when you tell your mother you've skinned your knee or dropped your favorite ring into the river—not when it happens but when you tell it and see your own hurt dawn on her face.

What if I had just let myself cry with her? Might I have been done with all the hurt of the rape right there and then? In that one moment she was open and ready to comfort me. Why did I refuse and cut myself off?

On another afternoon, four months earlier, I had come home from school and found her gone.

I walked in our lane, soaking up the warming April air, anticipating her greeting. Noticing that the car was gone, I told myself my father must be out on an errand. But already I knew something was wrong.

I walked through the house, though I knew no one was home, and out onto the porch where late-afternoon shadows were falling. I stood there, not knowing what to do, held by a fear.

After a while, I have no idea how long, my father came home, and I went into the kitchen to meet him. "Amelia has had a nervous breakdown and I had to take her to the hospital," he said.

I stared down at the red quarry tiles. Terror closed over my mind. How would I, or we, live without her for a single hour?

We were now in the care of *him.* I had no more use for him than she did. Every day she railed at him. She said she didn't think he would even get up in the morning if he didn't have to take us to school. He sat in his study all day and smoked. He messed up everything she gave him to do, was only capable of chopping vegetables. Now I had to step into her shoes as well as I could, and try to make sure that Alida did not get scared. But how could I stand to work with him? How could we bear to eat meals cooked by him?

Standing there in the kitchen, looking at the floor to avoid looking at him, I was looking over the edge of a cliff, losing my footing, wondering what it was going to feel like to fall through the air.

"What did she do?" I demanded. "What do you mean, a nervous breakdown?"

He was distracted, agitated.

"She was sitting there," he said, "In the chair by the stairs, and she just . . . went."

"What do you mean?" I said.

"She just started crying," he said, "and couldn't stop, and she wasn't in touch with reality."

I tried to imagine my mother doing this. I couldn't. It meant only that she had left us and gone off into a world where we did not matter.

A few days earlier she had been acting strangely. She took away a book I was reading and hid it, something she had never done, saying she thought it might be upsetting for me to read. It was *The Mysterious Stranger* by Mark Twain.

A day or so later she called me to her and said gently, "Is there anything you would like to have, as a reward?" with a strange, sweet note in her voice. She didn't say for what, but I guessed that she meant for being so good. It seemed as if all my efforts to help her had finally succeeded: she had finally noticed.

She seemed abstracted and dreamy, though, and I knew something wasn't right. Quickly I chose a sea green bottle resting on a windowsill nearby, something I'd never noticed before. After she gave it to me I felt as if I had taken advantage of her in a moment of weakness, even though all I had really wanted was for the strange interaction to be over.

Not allowed to see her in the hospital, I made a card for her. I tried to write on it something that sounded cheerful, but it was also meant to remind her that she must come home.

She did come home, just a few days later. She saw a psychiatrist for a couple of weeks and then, as well as I can remember, decided that she had recovered. I don't remember much about her homecoming.

Four months before her breakdown I had begun to keep a journal. When I was younger someone had given me a bright red diary for girls with gold-edged pages and a little lock and key. I tried it out but I already knew that people who cared about writing wouldn't use a book like that. So in January 1968 I tried again using a steno pad my mother let me have. I was fascinated by the green line that went down the center of the page. The pad was a grown-up thing and writing on it felt serious. I wrote in it the tasks I had accomplished during each day, the ways I had succeeded in being good.

When she came back to me from the hospital, she appeared capable of taking care of everything just as before. I told myself I could now go about my business and leave the running of the household to her. But I did not write in my journal again.

The last entry said something like, "Mom went to the hospital today. Fred said she had a nervous breakdown."

We both returned fiercely to our familiar daily life, but the orderly world I had tried to chronicle or invent in the pages of my journal was no longer convincing. Everything looked the same but I knew now that she sustained our world at the cost of tremendous psychic effort. There had come a point at which she simply could not go on. Although I already had the habit of saving the things I wrote, I destroyed the journal.

Years later, when I was twenty or so, I asked her what had happened then in her mind.

"I got really paranoid," she said. "I was very disturbed by the assassinations of Robert Kennedy and Martin Luther King, and the war, and I really started to think that it was a vast conspiracy. The more I thought about it the bigger it got until it seemed to include the whole universe. I remember holding that ashtray, the one from Fred's mother's shop with the curving divider that makes the yin and yang shapes, and staring at it and thinking that it explained everything.

"I was out of touch with reality."

"How did you get better?" I asked.

"By willpower," she said. "I was in the hospital and finally I just realized that I had to go back. I had children to take care of.

"I brought myself out of it by closing doors one by one in my mind."

Her heart has flown to mine, her arms have opened. She feels only my pain, the hurt child, the baby bird broken in the world. But thinking for her, before she begins to think, I know I must try to spare her this. I take it back, the hurt I almost gave her, and I pull away. I free her, I release her, and she drags herself, not yet fully awake, toward the business of holding herself together as mother. She goes on with the actions of mothering. She stays with me at all times, providing, with the presence of her body, a reassurance that is real. But her body is hollowed out by something. Inside myself a hollowness has come that echoes hers. Sensing this, I sense within her no spirit that can console me.

After she died my father revealed to us that our mother had had an earlier breakdown around 1960, when I was five years old and she was thirty-seven.

I think it possible that she was abused by her father, with whom she and her sister had lived in rural poverty in Alabama until my mother was four. In that year, 1926, her mother left him and returned home to Maryland, taking her girls with her. This had been an extraordinary act for her. She was a poor farm woman, my mother said. She did it because of the enormity of his wrongs, which my mother never spelled out to us. When we asked about the grandfather we had never met, she answered, vaguely, "Oh . . . he was the black sheep of his family." She once said that Mary had said that she would never forgive her father for what he had done to them.

Could my mother's "nervous breakdowns" have been touched off by early memories of violation recurring, perhaps even prompted in 1968 by my emergence into puberty?

What happened inside the mind of my mother, four months along in her effort to stay in "reality" and care for her children, when I came home and said, "Mom, I was raped"?

She must have struggled again during this time to close the doors of her mind.

I remember her saying to me a few days after the rape, "Fred and I talked to a psychiatrist about how you could get through this. He said that some people seem to be able to go through something like this and come out fine, and that the most important thing is that we should let you know that you are loved."

At rare moments my mother did mention "love." But in our family we did not directly use that word, or any words, to express affection and caring to each other. Hearing it made me uncomfortable. I wasn't sure why she was saying it to me or what she meant.

My sense, deep down, of being loved by her was in an abeyance since she had gone so far away in April. She might love me and I might "know" that—but what good to me was her love now that I knew that she herself was not all right? She was trying to act all right, but she was not sure. She wanted to let me know that I was loved but she was not sure. The psychiatrist, though, seemed to think our family could manage this with no problem, and she was trying.

She and my father were doing the best they could. They had no idea how far away from them I was, how far away from where they could reach me. I would not tell them.

I would be one of the people who came out fine. I knew I could.

She is afraid that she can't help me, that she doesn't have enough love. But she must make it seem to everyone around us that she is doing what she should. I help her, and together we show the right face to everyone. We act like mother and daughter. We talk some, she sleeps in my bed for a night. But while we do it each feels really that she is alone.

Was it something I had done to her, this rape? It was. I sensed it. The rape of me was also a rape of her and I was what brought it to her. Not raping her, exactly, but bringing *rape* down around her, the rape of her daughter opening a great darkness in her mind.

After her death my father also told my sister, who passed it on to me, that our mother had herself been raped when she was twenty-three. A man had broken in to her room at college. It must have been soon afterward that she had dropped out, as she had once told me, and gone to work in a defense plant to help with the war effort.

As soon as I came home that day and told her what happened she must have remembered her own violation. She must have felt pressure inside, a welling up of rage, pain, and loss.

She said, "Oh, honey." And held out her arms.

Stopping my tears I try, too, to close the doors of my mind. If I want to be strong I will not cry now. Being raped is a major emergency, like our house being on fire. I know what to do: pick up the phone, get the operator on the line. Don't wait, to cry, to fuss, anything. Stay calm and when the police come do as they instruct. We will do this together, my parents and I, doing the right thing as a family. I'll pull myself together like British people in bombing raids. I will make myself be as strong as I wish I were.

It seems emblematic of the lonely quality of relations within our family that Loch's distress about my rape would never be expressed directly to me but only in his single, sideways, mad act toward the outside world, riding down to Quarry Road to see if he could find the man. He was a tall boy for his age and strong. The noises he made when his body reacted to the news and he slammed out of the house were angry and violent.

I heard the sound of Loch's bicycle tires churning the gravel with the same sense of removal I'd felt when imagining him and Fred finding my body in a ditch. It was a sense born out of terror. I did not want to know that it mattered to Loch, more than I could ever have imagined, that I had been hurt.

For as long as I could remember Loch and I had fought over the food on the dinner table every night and all day over countless other things. We seemed to live as much as we could in separate worlds, and when we couldn't we were like two wild animals caged in the same house.

He had often tormented me. Lately he had not been able to hurt me physically but had kept at me with sarcasm. Anything new that I tried in the way of being female—clothes or ways of acting—he derided. And now he knew this horrible thing about me that was sexual.

When not angry or sarcastic Loch was always guarded. In a family where no one felt sure of being cherished he was the most estranged. The person he most needed to be close to, our father, he could never find. As Fred retreated further and further into his mysterious fog, Loch's rage and frustration grew more and more livid and desperate. He was like a smoldering fire most of the time.

We did not allow ourselves to see that he was angry a lot. Later, when he had one mental breakdown after another in his twenties, I wondered whether his instability would have been apparent in childhood if anyone had looked closely enough. To us at the time it was just Loch being Loch again. Alida and I tried to pretend that it need not affect us. We tried to divert his fury away from us and toward our parents.

Throughout our childhood, even when he was teasing and hurting me I knew Loch's real battle was with himself. He could have killed me, and may have wanted to, and he did not. He tempered his self-hatred as well as he could, turning it into a gruff tolerance, for me and everyone else. He had no idea how to express any affection for me, although I knew some was there. When I fought too deviously against him or tattled on him to protect or avenge myself I felt I was betraying him. As I heard him crash out of the house, I felt as though it was my fault that he was so upset.

I also felt a fleeting kinship with him. Even as I clung to my parents for whatever help I could find in that moment, I did understand that he too was trying to protect me, in his wild way, in the child-world of woods and back roads that we both possessed and our parents did not. He knew Quarry Road even better than I did and was as qualified as any adult to investigate there. He was doing just what I would try to do, were I able to at that moment, were I old enough—to go after the man, to try and find him. It was the same thing I was doing in saying to our parents, *We must call the police so they can catch him.* We both knew what right was, and how to act quickly and surely to pursue justice, while our parents acted stunned.

In my strange detachment at that juncture, in the middle of my fear, I made room in my mind for Loch to be raging and storming away. It would be all right that he did that, because I could be here, standing in the center, calm and collected, helping my parents. In this way I would not have to know that I knew, deep down, that Loch's reaction was true to the awfulness of what had happened. If I allowed myself to know how much he was caring about me in that moment I would have to know how badly *I* had been hurt. I could not let myself know that. It was easier to think of the hurt as something that had happened to him.

When I opened my eyes the next morning I saw through my bedroom window the same row of treetops I saw every morning over the roof of my father's study. Their outlines had been old friends. This morning they hung in the sky without meaning. The transparent glassy membrane remained between me and everything. Through it I saw the trees and sky, my room and all my favorite things, my mother in the room.

I remembered yesterday.

I didn't want to see anything. Maybe I could enfold myself in the white sheets for a long while and sleep until I could forget: forever, or until the summer would become itself again, my trees, my grass, my roads.

It was impossible, unthinkable, that I would get up.

But the detectives were coming to see me. They had questions that had to be answered and only I could answer them. It was late in the morning already. My mother was trying to rouse me, saying I had to talk to them.

"I don't want to get up." My voice came out low, fatigued.

"I know, honey. But the detectives are coming. You have to get up."

You have to get up.

Finally I sat up, stood up, put on my clothes. She helped me. I dragged myself, forcing my limbs into my clothes like dead weights.

It was the hardest task of all that time.

The two policemen met with us in our "library," a room that stayed dim and cool even in August. One wall was lined with books on jazz and American music and folklore. My father's record collection covered another wall, thousands of 78s in faded blue-green paper wrappers. We sat down together at the table my parents reserved for their writing projects and formal consultations.

One of the detectives was named Lou Rocco. He was not tall, but large and broad, his hair a black smudge. He wore a white T-shirt, not bothering with decorum on these hottest days of the year. I did not want to be near him. Sweating in his T-shirt, with his lumbering body, he reminded me of the man who had run up to me on the road.

The other detective, named Frank Goreski, was tall and slim, had dark brown hair that stood up from his head in a crew cut, and wore a clean white shirt with the sleeves rolled up. He seemed to lean forward, almost stooping, as if bending near to hear me better. He asked each question slowly and gave me time to find my answer. Something about him made me know that he felt what had happened to me. It was nothing he said. It was the tone of his voice and the quiet of his listening. He didn't just want to gather facts, he was also alert to me.

I did not forget the gentle presence of that tall, dark, soft-spoken man.

The questions seemed to go on for a long time. My parents sat quietly in the background. The two men, serious and quiet, listened to each word I said. No one had ever listened to me in exactly this way. This was an occasion for truth. I took care to make my sentences simple, clear, and to the point; to tell what I was sure of.

We drove to the courthouse in Flemington, the county seat, to meet with the county prosecutor, whose name was Oscar Rittenhouse. Rittenhouse, my parents said, is an old name around Flemington, the name of a Dutch family who had settled in the area and farmed it since colonial times. Around the walls of his office were shelves with thick books on them, law books. He wore a suit, something I was not used to seeing. Like me he was tall and wore glasses and looked a bit owlish. I could tell he was smarter than the detectives.

He shook hands with my parents. Then he shook hands with me. Clearly he recognized in me a kindred spirit.

He invited me to sit; I sat down carefully in the red leather chair facing his desk. My parents again sat quietly to one side.

"Now, Martha," he said, "I need to ask you to go over with me what happened to you on Quarry Road. I'm sorry to have to ask you to do this yet again, but it is important for me to get a clear picture of the crime. I need to develop my own understanding of what happened so that I can figure out the best way to find the criminal and bring him to justice. You can help me by answering my questions as best you can. All right?"

I understood exactly what he wanted, and why he wanted it: a clear story made up of facts, so that he could put the man in jail.

I was sensitive to his words more than anything else about him. The need seized me to express myself in his language, to prove myself to him through words. Just as I understood my father's words and could speak to him as a colleague, I would speak with Rittenhouse, as my parents had called him, man to man.

I had told it more than once to the detectives and I knew what I was going to say. I told it to him again. I was not, I told myself, very afraid of him. I could tell from the way everyone acted around him that he was the hero, the man who led the hunt. I could tell he was excited, like a dog after a scent. He was excited because I was able to speak clearly and well and I was ready to join him in his work.

I also sensed that he was going gingerly with me as if this case, this situation, might be snatched from him at any moment. Without me he could do nothing and he knew it. I would not refuse him. I would graciously aid him.

I understood too that his job was to see justice done, not to comfort me, and it didn't occur to me to mind that. It seemed as it should be or at least as it was supposed to be. There was a funny kind of emptiness about it, the way we were talking. I felt it vaguely, and a faint yearning for something more. I tried to make myself as real to him as I could by showing him my man-to-man spirit.

After questioning me he explained to us that what had happened to me was called "statutory rape" since I was under sixteen. Sexual intercourse with a girl of my age, no matter what the circumstances, was legally rape. This would make the process of a trial easier for us and a conviction likelier. I understood his logic, although it faintly crossed my mind that it was kind of funny that there might have been some question whether what had happened was rape. How could anyone of any age want what had happened to me? I was vaguely perplexed.

I don't remember having any thought that testifying in court about the rape was an ordeal I could choose not to undergo, might refuse to undergo. My parents must have felt some qualms. But they did not share them with me, having decided, probably, that to start doubts in me about the course I was now launched on could make things harder for me.

A week or so later my parents told me that the police had made an arrest. They had called to ask if I could come to the barracks and see if I could identify the suspect.

Inside the state police barracks, where the two detectives met us, was a large room with cinder-block walls and fluorescent lights. A long partition masked an area along the back wall. They led me quickly to a chair near this partition and explained to me that the man was sitting behind it. He did not know I was there. They wanted me to listen to him talking and see if I recognized his voice.

I sat down. I heard one sentence, low. His voice was not loud and not close to my ear. Another sentence. It sounded like he was reading something. It was something I had told them he had said to me.

"Don't drop your bike. Those are the keys to my house."

Then he wasn't speaking. It was over. I could not see him.

The voice test was over and I was not ready for it to begin. My ears had heard his voice as one might hear the call of a single low instrument in the midst of a symphony: a measure or two, gone before you're sure you've heard it. You'd even been trying to concentrate on the music, but you'd never heard this symphony before. My ears were also distracted and filled by the sound of my own anxiety, a hum.

The aura of this man, who might be my rapist, filled the space behind the barrier and threatened to spill out. The barracks held him inside it like a bomb.

I tried to act like this wasn't true. The policemen had him in their control; there was nothing he could do to me. Surely I need not be afraid of anything here. Yet his voice murmured to me of crime and betrayal, of terror in the clearing, terror in the barracks, and I could not clearly hear him.

I was very disappointed in myself. I had imagined something more like a scene in a movie or novel, his voice clear and unmistakable with its thick local rural accent. When he talked I would know it again. But it was not so simple, it turned out, to sit across a thin partition from a man who might have raped you and listen with a clear mind.

Angry at my own ears, I felt that everyone was disappointed in me. They were, in fact, frustrated. They wanted me to be sure. Did they know how much I wanted to be sure? Did they know how seriously I understood that I must not say I was sure if I wasn't?

The voice identification was no use. My father suggested we try a reenactment of the first moment I saw him. Maybe I could recognize the shape of his body or his manner of running.

They decided to try it. It seemed like a good idea to me, too.

As we prepared to go outside my father spoke up again.

"I can't do this," he said, in his grave, carefully not pompous way. "I don't know what I might do when I saw him."

They honored his request and he stayed inside.

Outside we stood on a little rise next to the barracks, my mother and I and the detectives. One or two state troopers in their black uniforms posted themselves nearby. It was another very hot August day. The sun was blinding on the bare building and the bare dirt.

There he was, not too far away, between two policemen, at the other end of the building. I looked away. I did not need to look at him ahead of time. It would be more like the way it really had been on Quarry Road if I only saw him when he started to run toward me.

Surely he could not try anything, escape or attack. But my heart raced.

They released him. He loped toward me from the right, not up behind me on my left as it had been on the road. He was wearing a white T-shirt, clean and blinding. He moved with an awkward gait, but fast, toward me.

I didn't know why but as soon as he started running toward me I was terrified. I felt like it was happening all over again. What I saw was something different; what I felt was the same as *then*.

He stopped running and faced me. I shrank from him like an animal in terror. I saw his face without a mask. I did not want to see it . . . I could no longer see anything . . . Horror, the glass pane, had gelled around me again.

He said, "Martha, I don't know you from Adam."

I could not remember. I could not remember him, or anything. I could not remember who I was or what was going on. I might die.

They had not intended him to speak to me. They pulled him back and took him away.

My mother and father and the two detectives now seemed far away and unreal, like puppets.

They asked me if I recognized the way he ran.

I had to say it: "No, I can't be sure."

What had happened on the road was no longer clear in my mind either. I could not say if he was like the rapist. I could not say anything about him. I only knew that I was afraid of him.

Someone, or all of them, must have seen my face go white, must have seen me shrink from him. I thought I was hiding it. I was trying to sound clear and intelligent. And I told myself I wasn't really afraid anyway, nothing had happened; I did want them to catch him, I just wasn't sure if this man was the one.

I had failed.

The detectives said thank you to my parents, and we all said good-bye, and we went home.

On that day my fear of the rapist was revived. I had promised the man in the clearing, deliberately lying, that I would not tell anybody. I had made and broken that promise with a child's persistent confidence in a secure world. He was bad and would be caught and any means I used to achieve that were all right.

As I repeated that I could not be positive that Frank Miller was the man who raped me, I hoped some adult would step in and help me to be sure. But this did not happen, and it dawned on me that I held the deciding card. And I could not decide.

I had never experienced such an uncertainty.

If I couldn't be sure, how could they know whether he was guilty? They had arrested a man who might not have been the one, and because I had reported the crime, this was my fault.

Frank Miller, wrongly accused, or the real rapist, out for revenge, might come to kill me, because I had broken my promise not to tell anyone. I was now living in a universe in which not only had this attack happened, but it might happen again.

The scenario of convicting the right man was equally terrifying. Even I, in my social ineptness with other kids, knew that if you squeal on someone who has hurt you he may be punished but he will make you suffer more for it later. He will hurt you again. He will find a way to humiliate you for being a coward, for turning to someone bigger for protection.

Not only could the world of adults not really protect me, I also had to protect them from knowing that I knew this. I had to pretend that I thought all their efforts were working and that I felt safe. I had to pretend to be more innocent than I felt.

If I shared with anyone how uncertain and scared I really was that the police might not be able to fix things, it might make it real. If I could keep my doubt to myself, the world would still believe that it had order, and that would keep it still somewhat safe. I alone suspected how illusory that order was.

My inability to identify him also arose from another fear: to recognize him would have been to confront the fact of him as a real man, not an enormity from another universe. I was afraid to imagine as human the hatred and rage that had been acted out upon me.

All these fears, which I tried to hold in secret, combined to make it impossible for me to see Frank Miller as the man I had encountered on Quarry Road. When he approached me outside the barracks, though, something about him—his heavy stride, his bare muscled arms, the dark, deadpan, stubborn look on his face—triggered a recognition in me that came out simply as terror.

Would it have been the same if Detective Lou Rocco, who also scared me, had reenacted the rapist's attack? No, because whatever fear he touched off in me I would have been able to see as "just a reaction," knowing that he was on my side. This guy they'd arrested almost acted as though he wanted to frighten me. He wasn't trying to act innocent but was almost leering in my face. He loped toward me as if he were trying to disguise his gait, not as if he were an innocent man being put through a repellent exercise. He loped toward me as if he knew he should act like he didn't know what was going on but couldn't help acting as though he were going to attack me.

My fear itself testified to his dangerousness. I don't think it was just the triggering of my memory that scared me, standing there on the baked dirt outside the barracks as he ran toward me. My sense was that he wanted, right then, to kill me.

In the stories I read the detective was usually a good, protecting authority figure. While pursuing the criminal he also uncovered people's secrets and solved their troubles. Before the rape I had been longing for such a presence, dreaming of a man who would stand with me, staunch and confident, an ally and friend. Now I had a real, obvious need for such a presence. As it happened there was none.

Soon after Miller's arrest they removed the detective I liked from his job. My mother told me that people were saying he had had a breakdown. He had been handling two or three other cases of teenaged girls being raped, she said, and it had been too much for him.

It sounded strange to me, the idea that a man would break down because of working on cases of raped girls. I didn't understand how it had been hard for him exactly. I hadn't broken down and I was the raped one.

In the back of my mind, though, this rumor sent me a small signal. I had felt him near me with sensitivity and concern as I had felt no one else. It fit that he would be the one to have a breakdown. I was sad for myself that he had gone from me and I was sad for him that his heart had broken.

I was sorry that working on my case and talking to me had disturbed him. I pictured him, with his thick black hair that stuck up from his forehead like a brush, his white shirt with the sleeves rolled up, and his stance of slightly leaning forward, framed against a picture window in a woods far from my own. With a small wordless good-bye I dismissed him to somewhere else in New Jersey. I understood that I would not see him again.

How did I respond to my father's inability to stay protectively near me after the rape? I refused him entry into my memory. I do not remember his presence clearly in any situation except when I first came home and asked where my mother was, not telling him what had happened, and when he fixed me a drink as we got ready to drive to the hospital. I don't remember if he came with us, and if he did, where he was when I was being examined. I had been screening him out in this way for many years.

When he refused to come outside the barracks with me and witness Frank Miller's walk, I knew his holding back had to do with his being a pacifist. Bravely, he had refused to fight in World War II. Not only did he not believe in killing another human being, he felt he must not let himself be put in a position where he might want to. I understood that even if he came outside with me his presence would not feel like much of a support. I felt a loneliness that was all too familiar. There were uniformed men standing around to protect me from Miller. There was no father there who could protect me from my fear.

Soon afterward I formed a strong resentment of what he had done. *Typical,* I thought. I kept hoping he would come through, act like a father, a parent, and sometimes it seemed like he was going to but then he didn't. I told myself, *Forget about him, there's really nothing to count on there.* But I couldn't stop wanting him to be there for me.

As the investigation proceeded he talked a lot with the police about locations and times, volunteering his ideas. I thought he was being officious. I noticed with disgust that in the midst of his own shock and devastation he seemed proud of the respect the prosecutor and detectives accorded him. I sealed him off further.

I did not see his rage toward Miller as a form of caring about me. It struck me as strange that he would feel like killing someone who had hurt me, when he never seemed to be wholly interested in *me.* His rage might be better than no rage, but wasn't it really anguish over something of me that he thought the rapist had taken? Could he tell that I was still me? How did he feel toward what he thought was left? I would never be sure.

Mr. Rittenhouse and my parents arranged a reenactment of my bike ride, to establish the times of my movements that day, especially the exact time of the attack. On the Pennsylvania side my mother drove alongside me, with a clock on the seat of the car, as I rode from Betsy Retivov's house to the river. I didn't mind doing the ride again. With her driving along I felt safe. I was even a little proud to be able to show her the roads and how many miles I had covered.

My father met me at the other end of the footbridge and followed me in a borrowed car as I rode and then walked my bike up Quarry Road. When I reached the site of the rape we stopped and he noted the time on his stopwatch.

I felt less safe doing this with him than with her. Still, it was better than if he were not there at all. In the silence between us I did feel a tenderness of his concern, which made me squirm inwardly and wish I didn't have to do this with him. The constraint between us was absolute.

When Loch rode on his bike down Quarry Road he found two vehicles parked in the track that led to the quarry: a pickup truck and Charlotte Tritt's Volkswagen. Charlotte, about two years older than Loch, lived up the hill from us on our road. Frank Miller, whom Loch did not know, was sitting inside her car talking with her. Loch stopped and looked at the truck. Miller noticed him and they had a brief conversation. Loch got back on his bike and rode to work. It was soon afterward that Miller was arrested.

My mother told me how they had caught him. "He was talking in a bar, the Forge and Anvil in Kingwood. He said he had seen a brassiere on the road and he thought it might have something to do with the rape that he read about in the papers. Somebody told the police, and they went to the covered bridge, where he said he had seen it. They looked around and they found your clothes."

If he were really the one, he would have talked about my clothes, not just a brassiere, my mind whispered. It probably was really him. It sounded convincing. But how could they be sure? As frightened as I'd been by Miller at the barracks, I could not think of him as the man who had raped me. I thought of him as *the man they'd arrested* or *the man who was on Quarry Road with Charlotte when Loch went down there.*

"It seems as though he wanted to be caught," my mother told me. "As if he knew he was sick and he was asking for help."

It turned out that there were some rumors that Frank Miller had molested other girls.

At another time she said, "Apparently he had this idea that he was helping out girls by deflowering them."

It was a little strange the way she talked about these things to me, as if I were not the person it had happened to, but someone else.

At one point I asked her if maybe I should have tried to run away from him or struggled more. She said, "No, it was a good thing that you didn't, because it was probably what kept you alive. You are lucky to be alive."

She was saying the right thing. She said it with a detached air of asserting a fact, as if she thought that would be the most convincing way to say it. She said it was lucky for me, not that she was glad of it and it was lucky for her too.

I still can remember the intensity of my yearning, as I stood by her bed and started to cry, to bury myself in her and yield to a simple childish grief. I remember also the knowing that arose inside and stopped me: I could not now go into the realm of her embrace where I might easily have gone, were I still simply a child. I had been exiled from it, by myself, or by her, or in a mutual pulling apart.

It wasn't only that I didn't feel sure of her strength or that I was trying to be brave and do the right thing. As I descended down toward the waiting, absorbing presence of my mother, I faced, in a split second of inarticulate knowing, that I'd received a hurt that was sexual. I'd endured an injury that (as far as I knew) happened because one was a woman, because one was no longer a child.

It touched my most private place, hidden from my family. No one must know, especially not her, about what went on in me in relation to that part of my body. I hardly knew what was going on myself. I knew only a deep reluctance to think or talk about that part of myself. In that moment, standing by her bed, just to say the word "rape," drawn out of me in great duress and distraction, was as far as I could go.

Paradoxically, in trying to act grown up and not cry, I was also refusing to let in the sudden, premature experience of womanhood. I was choosing to remain innocent, unmoved, unacquainted with my own harm, because I knew I was not ready to know anything concrete about the most private part of myself.

I had to disentwine myself from her arms. I could not find solace in what she was, a woman laden with sexual experience, her body soft with womanly fat and breasts. I did not want to join her in the sensual twilight. The physical sensation itself of her embracing me revolted me, and I had to turn from her body.

What did I know about sex at the time I was raped? She had tried, when she first told me about it, to speak in a tone of voice that would imply no shame.

"Martha?" she said one night, when I was eleven. "Can you come into the library? There's something we need to talk about."

She sat down in her usual chair in front of the fireplace, an old blue upholstered chair with many buttons in its high, curving back. I wondered what could be so important that she and I would need a private talk.

There was a silence while I got settled.

She said, "Do you know how a man and a woman make a baby?"

I had never really thought much about it. But suddenly I thought I might know.

"Yes," I answered. "I think so."

"How do you think they do?"

If I were wrong, she would think I was stupid.

"Does the man . . . put his . . . penis . . . in the woman's . . . vagina?" I said.

"That's right," she said, pleased. "How do you know that?" She was curious.

I squirmed.

"Well," I said. "I guess I saw some dogs doing it, once, and I kind of figured it out."

Not too long before that, on my way home from a walk down to the creek, I had seen two large dogs mating in the road. When the male dog mounted the female I felt a funny new curiosity about what he was really doing. It was faintly disgusting but also fascinating, and I was glad I was alone so that I could really watch them.

I had not thought about a man and a woman doing the same, but as soon as she asked me I knew that they did, even though I couldn't picture it.

"There are some other things you need to know about it right around now," she said. "Because you are going to be a woman soon."

She told me that once a month a woman's body prepares a nest inside for a baby, in case one was made, and if one wasn't, the nest drained out through her vagina and her body began building a new one.

"You'll be getting your period some time in the next year or two," she said. "If it happens, don't worry. Just come and tell me and I will show you what to do. Okay?"

She tried to speak of these matters gently and without prejudice, but I did not want to hear them. I did not believe her. I was fine just the way I was and I was not about to start bleeding from my crotch.

"Okay," I said, to make her happy. "I will." And forgot it.

It came in the late summer of 1967 when I was twelve. I had spent a night playing and sleeping in a hayloft with Alida and a friend of hers whose mother ran a riding stable. In the morning I ran into their house to go to the bathroom, and when I pulled down my panties I saw black streaks on them. But I didn't really see them. I simply pulled up my panties and ran outside again.

After I came home that afternoon I realized what must be going on and I told my mother. She led me into her bedroom and opened a small drawer in her bureau. She got out some sanitary napkins and a belt for me and helped me put them on. I was embarrassed. She asked me if there was anything else I wanted to know, and I said No, there wasn't. I might be menstruating, but I did not want to think about it. This was about a year before I was raped.

She believed that children should be allowed to go naked, and in the summers when we were small Alida and I ran around wearing only shorts. As we rolled down our grassy hill or played house down in the "pine clump," our small woods of Jersey pines, or got sprinkled by Loch's squirt gun, we didn't miss shirts.

I remember: a torrential summer shower, Loch, Alida, and me sitting on an old tin-topped table on our porch with all our clothes off, splashing and laughing in the hammering rain, our mother standing under the overhang and watching us, smiling.

Being a photographer, my father took many pictures of us as children. For years a picture he had taken of Alida hung on the bulletin board in the *Look* studio in New York, where his friends in the darkroom developed his film for him for free. In the photo she was about four and stood naked, holding a vacuum cleaner in cleaning position. She gazed straight at the camera with her dark, oriental-looking eyes, proud to be posing with the vacuum cleaner.

When I saw this picture on the bulletin board among the photos and notices people put up there for each other's entertainment, I felt envious.

Why had Alida got her picture there and not me? Years later when I mentioned it to her she spoke of it angrily. She had been furious at our father, and embarrassed and humiliated, from the moment she had heard that it was there.

I started wearing shirts because of something that happened one day when I was eight. Robin Remaily, a local musician whom my father had recorded at our house, stopped by one day, and as I often did I ran outside to see who had come. He walked in from the driveway, sporting a black leather jacket on his slender frame, and he stopped and looked at me. As soon as he saw me I stood still, shy, partly because I was always a little afraid of men and partly because I liked Robin. He was a romantic figure to me even at eight, with his black hair and eyes, his motorcycle, his wild fiddling, and his mischievous grin. He had taken me for a ride on his motorcycle once, a quarter mile down our road and back. It had been an exalted moment.

This time he *saw* me, as adults often don't see children and he had not seen me before. I could see him take in that I was not wearing a shirt. His look then became a little teasing and showed me that he was a man and I was a girl and I wasn't dressed quite right.

It suddenly felt acutely embarrassing and a little unsafe to be half naked. At the same time it dawned on me that the reason he wasn't interested in me was because I was just a kid. I ran in to my room and put on a shirt. I never went without one after that.

When my breasts began to emerge a year or so before I got my first period, I began to feel sore around my nipples and complained to my mother about it. She thought something might be wrong and took me to our family doctor. After checking me out he looked across at my mother and said quietly and casually, but as if the joke were on her, "It's just normal breast growth, nothing to worry about."

She looked embarrassed. She thought she should have realized that my breasts would be growing at this age. It simply had not occurred to her.

My breasts didn't grow very fast, though, and she did not think of buying me a brassiere. I found out that I needed one in the gym at Solebury one day, when I undressed for the first time with other girls and saw that they were wearing bras. Standing in my white cotton sleeveless undershirt, I hid myself as best I could. That night I pestered her to buy me a bra.

She did not think I needed one and seemed not to understand how I felt, no matter how many times I said, "But Mom, everybody is wearing one."

After one or two more episodes of misery, changing for gym class in that small locker room, I managed either to get out of gym or hide myself when I took my clothes off there.

When she finally capitulated she took me to the lingerie department at Bloomingdale's in New York, where, with a middle-aged saleswoman assisting us, I tried on different sizes until we found what seemed to be the best fit: 32A, the smallest size. My breasts had grown some by then but the cups of the bra were still a little loose. I was happy, though. She said I could have two. I chose a plain white one and a psychedelic one with a wild design of orange, yellow, pink, and green shapes outlined in black.

About a year later I found the lime green bra with white polka dots that I liked to wear under my red dress when riding my bike.

As I pulled away from my mother after the rape, partly to protect myself from having to know that my hurt was sexual, I didn't think that she knew about that part of my pulling away. I didn't even really know about it myself. She had not been exactly eager to help me become more sexual, and now it would be easier if we both acted as though I still weren't.

I knew that my father, on the other hand, was aware of me as a sexual being—as a girl, as a potential woman. Even though I was always angry at him, my sarcasm—which he tolerated and even seemed amused by at times—sometimes became, to my confusion, a flirtation. He knew what was happening to me, that I was growing up. He could see my small new breasts perfectly well. I felt a tiny delight in this and I felt ashamed.

At the moment of the rape I knew he was conscious of my hurt as sexual. In the days that followed I knew he remained exquisitely aware of it. It was an unbearable thing for me to know it, and that was part of why I had to keep him sealed off, keep him out of my world now.

It seemed safer to try to be as innocent as my mother wanted to pretend I was than to let myself be the young woman, now sexually hurt, my father could not forget I was.

A few days after the rape she asked me, "Is there anything you would like to have, that would help you feel better?"

She spoke tentatively, as if she wasn't sure it would help but felt she ought to try it.

The only time she had ever asked me such a question had been that day before her breakdown in April. This moment had the same awkward feeling except that this time I was the one who was in trouble.

She was saying I could have anything I wanted, offering me Christmas in August. I should be excited. Strangely, I wasn't. I was feeling lousy. I didn't want anything at all.

If I tried to explain this, it would mean trying to tell her what things were like inside me, and I already knew I couldn't do it. Better to go along with her idea. It might make her feel better, and it might even help me.

Suddenly I felt an urge to play with a Barbie doll. I thought I'd given it up for good but now I thought I might go back to it. My old one, now discarded in a closet, had got pretty beat up.

"Maybe a Barbie doll," I said.

I had a creepy feeling, ashamed of being treated like an invalid but not able to say no to it. I wanted the attention, I'd take it on any terms. But did the fact that I wanted it so badly mean that in some way I had let myself be raped on purpose in order to get it? Had I cooperated with him a bit too readily, been maybe a bit too resigned, too docile? My outfit too inviting?

For a brief unwelcome moment I felt uneasily how much more I really wanted from my mother. We both knew that her buying me the doll was not going to bridge the gap. She had only been able to ask me if I wanted some particular thing, and I had only been able to ask for a doll.

My mother didn't approve of Barbie dolls, though she let Alida and me each have one and grudgingly bought us their expensive clothes at torturously drawn-out intervals. We collapsed in laughter when we imitated Barbie, her slender hands held in a position of perpetual graciousness, her feet frozen in tiptoe. We knew she wasn't real, her legs strangely elongated and her breasts unnaturally large and high. Yet we were fascinated by that perfection, and the perfection of her clothes. She had a flounced sea green dress with a tight bodice for casual dancing, black slacks and a red-and-white striped shirt for lounging at home, a floor-length negligee made of pleated pink chiffon. Each perfectly fitting outfit transformed her, yet she remained lovely.

Playing with the new doll I tried to lose myself in the spell of her changes once again. But she looked younger than I thought she should, more like a teenager than a real woman. She lacked the feeling of remote maturity I'd loved. I felt foolish dressing her, as if I were trying to grow down, to go back to being a girl. The tiny bright outfits were ludicrous now, obviously just toys.

I played with the new Barbie only once or twice. I suspect I turned away from her not only because she was an outgrown toy, but because her form was sexy and her clothes affirmed that. I could not touch these things without ambivalence. The sexual appeal I had loved in Barbie and the sexual nature of what had happened to me made an impossible combination inside me. Unable to think about this contradiction, I felt it as nausea.

As much as I did not want to remember being raped, I had to. I had to make some place for it in my mind.

I never remembered it in terms of remembering "him," the man who raped me. I remembered a fleeting ugliness, a leaden force field, a shuddering of the universe. Yet the rape did remind me of certain other human experiences. I didn't think of the rapist as a man exactly, but I had to put the rape somewhere and I put it near the place in my mind where I thought of boys and men.

I seem to remember him, heavy and naked, the disgusting tip of his penis slipping against the skin of my thigh, his mouth's wetness on my small, immature nipple. What did it remind me of? I see my father having one of his tantrums. We aren't ready for the omelet he's just made; the toast is burning. His rage contorts his face into a child's, helpless under the onset of irrepressible emotion. These tantrums frightened me when I was very young. Later I learned to hate them, their tyrannic quality. By the time of the rape I felt merely disgusted by them because they showed me a father who could not control himself, could not hold a balanced stance in the world.

I always felt disgusted when near my father and my brother. Loch chewed with his mouth open because he had allergies and couldn't breathe through his nose. Fred sucked on his cigarettes, filthy objects that his fingers embraced, his large fingertips too thick with flesh.

On a hot summer day when I was eight my father had in a way exposed himself to us. On such days we used to turn on the hose and spray each other to cool off. He was the ringleader that day. He stripped off his clothes with appalling abandon, ran to the hose, turned it on, and began sprinkling himself with the nozzle. Trying to jump into our world, he danced and yelled to show us what a good time he was having.

"Ooh, this feels good," he crooned loudly. "Come on in!"

I stood there, transfixed by the sight of his body, hairy and beer-bellied, and the sight of his penis and testicles between his legs, bouncing and dangling weirdly in their nest of dark hair. I stood still, frightened. I did not want him to come toward me.

He just kept prancing and saying, "Oooh, it's cold, ooh, this feels good."

He wanted us to see him naked, to look at him and be shocked. That was what I felt. Probably he was just trying to play with us, thinking that because we were children we would not be bothered by his nakedness. But I felt he also wanted to be a bigger child than us, to show himself off. Even while he was scaring me I felt shame for him that he could make himself so ridiculous.

The rape fit more with this memory than any other. The rapist's thick body and chunky arms, and a feeling of murderous tension in him made me know instantly that I could not fight him, and this reminded me of being beaten in fights by boys. There had been times when I had felt completely at Loch's mercy, pinned, unable to move any part of my body. I had also been tortured by a boy two years older than me who lived nearby. From the first moment I met this boy, when I was five, it became clear that he was interested only in contests of will and strength, not in play. This boy wanted to hurt and bruise me, not only to win but to completely humiliate me. The realization came to me physically, in the shock of his urge to twist and squeeze my limbs, the crashing weight of his body on mine, hard, vicious, and impersonal.

When I fought with this boy, and with Loch, I did struggle, until I gave up. With the rapist I did not even try. I knew it would fail and might aggravate him. After a moment of helpless frustration I was overtaken by a sort of resignation and a certain willingness to go along with his sick idea, a feeling I had never had with a boy.

At the same time, dealing with him did seem like dealing with a boy. I promised him that I would not tell on him. I told him I was not a virgin, hoping that he only wanted a virgin. I tried to make a deal with him: *Don't kill me—I promise I won't squeal on you.* I tried to act with cunning to outwit him.

He imagined that he was initiating me into womanhood and I sensed that he was imagining it. He said, "I'm not going to hurt you." He had persuaded himself that what he was doing was required of him, was necessary. Sensing that if I played along with this scenario he might be able to avoid killing me, I answered his questions—*Are you a virgin? Fooled around with boys before?*—as if they were meaningful in relation to what he was doing.

I knew it was a travesty, but in playing along with it I had to really let myself believe in it, live it. This happened easily because I had no alternative scenario. It would have been right for him to do nothing, because I was too young. I knew this clearly. It would have been right, instead, later to be initiated with great gentleness. I had never thought about that one way or the other. So in letting him become my initiator, even though only playacting, I was participating in a myth that was entering my mind before any other myth of initiation had had time to arrive there. And the terror and shock had opened a raw place in my mind where anything could lodge. In that moment I gave him complete authority over my mind and my imagination, the authority to be giving me the first experience of sex, to define for me what sex was. He became my teacher.

In the minutes in which he did not talk, gave me no instructions, no guidance, but simply pressed his sharp member against my small dam of flesh until it tore, this teaching happened: the silent instruction of his action. And this became a pattern in my mind of what instruction might be. I had loved my teachers. Now came this one, not a boy who at least I could sense as caught, in some way like me, in the struggles of childhood, but a grown-up who taught me by doing to me.

August was coming to an end, and soon I would be going back to school. I looked forward to that and tried not to look back to August 13. Because Solebury was in Pennsylvania where the local papers had not published much news of the rape, and because many students and teachers were not around in the summer, school would be like a world in which the rape had not happened. This would make it easier for me to think of it any way I liked.

I was excited about beginning my sophomore year, my third year at Solebury. Normal life would begin again. I poured myself back into the routine of the first days of school that I liked so well, the round of classes, the daily contact with girls and boys whom I already knew, singing in chorus, playing my flute. I knew I had impressed all the adults with my cool demeanor. It was a pretty big adventure to be able to tell about if anyone asked me about my summer. I had been questioned by policemen and written about in the newspapers. I had lost my virginity. I had joined the adult world.

I didn't know who at the school knew, or what anyone thought about me having been raped. I always wondered. Was there a certain care some people took when they asked me how I was, a keener look at me than usual? I couldn't tell.

There were some people at school I tried to avoid. The worst was a limp, small, nasty boy who led the other boys into low states, I thought. One of the best things about skipping eighth grade had been getting away from him. One day in seventh grade he had come up to me and said, "Fuck you! . . . on the other hand, who'd want to?" He probably tried this joke out on quite a few people, but I could not forget how it had felt. He seemed to have secret knowledge of my worst fear. No one would want me.

Coming back to school after the rape, I thought to myself, *Well, he was wrong. Someone did want to fuck me, and they had done it.* This thought gave me a curious, shameful pride. Whatever else had happened, he had been proven wrong. Shamefully, secretly, I wanted him, and everyone else, to know it.

I did not understand that I didn't need a special story to earn friends. I did not understand that I might already have friends, if I could let myself be befriended.

One morning in the first week or two of school my new French teacher asked me to stay after class a moment.

"Could we talk?" she asked. "Let's walk over to the pond, where we can be private."

We stopped and stood together by the pond.

"The boys were whispering in class," she said. "I asked them to tell me what they were talking about, and they told me it was that you had been raped." She raised her voice. "I told them to cut it out." She tried to speak more calmly. "But I wanted to talk to you too and see if you are all right. Did this really happen to you last summer? Are you okay? Is there anything I can do to help you? Is there anything you would like to talk about?"

This was the last thing I had expected from a teacher. I answered quickly.

"Yes," I told her. "It did happen last summer. But it's okay, I'm fine now."

She questioned me about how things stood. I reassured her that my parents did know about the rape, the police had arrested someone, and the trial was coming up in the spring.

It seemed odd to me that she was so concerned, as if there were still some possibility that I might not be all right. I thought she did not know how strong and grown up I was, or how open and honest my parents were, not trying to hide the rape like someone else's parents might.

I realized I had heard the boys whispering in the background. But I'd trained myself to ignore their mutterings. It hadn't occurred to me that they would be whispering about me. In the back of my mind something moved, a moment of surprise. I hadn't thought my rape would be a joking matter, even to them. *So that's how it is.* I now knew what some of the people around me were thinking.

But I didn't feel angry at the boys. What they were doing, I recognized; what my teacher was doing was strange. Because they belonged to me in a way she could not, I could not be protected by her anger. Did she see my thoughts in my face? I don't think she realized that finding out what they were doing mattered far more to me than finding out what she was feeling. I could not tell her that. I could not disappoint her in her righteousness.

I remembered her outburst, though. Through the years of trying to forget about the rape, this memory subtly reminded me that my hurt had been serious.

For me to open up to her at that moment was impossible.

I did dream of opening up to someone else—Allen, a boy in my class. Lying in my bed I imagined telling him about the rape and crying on his shoulder. He would be wearing his brown wool jacket over a dark sweater, which made him look more grown up. A look of concern dawned in his eyes as he listened to me tell him, with brave directness, about what had happened to me. Slowly he realized how awful it had been and simultaneously he realized that he loved me, surprising himself. When I saw him looking at me with such tenderness I burst into tears, unable to help myself, and he pulled me to him to cry on his shoulder.

Allen as I knew him was not suited for this role: his round brown eyes had never met mine. He was always fooling around with his own friends, other boys. We rarely had conversations, and when we did it was to gossip about teachers and other students he knew.

In some oblique way a few words were exchanged between us about the rape. I knew that he was not totally devoid of any concern for me or interest in my adventure.

One afternoon that fall my mother asked me to come in to her small "private room." She had claimed this room as her own and fitted it out with my grandmother's drop-leaf desk, a bed, a remnant of rug, and a small abstract painting she had made, her only painting. She rarely invited us in. I dreaded what I might be about to hear.

"I'm a little worried that you might not really be all right," she said. "Since the rape."

I was startled.

"You haven't been talking about it at all. Are you really all right? Is there anything you'd like to talk to me about?"

She spoke awkwardly, uncertain of her ground.

I looked at the floor.

"It's okay, Mom," I said. "I'm really all right. I've been talking about it to my friends. And I cried on Allen's shoulder some."

As soon as I could get away from her, I did. If I turned to my mother for help it would be an admission of defeat. Far better to pretend to her and to myself that I was going to make a thriving social life for myself. In school would lie my salvation. In that world I must become wholly absorbed.

The part of the lie that mentioned Allen also felt more like an exaggeration than outright invention. Surely Allen, if he let himself, could help me far better than she could. I so longed for the time when that might be true that I pretended it had already come.

I also was trying to impress her. Instead of worrying about me and trying to comfort me, I wanted her to respect me.

A part of me still yearned for the care she was offering. I could not look her in the face, could not yield to what might happen if I did. I half turned from her, trying to hide myself. If she wanted to look into me and think about me being raped, I would not let her. I knew deep down she was trying to give us another chance. I could only feel myself refusing, and then guilty about the refusal.

In all our dealings with the rape our relationship had this same strange formality.

Physically, yes, she was near me—with me in the car, at the hospital, at the barracks and the courthouse, as if she hoped I could be reassured by her silent presence. Of course I was somewhat reassured. But most of all I sensed her uncertainty. She was keeping quiet because she too was like a child in the presence of the law or the doctor. Talking to me at home she seemed to understand what these men were up to. Her readiness to express her opinion of them awed me. But I also sensed how little she felt able to stand up to them when she was on their territory. She reminds me, in my memory of her demeanor, of a stout farm woman in a French story, coming to Paris on a legal errand once in her life.

Caught up in events that felt bigger than she was, it was as if she felt she had to let others rescue me, these men who would take charge of me and do what should be done next.

I lied to my mother and my French teacher (and myself) when I told them I was fine. What might I have said if I had been able to speak the truth?

I'm scared that Frank Miller wasn't the rapist, and if he's not convicted he'll come after me, since he knows he was arrested because of me. I'm scared that the real rapist who may be free out there somewhere might come after me too because I told on him.

Why did he do it?

Why don't I feel like my family loves me?

What is it going to be like to testify at the trial?

How come people at school still don't like me?

How would an adult woman put these things into words? (I was trying to be an adult.)

How could I talk about the end of everything, after which, strangely, nothing seemed to have ended at all? What kind of intimacy, or language, would have made it possible to share such a thing?

No one knew me that well.

The preliminary hearing was a small event, a simple step, Mr. Rittenhouse told me, as I sat in the red leather chair in his office again, the day before the hearing date.

"In the courtroom will be only the judge, and the grand jury," he said. "The public are not admitted. The purpose of the hearing is just to establish what happened, so the jury can decide whether Frank Miller should be indicted. Just answer my questions as clearly as you can. It won't take long."

He gave me a transcript of what I had said to him in August and asked me to read it to help myself remember what to say the next day. As I read my own typed words the events felt very near, as if they had just happened. It was something that was happening again, or something that was, I now grasped, continuing to happen.

Rittenhouse asked me the same series of questions over and over so that when I spoke in the courtroom there would be no surprises. As I gave my answers, each one the same as it had been before, I began to realize, faintly, that we weren't just preparing, we were rehearsing. He and I were going to perform for the people in the courtroom. I had a faint sense that something was going to be repressed—that there were parts of the story that he wanted to make sure I didn't tell, or ways he wanted to make sure I would not act.

I had felt that I was the natural author of this story, the right teller of it, and I was discovering now, in a silent, inchoate way, that I was not going to speak as myself to the public.

I was offended, too, aesthetically, by what he was doing to my story. He was making it boring. All the intensity and color of what had happened to me—the terrible, numb fear, the physical hurting, the appearance and disappearance of the rapist like a thunderbolt or ravaging beast of prey—all that was reduced to a plodding account of times, locations, and actions told in words like "come" and "go," mostly restricted to the answers "Yes" or "No."

When I came to sit in the stand in the echoing courtroom, empty except for the jury in their box, I was able to rattle off my story and not think about what I was saying. I was curious to see what effect it would have on its hearers. I was no longer curious about what it said.

I reached the point in my routine account where the man had "dragged" me into the woods across the road, and I paused. Mr. Rittenhouse chose this moment to impress upon the jury the seriousness of what had happened. In a bold voice that startled me, he asked, "And what did he do then?"

For an instant I sat stunned. He had not asked me that question when we were going over it together. I was perplexed, then frightened. I did not want to say the word "rape." I was angry, too, for I realized he was deliberately making me say it.

I said quickly, in a frightened voice, "He took off his clothes and he raped me."

On the word "rape" my voice came out in a squeak.

I blushed, and would have cried. But I was determined not to. And I was angry at him.

Allen asked, "Where were you yesterday?"

"I had to go and testify at the preliminary hearing for Frank Miller," I answered.

"Were you scared?" he asked.

"It was okay," I said. "Except for one part, I was telling about how I was riding my bike home, and how he came out of the woods behind me, and dragged me back into the woods, and then the prosecutor all of sudden said, 'And what did he do then?' and I was really embarrassed, and I said, 'He *raped* me,' like that, it came out in a squeak."

A day or so later Allen and I were standing around with one or two other boys, his friends. The topic of the hearing came up. I might have brought it up myself, trying to show off.

"And then you said, 'He *raped* me,' " Allen said, mimicking my squeak as I had mimicked myself when I told him.

They all laughed.

Silent, trembling, stricken with shame and rage, I turned away.

Somehow, sometime that fall, despite our differences, Allen and I managed to get ourselves into a place where we could explore our interest in each other. Loch had left for college that fall. One afternoon Allen came to our house to wait for a ride. We came together, without saying a word about it to each other, in Loch's empty bedroom.

By silent consent we lay together on the bed, neatly covered by my mother with a striped Indian bedspread. I was wearing a brown turtleneck with my jeans. Under it I had on my psychedelic bra. I lay down casually, facing the wall, unable to look at him. When he lay down beside me I exulted, I winced, and I felt as though I would die of suspense.

For a brief moment we embraced awkwardly. I began to hope for the satisfaction of my deepest longings. Now maybe I would be rescued. Now maybe there would be someone I could cry with about whatever was troubling me. Now maybe I would have a boyfriend.

I was completely unprepared for what happened, his small, warm paw creeping up under my shirt to touch my breast.

He did it quickly, before I realized what he was doing.

It felt strange, unwelcome, and most of all, unreal. He wanted something I had never thought about.

I had yearned for his touch upon my body: warm hands grasping my arms, my shoulders, encompassing my waist, caressing my hair—all these embraces I had dreamed. His first touch there, upon my breast, was an excruciating mixture of something I wanted and something I couldn't stand.

I pulled his hand away and said, "No."

I was angry and didn't care if he knew it. I also hoped that he would stay with me. But he withdrew. We got up and left the room without talking. I did not realize how wholly he had withdrawn until the next day. Still hoping that we might become a couple, I ventured to sit next to him at lunch and tried to talk to him as if we were friends. He ignored me and behaved as if he did not know me.

Allen's trying to touch my breast did not make me think of the rape, then or later. When I compare the two experiences, though, I see that when his hand crept under my shirt I did feel something similar to the raw creepiness I had felt when the rapist touched my nipples with his mouth. I was not terrified when I was with Allen, but both touches aroused the same perplexity: *Why was he doing it?* Why someone would want to touch me in such a way, especially without asking me, or me asking him, was beyond my understanding.

If I had not had the rape, which had combined such touch with such terror, would I have reacted to Allen's touch with such a blanket refusal? Would it have hurt so much that he was not going to give me the reassurance and help I wanted? Or might I have yielded a little, to a soft erotic thrill, and later looked back on it with a smile at our fumbling and confusion?

I wanted to be held and comforted badly. I fantasized about it every night. The man-god would come in my window, lie next to me, enfold me in his arms while I slept, and gaze on me and my lovely body all night with reverent tenderness. Sexual arousal and the desire for sexual touch had not yet happened. I was simply still dreaming of the father's care I had not been given, but I thought these fantasies were preparing me to be with men. I had been dreaming of this kind of attention before the rape, and I didn't think of my wanting it now as having anything to do with having been raped. I did not think I still had any pain, though I did wonder sometimes whether I hurt in some way I couldn't really decipher. I was noticing that I had not cried about the rape at all, and this seemed odd. I had not let myself cry with my mother (or Allen, after all). I thought maybe I should try to finish up that crying with someone else.

There was a new girl in my biology class, Eleanor, known as Nora. Like me she was tall and thin and had straight hair that would not hold any shape. She seemed serious and quiet, too, like me. She spoke of her father's new wife with pragmatic irony. I hoped we might make friends. We began to get to know each other, and after a while we arranged for me to spend a night at her house.

I was surprised by her bedroom, a small upstairs room that seemed bleak to me, its plaster walls in need of repair. I imagined that her father was treating her as an afterthought as he lost himself in his new romance.

As we were falling asleep she told me about how hard it was to live in this house with this woman who was not her mother, hating to have to show respect for her, and hating *her.* As I listened I decided that I would tell her about the rape. Maybe I would even be able to cry about it. Even as I decided I felt ashamed. She was sharing her secrets with me spontaneously, while I had a script inside my head: a carefully refined fantasy of being consoled.

Sure enough, as I began to tell her about being raped I could feel her withdrawing, as if she could tell that I was trying to take advantage of her. I kept talking, though, and was able to build up enough feeling of distress so that finally I cried. Nor could I stop myself from trying to act out my fantasy to the end. When I finished with crying, she asked me, almost impatiently, as if trying to disguise her skepticism of my performance, if there was anything she could do to help me feel better. Unable to stop myself, I asked her if she would get me a glass of chocolate milk. (Chocolate milk was something my mother never had in the house.) Grudgingly she went downstairs and brought it up to me. Hating myself for taking advantage of her hospitality, for not being able to control my selfish drama, I drank it up.

One day in English class our teacher asked us to write a poem about something that was on our minds. I wrote my poem about being raped. *This'll wow them,* I thought, when the idea came. I knew the subject was unusual and shocking, but it didn't occur to me that I was taking a big risk. I had a strange, innocent sense of my own power, almost as if having been raped had given rise to a rashness in me that hadn't been there before. How could testifying in a courtroom or writing a poem compare in difficulty to the rape itself, the adventure and the torture that I'd come through so well? If I could continue on as myself after that, what couldn't I do?

The poem brought itself into being quickly and surely. As soon as I finished writing it I knew it was great. I had said it, what being raped had been like. I couldn't wait to read it out loud. When my turn came I took a deep breath and began, my heart racing.

As I read, I began to understand how unusual the poem was. My words gathered power as they lined up to come out of my mouth. My voice faltered as I realized that the poem was deep and raw, and that I had listeners, and who they were. I became my own listener and began to feel what it was to hear such a thing. But I kept reading, in a shaking, proud voice.

When I stopped reading, heated and inspired by my own words, everyone sat transfixed in stunned silence.

My face turned red, and I looked down at the table.

In the moment before shame swept over me I knew, first, triumph; then shock. The silence that fell was not just my classmates and teacher shaken and uncomfortable. My own heart stopped and my own mind was disturbed by what I had said.

In the instant that the room filled with discomfort, I tasted a terrible defeat. I sweated; I blushed. I had spoken aloud about something that was sordid, private, and too sexual for English class. No one wanted to hear it. Being raped didn't entitle me to any special attention and didn't change me from being an uptight, smart girl who did not seem to know how to be friendly.

the poem

!what is this
some kind of a joke I have a sense of humor
Remember the face
   remember the face this is not a joke
what   meeeeeeeeeE
are   to
they   do
going   to

get your Big hand off my
      mouth. Im not gonna scream.
         . Im not gonna scream.
         . Im not gonna scream.
   will you listen to me
Ffinally I can breathe there is not a gang but one
                    rape
I know What This is this is a

There is no one back here
  if
  I screamed no one would hear me
if
he kills me   I am dead
    I will die

PLEASE DON'T KILL ME?
beg
not to be a virgin is
    like   a gap
    a tooth missing
        you know??: you :

BRUTAL

I wrote the poem on a sheet on ruled loose-leaf paper. On the back of it I wrote:

> On August 13 last summer I was approached and attacked by a man wearing a stocking mask. I was walking my bike up a back country road not far from where I live. A man has been arrested and indicted. There has not yet been a trial. I am not looking forward to it.
>
> I am thirteen years old.

In the back of my mind I did think about the virginity I had lost. Before the rape, at twelve or thirteen, I had thought of my virginity as a gift of love, a mysterious possession I would bestow on the right man. I was pretty powerful, no passive girl. *I* would grant *my* virginity to the most deserving suitor, not just the first one who asked. My first real lover, the one to whom I gave all of myself, would be also my rightful consort, my ultimate and true life partner.

After the rape, all this became confused. As it turned out, the breaking of the hymen was no big deal. A small happening, a part of growing up. It didn't hurt that it was gone (I announced this discovery in the poem), and it had had no useful function.

At least that's over with.

I even felt a certain pride that I now knew what intercourse was. What none of the girls in tenth grade knew yet, I knew—some of. I knew what the hymen felt like afterward, the soft wall of flesh that remained now split and obsolete in two halves secretly inside the opening of my vagina. I had become a woman in some sense. Whatever else it meant, not being a virgin meant being advanced, moving ahead.

I need not be changed by this rape. If I go ahead with my life as if nothing happened, I can be as if nothing happened. I know I've lost my virginity. I don't need to worry about how I lost it.

Yet I'd once thought that how I would give it up was very important. With Allen I had still felt a certainty that I was not ready for a lover. So was I still a virgin in some way? Did I still want to be? I did feel a wistful sense of loss of something, I wasn't sure what.

In a fairy tale a girl's feet are cut off by a giant, but at the end of the story after her many trials the fairies put them back on and she is as before. I brought this yearning to the rape, this wish and hope that I could be wholly restored by magic power. Trying not to think about it, trying not to think that anything was lost, I had a vague imagining that I can only faintly remember. A fairy godmother, or some such being, could restore my feet, could make the sacredness of my virginity—the integrity of myself—be not finally gone.

In the back of my mind I noticed that it did not seem to be happening.

Eventually I decided that I was being restored by a power that operated in ways I couldn't see or know. The magic would work while I went on with my life and acted as if nothing had happened. With this pretending no one disagreed. No one dared disagree. If they dared to suggest otherwise, it might not happen. They themselves, the adults, believed in the same magic.

Yet I did wonder why I was not being helped. Some part of me knew that I needed help in reality, not just from the fairy world.

It was a child's logic; a mixture of various impulses—wanting to ask for help, not wanting to know that I needed it, not believing that even if I asked for it I could get it. This inarticulate logic fed my more conscious conclusion that my urge to share my experience with others was stupid.

Who, anyway, could have promised me that, having lost what I had lost, I could be sexually healed?

Only a fairy.

I went on wordlessly affirming to myself that I would be, somehow, magically healed.

I had to miss two days of school to go to the trial, starting March 13, 1969.

The night before our first day in court, my mother helped me pick out my clothes. She explained to me that it was important that I appear serious and proper. I had never known her to show such a concern about what to wear.

I wore my favorite dress, which she had sewn for me out of an Indian print bedspread. It was a soft pale green and had bell sleeves. Black elephants marched in a wide border around the skirt. The hem hung, softly fringed, just above my knees, somewhat lower than was fashionable. It seemed to both of us the best choice for the courtroom. With it I wore cream-colored tights and her pair of pale brown suede shoes, which were a touch nicer than any of mine. It was the outfit I would have worn to go to a concert or a play in New York, or Princeton.

The next morning we drove to Flemington and walked up the steps to the courthouse. Mr. Rittenhouse met us in his office and led us down an imposing hall to a room where he asked us to sit and wait until we were "called."

We had to wait for a long time. We did not talk much. My mother knitted. I fidgeted.

When I was finally called I walked with her toward the doors of the courtroom with my heart pounding. I was going to be the first witness. I knew that all eyes were on me as I walked down the aisle and went to sit with her in the place reserved for us. The room was full.

I watched Mr. Rittenhouse make his opening statement to the jury. He walked back and forth in front of their box, but not dramatically as on TV. He told them slowly and quietly about the rape and what he claimed Miller had done.

His description seemed strangely remote from me. What had happened to me, the appearance of a man out of the trees, the lying down in the sunned clearing, the penetration between my opened legs, had happened in my world. What he was talking about—Miller's location just before and just after the rape, where he had gone in his truck, how it could be proved that he had had time to commit the crime—was in another world.

Near the end of his talk Mr. Rittenhouse said that Miller had "perpetrated" the act. Not recognizing it as a law-enforcement term, I thought it sounded like something out of a nineteenth-century romance novel. I thought it was the only reference to the terrible nature of the crime that Mr. Rittenhouse allowed himself, and to me it sounded faintly foolish. I was embarrassed for him.

When I was called to the stand my heart pounded harder.

This was not going to be my first time on stage. I had always enjoyed acting in plays and reading aloud. But this was not like any stage fright I had experienced. I did not know exactly what Mr. Rittenhouse, and especially Mr. Edmund Bernhard, Miller's lawyer, would ask me. I was not looking forward to telling about being raped. I was frightened of having to be in the same room with Miller. I could tell that my voice would not come out strong. I walked to the box and sat down in the chair. The hinged door was closed and latched in front of me, locking me in.

In that moment I realized where I was: isolated, exhibited for everyone to see. The judge sat disturbingly close to me on my right, behind his high counter. The two tables of the prosecution and the defense were just below me. The twelve jurors, their middle-aged faces alert and impassive, sat in two rows below me on my left.

When I remember the trial I see the courtroom from this perspective. I sense tall windows in the faraway wall on the right, windows that begin at the back of the room where the audience sits in rows, and end behind the judge. I have an impression of the table where Bernhard and Miller sat. The area around it seemed menacing. As I sat in the box I strove to ignore this feeling, telling myself that there was nothing Miller could do to hurt me in this room.

He was wearing a suit that made me uneasy because in it he looked so much neater and more contained than when I had last seen him, confronting me outside the barracks. His appearance confused me, as no doubt it was meant to confuse everyone in the room. He was not the heavy man who had loped toward me with a lunging step, his head rounded by the stocking mask into a naked and primal shape. He sat quietly at the table, his hair neatly brushed, looking at papers through his glasses. How could he possibly be the same man? My doubt of his guilt grew.

I sensed the captive quality in his silence, though. His attorney must act for him and he must watch. And I sensed something else: it was as if he were a stuffed bird, sitting there. Someone had tried to force something out of him, replacing it with cotton. Nothing much was left. He was no longer a real man.

The court officer came and held out the Bible for me; I put my hand on it. He mumbled something. The words of the oath sounded empty of meaning. I had thought they would inspire me, but I was numb. I said "Yes," and he was done.

I was alone.

In the back of my mind I felt surrounded by people who meant me well. I could sense anger and sympathy rising up in the women in the jury and in the audience. I could feel some concern for me in the hush of the room, which created a great distance between me and the others.

I felt the curiosity of everyone.

The name of the judge was Thomas Beetel. He was not what I had thought a judge was supposed to be like, a kindly father figure who would make everyone in the courtroom feel somehow safe, especially me. He was an ordinary-looking man, middle-aged, medium sized. His impassivity surprised me. He even seemed a little bored. He too was remote from me—too close to me, yet isolated, in his dark tower in the middle of the room. Around him hung a gloom and loneliness: his power. He was sharpening his mind the way you'd sharpen a pencil.

Mr. Rittenhouse came and stood facing me.

"Now, Martha, if you would, please, could you tell us what happened when you were walking your bike up Quarry Road on the afternoon of August 13."

The words came. I'd said them many times before. My voice came, trailing along reluctantly, barely audible.

The judge leaned over and asked me to try to speak louder. I tried.

Mr. Rittenhouse was not with me as I was used to him being with me. He was performing. I had not been prepared for how remote this would make him, how alone I would be out here with him. His respectful and careful demeanor had always reassured me, and I had imagined I could hold on to him for guidance. Now he had turned into a stranger. His voice was pitched toward them—the judge and the jury, the audience—with no overtone of any connection with me.

We were performing together, and he had to rely on me to remember his instructions. He depended on me now to come through on my own. He could not prompt or encourage me. He could not signal to me with his eyes.

In fear, with dry mouth and stiffened back, frozen in a position of decorum, I tried to come through for him, even though I knew it wasn't for him, really. The questions led me on; I fastened my mind to them. My voice sounded high, almost noble, in the huge space around me. As loudly as I could I spoke my single syllables, Yes and No. Mysteriously, my beautiful dress made my sitting and talking powerful. I even began to feel proud of myself.

Mr. Rittenhouse had explained to me that during cross-examination the questions might get a little difficult. All I had to do was continue to tell the truth, and I'd be fine. But when the time came for Mr. Bernhard to cross-examine me I sat and waited in the witness box with fear.

The danger I sensed in Miller seemed also to inhabit Bernhard. He was short; his clothes bulged. He was as sharp as Rittenhouse but in a different way. An inner dynamo seemed to inhabit him as he moved around the courtroom, officious and rotund. When he stood by the rail his face came close to mine. He looked at me with hard intelligent eyes. Small and slightly bulbous, they seemed to glitter with an impersonal malice toward me as he spoke.

As he questioned me, my fear made it difficult to think and open my mouth. As I answered him slowly, Yes and No, I began to feel that he was trying to twist all our ideas around, playing with truths we had not even thought of questioning. He was trying to make this happen through my mouth. I began to discover that I was no longer as reliable or clear as I thought I was about what I knew.

He was my enemy.

I felt as if I were floundering and might drown. I grew sullen, or tried to say something of my own. I felt insulted by his attempts to suggest that what I said could not be relied upon, if only because I was a child.

But I held to my story, to what I remembered. I kept on answering straightly. I was fenced in, on the stand. Here, despite the real and silent drowning that was going on in me, I could fight back, and I did.

On the evening of the first day my mother and I again stood in front of my closet and considered what I should wear.

"Maybe I could wear what I wore today," I said. It had worked for me.

"I think you'd better pick out something else, honey."

"Why?"

"Well . . . I have a feeling that that green dress is . . . too attractive."

I was very surprised to hear these words come out of her mouth. She had never said anything to suggest that she did think I was attractive. I was thrilled. But in the same breath she seemed to suggest that such attractiveness might be wrong, at least in the courtroom. I have a distinct feeling that she was reacting to some of the questions that Mr. Bernhard had asked me, revising her idea of what would go on in the courtroom. I did not want to explore in my mind the implications of what she was saying.

Dutifully I looked through my closet and chose an outfit I wore on school days: my red, white, and blue plaid skirt from the thrift shop, pleated and short. I tucked tightly into it a white blouse she had sewn for me, edged with lace. The outfit looked fine—neat and pretty—and I did not want to wear it. The jury, the lawyers, the judge, and the audience would all see me as younger, unsophisticated, a schoolgirl in a plaid skirt. I did not look forward as much to the second day.

My parents attended the remaining days of the trial without me, while I went back to school. I think my mother wanted to spare me having to be in the courtroom any more than was absolutely necessary, especially when Miller testified. The local papers reported on the trial. Each evening I read those articles and she told me how the case against Miller was unfolding.

Charlotte Tritt testified that when Miller sat in her car with her on Quarry Road that day, he had talked with her about sex. She said that she had not responded to him in any way.

"Bernhard tried to make it look like Charlotte was a tramp," my mother said, "Or that she had been carrying on with Miller. But Rittenhouse objected and Bernhard wasn't able to go very far with it."

She sounded disgusted and angry about Bernhard, and bitter, as if she were saying to herself, *I should have known it would be like this.*

I had testified to exactly where I was when I was attacked and the route I had followed to get there on my bicycle and to get home afterward. Betsy Retivov testified to exactly what time I had left her house. Mrs. Michel, a neighbor, had seen me walk past her house on my way home and had noticed the exact time. The time it took for me to ride my bicycle from my teacher's house to the rape site and from there to home was established. From these facts it could be known exactly what time the rape had happened.

Miller admitted that he had seen me walk past his house and on up Quarry Road. As soon as he saw me, Rittenhouse claimed, Miller had got in his truck and driven around a small triangle of roads to get ahead of me on Quarry Road. He had pulled his truck into a spot among the trees ahead of me, hiding it. He had sneaked down the gully that ran along the road and crouched there waiting for me to pass. When I had walked a few yards past him he came out on the road and began to run up behind me.

The time when Miller had admitted he was in Raven Rock and had seen me ride by, and the time my brother had found him with Charlotte later, were all established by witnesses. Mr. Rittenhouse was able to prove beyond a doubt that it was logistically possible for Miller to have committed the crime.

As a kind of math problem Mr. Rittenhouse's reasoning seemed to me to work. But I could not connect or reconcile it with what I remembered. How could I not have sensed the presence of a man deliberately parking his truck ahead of me and creeping a long way down in the gully to do what he had done?

In the courtroom Miller had seemed an ordinary person. I could not—or could not bear to—connect him with the rapist's voice, his urgent, anxious wheezing, the touch of sweating skin, the stabbing between my legs, the vanishing of the figure from the silent grass.

My mother, and Mr. Rittenhouse, had explained to me that if Miller was convicted, it would be on the basis of "circumstantial evidence." I worried about this circumstantial evidence. It happened that Frank Miller fit the circumstances. Couldn't there be someone else who fit also?

I imagined another: a ruthless, heavy, masked man who struck and vanished, a man who dwelled in the night and had no home, no friends, no family. (Frank Miller had a wife and two little girls.) That man might still be out and about.

At the end of the trial came a surprise, the testimony of a couple who had been friends with Frank Miller and his wife. The husband testified that one day a few months back, after Miller had been indicted, he had sat down with Miller alone in a bedroom during a visit between the two families. He had asked Miller straightforwardly if he had done it. Miller, he testified, had not spoken but had nodded, lowering his head slowly, once.

Mr. Bernhard, my mother told me, had suggested that Miller's friend was trying to get revenge on Miller because Miller had been having an affair with his wife. It was not clear whether such an affair had taken place at all, but Mr. Bernhard tried to make it look that way. The friend's wife was also called to testify, at the very end, to back up her husband's testimony about what had happened in their house that day. There was clearly very bad feeling, my mother said, between the Millers and the other couple.

This surprise evidence did not convince me more than any of the rest. Bernhard had a great power over my mind. He had caused me to doubt even myself. Maybe this couple really was out for revenge on Miller. A single sinking of the head was not an admission of guilt.

In her reports to me my mother seemed to be trying to refrain from telling me her own opinions. She seemed to be trying to give me a careful and accurate account so that I could form my own ideas about it. She did not express anger toward Miller or even act as if she were sure he had done it. Did she assume that Miller was guilty? Did she assume that I thought so too? Is that why I hid from her the depth of my doubt? I think she thought I understood more than I did.

On the fifth day the jury began to deliberate. No one knew for sure what they would decide.

I wanted them to convict him. It would help me to be sure of his guilt. If they didn't convict him everything would be worse. He would be free. He might come after me.

That evening she told me they had found him guilty. I found I was still not convinced. New doubts sprang up. A jury was just as capable as a prosecutor of being wrong, I realized. She told me she had heard that Miller planned to appeal. Maybe that meant that he really was innocent.

The judge sentenced him to the maximum sentence, fifteen years. She said everyone thought the judge had done the right thing.

When Miller was released, I calculated, I would be twenty-eight, the age that he was now. This fact linked us strangely. When I was twenty-eight, though, I would be a grown-up and would not have to worry about him.

The end of the trial put an end to a certain kind of talking. My mother and I and others had had to talk about the rape whether we found it easy or not. A dialogue, however minimal, had been going on. Now the rape was in the past. To mention it would be to bring it up again. To bring it up again would be to suggest to myself or others that all had not been attended to.

I did not mention it.

After the trial ended, my mother and I would never speak directly to each other about the rape again. My father and I never spoke of it at all. Perhaps he thought about trying to let me know that he cared, but did not then trust himself not to be clumsy and cause me further hurt. I think he imagined that as a man it was not right for him to bring it up with me. Loch and I never spoke of it.

Alida asked me about the rape years later when we were in our early twenties. She wanted to know what had happened to me on Quarry Road.

They had told her that I had been "attacked," she said. No one had ever told her what that meant. I calmly told her exactly what had happened, trying to tell it in a way that would satisfy her curiosity and reassure her that I had come through it all right—not realizing then, in my twenties, that in responding to her fears about the rape I was trying to give her a caring attention I myself had not experienced.

When did the silence begin? It began when the rape began, on the road, and in the clearing.

The silence of my quiet dusty road changed in quality, the change ushered in by just a few sounds: the crunch of his feet behind me on the small stones. His first words: *Don't drop your bike.* The softer sound of the bike being laid down by him on the side of the road. Then some sound of his feet crossing the road with me, some rustling and crackling as he pushed through the undergrowth.

The silence grew deeper, became an abyss, a void; and grew shallower —hearts rattled, breaths quickened into gasps.

When he raped me it was done in silence. Maybe the trees turned away, unwilling witnesses, and in a dark metamorphosis bowed down into a hedge of wild horror. Maybe there was a roaring in my ears of darkness. I think there was. In the clearing darkness fell, a terrible eclipse lasting twenty minutes.

When he went away, I was counting out loud, my clear voice measuring time. Then I stopped. I listened for him, did not hear him. The silence then was me alone in the clearing. The grass lay flat in the bed he'd made and stood up all around it, washed in sun, and the light and shadows of the grass beat around me like the heart beating of the world. The silent grass, my familiar grass, was shocked, stunned, and at the same time completely unaware. It received my blood like a blank page receiving the printing of a word, impartial and absorbent. My blood went where the bugs had their shadowy passages, their small caves between the bright arches of grass stems, small to us but huge to them. The blood fell into the silence.

The shock of having been raped was a loud, dreadful stillness in my ears, the removal of all usual connection between the senses and the mind. Me getting up, me walking home, all this happened in that silence also of shock.

Did this silence ever "wear off"?

I say no, I say it simply faded into and was transformed into other silences.

I see it as a painting. *After the Rape,* a medieval arrangement. The girl, wounded and bloodied, lies across a bed. Beside the bed, leaning over her, stand her mother and father. Her brother stands helplessly by, his face contorted with a desperate, concealed pain for her. Her sister, locked out of the room, is leaning up against the closed door to hear whatever she can. In a wider circle just beyond the parents stand the doctor, looking concerned, and the two policemen, watchful, rural, and alert for the moment when the child may be questioned. Outside the house the rapist runs, his hands and penis dripping blood, his terrified face stark against the long grass of a field in August. Beyond the policemen and doctor in a more removed circle stand the judge, looking on with distaste; the prosecutor, smart as a whip, determined, enraged and joyful with his bundle of evidence; the defense attorney, pudgy and conniving. Sitting in their double row along a wall, the members of the jury look cornered, uncomfortable, awed by their job, and determined to do it correctly. Charlotte Tritt sits in her Volkswagen, a young country girl, smoking a cigarette, nervous. The girl's schoolmates are gathered in front of a schoolhouse, talking among themselves, silent among themselves, making lewd comments, uneasy.

Members of the community make up a little group in front, surveying the scene and gossiping. They are outraged and highly curious.

Everyone is concerned, but in a fixed pose. They seem to stand together but they are not really alive, nor are they meeting each other and sharing in each other's pain. Instead they stand silent, as pictures do.

Standing in the clearing after the rape I was released from my ordeal. I was alive. I had survived. The regular world, which I then embraced with a wild drive to recapture a sense of safety and protection—the law's protection, the familiarity of my family life, of school—all that then became dangerous to me in ways I did not imagine or understand. The greatest harm to me lay in the silence that hung in all these experiences, the silence fed by the inability of those around me to speak in any intimate way about rape.

I am talking here not about shame, exactly, not the feeling when I spoke to others about the rape that it had been stupid to try—which I did have—but also the sense simply of being the possessor of an experience that others do not want to know about. Others do not want to live in a world in which these things happen, the world in which you now must live. They hang back at the gates with a natural, an almost animal, shrinking. You understand perfectly well their shrinking, for you are also like them. But you do not know how to be what you are now.

In the silence I had to guess at what was going on in others' minds and at what was supposed to be going on in my own mind. I made more than one guess at once, and I honored them all, for any of them might be right. I didn't think, *I am guessing.* I felt, *I guess they . . .* and decided it must be so, trying to make up some sense of certainty.

Another idea throve in the silence: the idea that it was necessary to keep silence. This idea kept guard over the silence itself, kept all my other guesses hidden, even from myself.

My guesses or interpretations had nothing to do with facts or sureties. They were as true as a primitive painting in its representation of some true world. They were fictions, things I made up, but they were not wrong. Misguided at times, but never without their own logic.

Everything that I imagined became truth, because I believed it, and I lived it as if it were true. I became what I imagined, in the moment I imagined it, and by accrual of these moments.

After the trial that spring, for the first time I began to doubt the importance of school. I became enthralled with Suzanne, a sophomore like me but two years older, sophisticated and comfortable with boys. I felt lucky when she invited me to spend a night at her house and we stayed up late talking in her bedroom. I was fourteen and wanted to be her: sexy, relaxed, poised, sixteen. I wanted a boyfriend so badly it was like a physical ache in my chest.

In our English class a senior girl, trying out teaching, assigned us to listen to and read the lyrics of the Beatles' *White Album.* Suzanne celebrated the advent of this album with cool reverence. I had never understood what the Beatles were about; now Suzanne taught me how their lyrics worked as poetry: mysterious, glinting with allusions.

> Take these broken wings and learn to fly. . . .

"Blackbird" reminded me of my brother, tall and awkward, with his long dark hair and dark expressions, sensitive, angry, and disturbed. When I heard the song, the blackbird was he, as if he lived in the trees outside our family's window and had never really been let in. He had had to go further away from us that year, to college in Hiram, Ohio.

For years my parents had worried over him as he struggled with his subjects at school. His grades were never really poor but there was a sense of tremendous frustration to his efforts, as if his mind was mysteriously handicapped, a problem that seemed to be expressed also in his stuttering. Dimly I knew that at school he was strangely disconnected from everyone, as if he were stuck in his own world and did not know how to get out. He receded into the background, unnoticed.

My parents were relieved when Hiram accepted him and gave him financial aid. They were not able to drive him out there in our old car or to pay much of his tuition. To get home for vacations he had been getting rides with other students or hitchhiking.

I worried that he might not be able to get good enough grades. If he didn't he would lose his student deferment. Then he might be drafted and have to go to Vietnam and be killed. I was sure that he would be killed, because he was having so much difficulty just managing regular life.

The song spoke to me, too: an encouragement. I felt like that blackbird, even though no one knew it. Was I in a way like that wounded one?—singing, but crippled, and needing the encouragement of this song to keep trying to learn how to be in the world with everyone?

Maybe learning that was more important even than my English class. One day I skipped it and hung around with a group of boys and girls who were just hanging around. Missing the class I loved, I felt a strange mixture of loss and a new, guilty power of choice.

Was I somewhat more frightened of everyone, that spring, than I was before it all happened? Would I have been more able to see learning to be with people as something to do in addition to my schoolwork, instead of something so difficult that I could only manage one or the other? The rape and people's reactions to it must have made me shakier.

Like any tenth grader, my struggles were mainly about school and friends. I was two years younger than anyone in my class, and I had trouble understanding what was going on with the people among whom I wanted to be included. I did not want to think of the rape at all now, except as something very bad that I had come through with flying colors. I managed almost completely to forget about it.

Because of the silence it's difficult, impossible really, to look back and see exactly what went on within me regarding the rape over the years. But certain incidents did remind me that it had happened. I tried not to notice them. But they could not be avoided, and I remembered them. Now they appear to me as flashes of truth, small signposts, clues to what my mind was doing—a few isolated moments in the complicated unfolding of my adolescence when my mental barriers opened and consciousness of rape broke through.

The first time it happened was in June of that school year. I was up unusually early and had slipped outside to the kitchen terrace after breakfast to sun myself on the first stone the sun had found. It was going to be a hot morning.

A figure wearing a plaid shirt and pants walked out of the woods onto our lawn. As it emerged from the trees I was washed in sheer, blinding terror. It was *him,* coming to get me at last. I knew I would be killed there in an instant on the grass, a single moment as blinding as the sun. My heart surged in my ears, drowning out my thoughts and freezing my voice. I felt I should try to stand up, get inside, and hide, but I sat paralyzed as in a nightmare.

A few seconds later I recognized the figure as our neighbor, Judy Galuska. She had come along the path from our garden, where my parents were working. She had asked them to lend her a tool and was crossing our lawn to reach our cellar door where the garden tools hung. It was the most normal thing in the world.

My relief was as strong as my terror. The world had become wholly monstrous and in an instant become familiar again: the lawn, sparse in the shade of my beloved dogwood trees, which had masked Judy's head as she walked under them. I had never felt so glad to discover I had made a mistake.

I told myself that my fear had been misguided. No one was going to come after me. Frank Miller surely was the one. I decided I would not let it happen again. I would not mention it to anyone either. I would keep it to myself, that sudden feeling of defenselessness. That morning I decided I was going to think of the world as incapable of attacking me again, and of myself as invulnerable. I would cover up my fear with a mask of fearlessness.

Later, walking alone on deserted city streets, I would summon up a feeling of invincibility, of having paid my dues, given up what could be taken. It did not occur to me until twenty years later that my sensitivity to the men around me, on the street or in the woods, could actually be valuable.

In July a family friend, Len, told my parents he was going to Greece in August, taking his five-year-old daughter with him. He had wanted to go all his life. My parents decided at the last minute that they should send me with him. I could help out with Rose, and he could keep an eye on me. They couldn't really afford it but they wanted it for me.

It was a glorious surprise. I'd been talking for weeks about how much I wished I could go there. I was very excited about the Greek art and history I'd been studying in my ancient history class.

At the end of the school year I had also read, in English class, *The King Must Die* by Mary Renault, a novel based on the myth of Theseus, who had led Ariadne out of the Minotaur's labyrinth. In the sequel, *The Bull from the Sea,* Theseus conquers the Amazons and captures their queen, Hippolyta. He loves her for her kingliness, which matches his. In a stormy love scene she surrenders to him after a fierce emotional battle with herself and weeps in his arms, not surrendering her warrior nature but responding to his. This scene captured me completely. Greece was the place where the gods had lived and these things had happened.

I was glad too that I wouldn't have to be at home in August, on the first anniversary of the rape. I would never forget that it had happened on August 13, a Tuesday, at around four o'clock P.M. As the anniversary came closer I was feeling a gathering dread. I didn't want to have to think about the rape again, but I knew when the day came I would have to. Everyone in my family would too. I was not looking forward to the awkwardness. It would be much easier to be somewhere else. My parents may have shared that feeling. I wondered, as we made plans, if they were aware of the anniversary too. I thought maybe they were hoping it would help release some of the bad feeling of the rape if I could have new experiences in another place.

Our hotel the first night in Athens overlooked a market street. Men shouting below our wood-slatted windows woke me at dawn. I felt a surge of passion for just being alive, something I had not felt for a long time. I went downstairs into the street alone. I found there the overwhelming sun, men with carts, kittens running back and forth among pieces of garbage.

Shopkeepers ungated their windows with a tremendous clanking, trucks rattled and honked, all the sounds richocheted against the walls that leaned close in. I bought myself breakfast in a little store that sold dairy products. Twenty years later I remember the taste of that meal, which I ate standing up: the fresh yogurt from a large container behind the glass front of a refrigerated counter, some white sugar poured over it, a peach. The man who handed me this food out of his white cooler smiled at me as if he were making a toast.

I explored the streets around our hotel, parading in a new dress my mother had made for this trip. Vendors murmured to me on the street, inviting me and other passersby to look over their wares. I was rewarded, as I passed a café, by the welcoming calls of men.

To be able to have this effect just by walking by! I had been right to guess that the slender form I'd inspected many times in my mirror really would inspire men. The dress had long sleeves but I felt only pleasure in this dry Mediterranean heat. I felt that they were rightly admiring me and I felt no threat.

A few days later, in closer encounters, I insisted to myself that I was not afraid. I had ruled out any further mishap. I couldn't be raped again as I had been. I could not be further soiled. Or I might as well be further soiled, since the damage had already been done. It seems sad, a certain hardness developing in me at fourteen.

We stayed on the island of Paros for two weeks, in a tiny apartment with a balcony that overlooked a whitewashed alley. I had brought my flute with me and in the evenings I stood out on the balcony and played it in the velvety air. It felt right and pleasant to sing without words to my neighbors there. One evening a young man stopped to listen and we began a conversation. He was studying to be a dentist, he said. He was not very tall, and looked unassuming, but was solidly built under his suit. He had the gentlest voice I had ever heard.

"I will teach you Greek," he said, looking up at me with dusky eyes that held a surprising, gentle yearning. He invited me to go swimming with him, later, at ten o'clock. Thinking he meant ten o'clock the next morning, I agreed. He came by later that night and asked me to walk with him. I refused, certain that he had meant the next day. Finally, he went away. The next morning I waited on the porch in vain.

Len's friends on Paros, Gene, a photographer, and Beverly, his girlfriend, said that probably he had meant ten at night. They laughed at me because I knew so little about men and because I was taking a Greek man seriously. Len paid no attention, which was fine with me.

At the beach I met a boy, somewhat younger, who asked me to have dinner with him. He took me to an expensive restaurant overlooking the ocean. We ate shrimp, which were delicious. He didn't take much trouble to talk with me, unlike the other young man. When our dinner was over he led me out into the night, away from the lighted street and across a deserted stretch of beach strewn with sharp-edged boulders. Finally at a low stone wall he stopped. Before I had time to think he began to caress me, his hand sliding across the inside of my thigh just above the hem of my dress. For a moment I stood still, startled by a strange flickering in my leg, a quick stirring of something in response to his light touch. It disturbed me. I pushed his hand away. His hand returned. I pushed it away again. We argued about whether he was entitled to touch me. Since we weren't speaking each other's languages it was an argument conducted through tone of voice. I said loudly, several times, "No." He objected. I tore myself away from him and stumbled back through the rocks toward the lights of town. He let me go and trailed behind me pouring out complaints.

I was upset, angry, and a little scared, but it did not occur to me that he might have forced himself on me.

As soon as I got back into town I went to Gene and Beverly's.

"You're pregnant," they joked, as soon as I walked in their door and they looked at me.

I told them the whole story, breathlessly. They laughed, as if they thought I was telling them for their entertainment. To them what happened was adolescents fumbling with sex. They saw no harm. I felt ashamed. I guessed that I ought not to have been so upset by the boy, or at least I ought not to have allowed them to see me upset. I left them quickly. They did not know I had been raped. I would not have wanted them to know.

A few days later came the anniversary. I woke up wondering what the day would be like, wondering what I would feel. I was glad to be in this other August, in this dusty, sunny, friendly land. The rape was safely far away from me. Len had the idea of taking a bus trip around the island to check out the other towns. We rode the bus together to the first stop. Standing in the little square of a tiny village, suddenly I realized I didn't want to get back on the bus. I wanted to walk back into the main town by myself. Len agreed to my idea and went on alone to the next town. Gene had told us we could hitch rides on the island roads, and we thought I could do that if the walk was too long for me.

I was wearing shorts and a shirt, dressed for exploring. In the back of my mind I knew I was taking this walk because it was the anniversary of the day I was raped and I wanted to be by myself. Around me were small, low hills, deserted in the heat, sparsely sprinkled with harsh grass. I passed an olive grove; I had never seen olive trees. Their gnarled, stumpy trunks with their murmuring leaves made shade over an entire hillside, transforming it. I reminded myself that the olive branch was the symbol of peace because an olive tree took twenty years to bear fruit. I passed a tiny outdoor shrine, a little chapel brilliantly whitewashed, and a little spring by the road, a single faucet dripping water into a puddle in the middle of a desert. Entranced, I also felt at home.

Here I was, free on this island, where whitewashed buildings tumbled down to the sea like a fairy town, and that sea, adorned with necklaces of pure white foam, was so blue it hurt. The gods and spirits were palpable here. I felt open to their presences. I didn't want to even notice it, but I knew I'd chosen to walk for miles in the heat also as a way to distract myself from the pull of the memory of the summer before.

When I had finally walked myself out and exhaustion had driven away that danger, I decided to try to hitch a ride the rest of the way into town. I was feeling proud of myself. I had walked a long way, nearly seven miles. I had survived this day. I had lived it and not let myself be dragged down by it. I'd fought and won this second round, aided by gods and olive trees. No one would ever know how glad I was of it. No one knew how, in July, I'd been dreading August's approach, in 1969.

A man came around the curve on a black motorbike and stopped for me. He wore a black leather jacket and his stiff black hair stood up in a small-town cut. Up close, I saw some lines in his face; he was middle-aged. Mounting the bike behind him, I clasped my hands around his middle as he directed me. I hadn't pictured myself riding home on the back seat of a motorbike, so intimately bound to the one who gave me a ride. But another might not come, and I was very tired. I would not be afraid.

After a mile or so, a matter of minutes, he stopped at the outskirts of the town. I got off and thanked him. He invited me to come home with him to have dinner. When I said thank you, no, he repeated himself. He pled with me. He looked as though he could not understand what was wrong with me, that I said no. I said it again. Finally, as he continued to press me, I turned and walked away. It was rude, I knew, but how else could I make him believe that I meant no? Behind me he raced his motor disconsolately and then buzzed angrily away.

I walked home, feeling guilty. Maybe I really shouldn't have got on his bike. He had probably thought he could seduce me, as the two others probably had.

But it was great! I had fought him off, had made him go away! That man, with his black clothes and machine, had brought me a whiff of the rapist. But I had spurned and repelled him.

This was a small, slight idea—that I had encountered the rapist again and in the encounter had freed myself of some hold the rape had on me. Years later a similar idea would recur, twice, with men I was strongly drawn to.

I walked down through the town to our apartment. Soon I would tell Len and Gene and Beverly how far I'd walked and how boldly I'd dealt with the man. This time we would all laugh—at him. Soon after, since evening was coming on, I could forget what this day was and would be in no further danger of wanting to bring it up.

In my journal that night I did mention the anniversary. I was keeping my journal of Greece as a long letter to my family, fighting off homesickness and guiltily trying to share this expensive adventure with them. I knew they wouldn't have forgotten the date, so why pretend? I tried to mention the matter in an offhand way as if we all took it for granted that we would think of it and when we did it would be with a certain self-congratulation. Well, Martha's made it through a whole year and she's fine. We pulled through it together. Good for Martha and good for us. It was safe to bring it up, at a distance of a few thousand miles, in writing.

Tuesday, August 12—Afternoon

Len and I got up early this morning to catch the bus to Lefkes, a village on the other side of the island. We hung around there

> awhile, I took some pictures. After stopping at a taverna for some krema and cherry soda, I started on the road back to Parikia while Len went on to Pisa Livadia.
>
> Well, I walked seven miles. Around the sides of mountains, across dips, over beautiful Paros countryside I walked. I realized that a year ago tomorrow I was walking my bike up a lonely road in New Jersey, coming back from visiting the Retivovs. It struck me suddenly how long ago that really was, and how fast the days had passed for me.
>
> Now I am preparing for the departure, washing clothes and packing. I am excited about leaving here, and going places I've never been before.

That fall, when I returned from Greece, Solebury was in financial trouble and could not offer me a scholarship. Instead that year I attended our local public school, Hunterdon Central. It was housed in one gigantic building, a sprawling complex of tiled corridors lined with a thousand lockers. Solebury had two hundred students; Hunterdon Central had fifteen hundred. Between classes they all noisily flooded the halls. Lost in the shuffle, I spent almost all my days there in silence. If I had found the social rituals at Solebury confusing, here I was paralyzed. I rarely spoke to anyone. Homeroom was a holding tank where the students gathered every morning to pledge allegiance to the flag and listen to announcements through a round speaker in the wall above the blackboard. I couldn't see how to start a conversation with anyone in homeroom; there was no time.

Gym class, with mostly older girls who talked fast and loudly while casually undressing and showering, was an agony of nakedness before strangers. Waiting in line in the hall outside the lunchroom, older boys in their short athletic jackets horsed around and called out obnoxious remarks to passersby. I was terrified that they might turn their attention on me. Every day I ate without companions in a giant cafeteria where Crosby, Stills and Nash sang tinnily from speakers high in the cinder-block walls. Sometimes I spoke briefly with a teacher after class.

I struggled each morning to put together outfits that looked like everyone else's. It seemed I would never quite succeed. I imagined that if I could only do that I might somehow make friends. Obsessed with my hair, I began to rise at six-thirty to get a shower in before the school bus came. I did it as often as I could get away with it, trying to ignore my mother's anger. She said we could not afford to use that much hot water. As I washed my hair in the morning cold I cringed in the shower, knowing she was angry.

"Why don't you wash your hair at night? Then you wouldn't have to go out with it wet like that and catch cold."

"It gets greasy if I wash it the night before. It doesn't look right."

"It looks fine to me. I think you're putting too much hot water on your scalp, it's not good for it. The doctor says your hair may fall out, later."

She did not realize how close I came to really believing her. I might be punished later for wanting nice hair now. I was a slave to my craving to be beautiful, a secret addiction I could not rein in. She did not know how I struggled to liberate myself from it, how I wished I could rise above it and please her. I would be a better person if I did not let myself think about how I looked. I would be pure. My innate beauty would shine forth. I tried to believe this wholeheartedly. Yet when I looked in the mirror I did not see an inner light glowing.

Spring came. An event was planned at the school, a day for everyone to exchange ideas about the war in Vietnam and the problem of the environment. Mr. Falcone, my favorite teacher, asked me one day after class if I would be willing to join a panel discussion planned for the whole school to attend in the main auditorium. He thought I should do it because I was "articulate." I said I would.

Then Mr. Falcone told me that one of the panelists would be the Flemington lawyer Edmund Bernhard. My heart sank into my feet. Of course, I could not tell Mr. Falcone that I had met him before.

That night I told my mother about the panel and said I wasn't sure if I wanted to be on it. She asked me some questions. What was I actually afraid of? How bad was it really? Did I want to do it or not?

Of course she couldn't tell how much I didn't want to do it. She didn't really know what the rape and the trial had been like for me, because I hadn't wanted her to know. I still didn't. So I thought I'd better go ahead and do it. I could manage it. Maybe he wouldn't remember me. Besides, he'd only been doing his job at the trial. He wasn't supposed to have anything personal against me.

I had hated him, though, with his small eyes. Why had he been chosen to speak as an example of thoughtful citizenry? I did not want to ever see him again, much less to share a table with him in front of fifteen hundred teenagers.

When the day came I got through the event. Mr. Falcone introduced Mr. Bernhard to me in the general round of introductions before the panel. He showed no sign of recognition. Was he acting somewhat more distant than he would if he really did not remember me? I tried not to think about it.

When my turn came I spoke as eloquently as I could in a little speech about the revolution that my mother was sure was coming. I could tell that the audience thought I was weird, but I was determined to offer them our family's truth. The moment was fleeting. It would be hard to say what caused the roaring in my ears: the size of the audience, larger than any I had experienced before, or the terror of sitting a few seats away from Edmund Bernhard.

The next fall, Solebury was able to give me a large scholarship. Sixteen now, I walked back onto the campus shy but ready. Suzanne greeted me, smiling, as I came out of the tiny bookstore in the old "barn" with my new books in my arms.

"Mala Sundstrom was talking about you," she said. "She told me she saw you, and you're going to be in her art history class. She said, 'I'm so glad Martha is back. And she's so beautiful!' "

Starved for Solebury things, the small classrooms, my intimacy with teachers, everyone's excitement about the great change happening in the world, which no one at Hunterdon Central had heard about, I threw myself back into life there. I went to Callanan, one of Solebury's most loved teachers, who was acting as headmaster that year, and talked him into teaching me Latin in his office with another senior, a boy named Chris.

Callanan never acted as if he were teaching things he already knew. He seemed to be taking you along with him as he expanded his own learning. In his classes you took yourself seriously. Somewhere in the middle of reading Cicero's letters something happened in my learning, in an hour I would never forget. These Latin words, which I had memorized and tried to put together for almost four years, knowing them mostly as a puzzle, suddenly became for me a breathing entity, a *language.* Suddenly I could sense the meaning of a whole sentence at a time. These letters became *letters* an actual man wrote to those he cared about, in language that acted very much like my own.

Gradually Chris and I made friends as we struggled over our Latin assignments together. One day in the spring it dawned on me that I loved him. A group of us spent an evening at the home of the biology teacher and her husband. I wanted to sit next to Chris, close enough to be touching. Why couldn't he lay his hand on my arm? Driving home with three of us in the back seat I managed to lean my leg against his, and in that instant felt a sweet, hot sensation all through my body.

My dreams of kissing Chris were untinged by any doubt of his goodwill. He continued to be friendly, calm, and affectionate. He never could bring himself to kiss me, even when finally in desperation I asked.

A few weeks later I told another senior girl about my love of Chris and its disappointment. She said, "Have you ever thought about Andy? I think he likes you."

Andy was shyer than Chris but didn't seem to mind spending time with me. We arranged the second movement of Bach's Italian Concerto as a duet. He played the harpsichord, I played the flute. We got permission to perform it in the school's annual arts festival.

After the concert in the school gym, excited by the music and applause, and spring, we decided to go for a walk in the moonlight. I knew if he was going to touch me it would be that night. My parents had come to the concert and were waiting outside the gym to pick me up. But if I left him for a moment, or even if I asked him to wait for me while I talked to them, he might change his mind. So I just stuck with him and refused to think about my parents or anything else.

We walked out past the pond, across the fields to the edge of the woods, and back, without saying much. He had arranged to spend the night in a room on campus since his home was a long drive away. I asked him if I could stay with him. He said he wouldn't mind. We spent the night illegally together in a tiny attic bedroom the nurse used sometimes for sick day students. He sat down on the bed, leaning against the wall. I managed to sit on the bed too and lie back against him, so that we were not lying down together but both half sitting. I leaned my head back awkwardly against his neck. Neither of us could say a word. I thought he might have kissed me, once, on the very top of my forehead. I could not be sure. That, if even that, was all. We never spoke of it. I don't remember exactly how or where I slept, or if I slept at all.

I never told Andy at what cost I was staying near him. The next day a teacher told me noncommittally that after the concert my mother had come into the library, where he was serving night duty, in a fury. She had demanded to know where I was. He had been unable to tell her. Finally she had given up and gone home.

I called her that afternoon after classes were over and said casually, "I'm ready to be picked up."

My father brought me home as usual. When I came in the door she treated me to a single scathing remark.

"Don't ever not show up to be picked up again."

It was my biggest and most dramatic rebellion ever. I was appalled by my own cruelty. I had driven her to distraction, to a mad rage. I had hurt her deeply by ignoring her. But it had been wonderful to stay out with Andy all night. How could I have done so well and so badly at the same time?

We both knew what staying out all night might mean but we did not dare speak of it. She did not ask me what I had done, and acted as though what I did was my business, as long as I had the courtesy to tell her my plans. It never occurred to me that she was probably worried about me, perhaps especially because I had already been hurt once so badly.

That spring I began to stay on at school for dinner, beginning to feel a widening of the world and of the range of my powers. I sometimes sat at the table of one of my teachers from sophomore year, Knight, with mixed feelings. He talked the most scurrilous gossip anyone knew, discoursing freely on the politics among the teachers and sex among everyone. I wanted to know all of it and I did not want to know any of it.

One evening he got onto the subject of which girls at school were not virgins. I saw a chance to try to join the social life at the table. I also wanted to spoil his game.

"I'm not a virgin either, of course, you know, Knight," I spoke up. "Remember? I was raped when I was thirteen."

It did stop him, at least for a moment. He hadn't expected it. He mumbled, "That doesn't count, of course," and went on to another subject.

I was embarrassed as soon as the words came out of my mouth. Yet something in me had insisted on telling him. I had lost my virginity, but not in the way anyone else had. Was I still to be considered virginal or not? If anyone would know maybe Knight would. And I was still, in spite of myself, proud of my rape, wanting to think of it as a kind of achievement even though I wasn't sure if it was.

My thinking of myself as having been raped was drawn to the surface that year only by that incident, not by my spontaneous attractions to Chris and Andy. Knight's frank sexual talk forced me to remember. With Knight I wanted to show my sexual sophistication. What I wanted with Andy and Chris, while I was beginning to feel some sexual feeling, was not much different from what I had wanted with Allen two years earlier—to be touched and loved by someone kind.

It would be years before I would feel such tenderness toward any male as I had felt for these two boys.

I would rather eat a bad meal in the school dining room than go home for dinner. I didn't want to participate in whatever was happening there. I couldn't have told you what it was that I sensed in the house: the coil of my parents' troubles tightening. They were worried about Loch, they were worried about money, and it was my father's fault. He wasn't working enough. Her main resentment was probably his drinking, which was getting worse. She was at war with him, her argument with him never resolved, her anger never finished. He cringed and flattered her, would say anything to try to pacify her, but would never face her head on. All I understood then was that home was beginning to feel impossible, a place of trouble and loneliness where I could not breathe.

Each night she made an inspired meal as if that could keep things as they had been, make up for Loch being gone now and maybe not going to be all right, make it not happen that soon I too would go away. But the beauty of her created world—her gardens, the sun pouring into the big room where Alida and I had sewing and art projects going alongside her piano, the kitchen with its big pegboards hung with seasoned pots and pans—could not hold me. Her power was waning. Guiltily I avoided helping her whenever I could. When I did help she was not satisfied. She was unhappy in a way that I could not solve, but could only try to get away from.

She and my father did not know what I should do about college. There was not going to be any money to pay for it. I would have to find a school that would give me full financial aid. They hoped I could, as I was third in my class at Solebury. There was some doubt in everyone's minds—my parents', my teachers', and even my own—whether I was ready for college, since I was only sixteen. But no one could think of a good alternative. I sensed that it would not be good for me to stay with my parents in the thickening gloom of our house. School was the place where I was managing to have relatively happy and lively days.

I applied to three colleges that offered courses in Greek and anthropology. I longed to learn Greek, the language of the *Odyssey.* I wanted to become a classical archeologist, to go to Greece and Italy and dig up ancient ruins, to touch vessels the ancient ones had touched.

Years later my mother told me that she had worried about my going off so young but had decided that the best thing was simply for me to "get out of there"—the house full of gathering bitterness.

I went to Trinity College, in Hartford, Connecticut, a small liberal arts school that had been recommended to me as having a strong classics department. I arrived there alone, lugging a tightly packed suitcase a mile from the Hartford train station. As I unpacked my things in my tiny, bare dorm room, I felt a sinking feeling. I saw other students unloading boxes from their parents' station wagons, running out with their mothers to pick up cheap bookshelves and curtains. My family felt far away, like a gypsy caravan camped out in the night. They would not be able to tell me how to conduct myself inside these stone and cement buildings, dorm and dining hall. The home I had wanted so badly to leave was now really gone.

It was going to be all right, though. I would perform beautifully in my studies and my teachers would like me. Best of all I would have boyfriends, lovers, men. I liked to say it: "men." I would make a leap to adult forms of love. I would become a sophisticated and sexy woman.

Trinity had converted to coeducation only two years earlier over the strong protests of its alumni. Women were still a minority on campus. I was glad. It did not occur to me that a strongly male institution might not be a nourishing environment for me. I simply thought that among all the men I couldn't fail to find one who would fulfill my dream.

Someone told me that some of the older students called the freshman handbook, which contained a photo of every new student, the "pig book." They looked through it together, rated the faces of the girls, and decided which ones they wanted.

I was in fact up for grabs. I went to bed with the first man I met who was interested. I chose him because he was tall, blond, and twenty-three, more of a man than the freshman boys or classics students I'd met, and because he had a knowing air about sex and was willing to initiate me. After we made love he told me that I had been wonderful.

"You will have thousands of lovers," he said. I was thrilled.

I knew my mother was worried about me when I went off to college. In my mind's eye she stands in a room of the house in a falling light, holding a serving spoon in her hand, drying it with a towel. She is in the midst of her day of chores, hanging out wash, working in the garden, preparing food. Maybe she's just gotten up from her afternoon nap and is groggy, dreading the beginning of making dinner. It's just a pause—she sees me, *Martha,* young, tall, and serious about my studies, and she wonders if I am all right. I, walking down an elm-hung path, carrying a pile of books, with my shoulders hunched, am taken aback for a moment and also pause. I am no longer sure I want to go to the library, or anywhere at all. It's as if she is calling me home, as if she wants to hold me and keep me—and I want her to.

I wrote her a letter and casually mentioned that I'd been to Planned Parenthood and obtained a diaphragm. I was proud of my responsible act and thought she would approve. She wrote back, "Your announcement of getting a diaphragm sounded like a girl announcing that she had earned a varsity letter. There is more to sex than having a pleasant companion, and it takes years of living to know it."

Shocked, I showed her letter to the student resident assistant in my dorm. She admired my mother's directness and told me she agreed. Yet I never understood what my mother meant, especially by the words "having a pleasant companion." That sounded pretty good to me. Perhaps she meant to caution me. Instead her letter was both a reprimand and a punishment, her anger sizzling through the mail.

Home and the increasing troubles of my family pulled on me strongly that fall. Just before Thanksgiving my parents called and told me that Loch had had a breakdown. He had walked around the Hiram campus naked, out of touch with reality. They would have to drive to Ohio in our '57 Chevy and bring him home from the hospital where the college had put him. They arranged for a neighbor to pick me up at the train station in Trenton so that I could still come home as planned and stay with Alida.

Alone in the house for a day or so, we wondered what was going to happen. Alida was fourteen and I was sixteen, but now I was the older sister home from college. I tried to act confident and in charge. We did not want her to be alarmed.

It was never clear to me what happened to Loch that fall. He had been struggling with his studies, unable to choose a major until it was almost too late. By Thanksgiving he had gotten himself into a bind, at risk of not passing all his courses. Like most students during that time of unrest, he smoked a lot of marijuana, maybe more than most, and he was someone who probably should not have smoked or drunk alcohol at all. Years later he hinted to me that he thought someone had put LSD in something he was drinking that had triggered his delusions.

It was a dark Thanksgiving. My parents were distraught. My mother managed to prepare a Thanksgiving dinner and we managed to eat it, sitting around our table like orphans without any idea of what was going to happen to all of us.

Returning to college I discovered that my new lover had lost interest in me and moved on to someone else. I was devastated. It turned out it wasn't so easy to be sophisticated about sex. I began to have trouble doing my schoolwork. I began to wonder if I might be going to have some kind of breakdown like Loch.

I tried calling home, hoping my parents could help me, longing for reassurance I thought I might get just from their voices. I could not tell them everything, though. I dropped some hints. But I could not find words with which to talk about my emotional self. They listened, but I sensed that they wished I would not disturb them now with problems they could not understand or fix. The calls ended with both sides frustrated.

I managed to finish my first semester with As in six subjects.

My first lover had been a sexual adventurer, moving swiftly from one conquest to the next. Following his example, I began going to bed with a succession of different men. I persisted in seeing each encounter as an opportunity, a possible romance, even though it kept not happening. I had a wild yearning for my partner to offer me love (imagining that my yearning for it *was* love) and a strong craving for approval, the admiration that I'd discovered I could get from men simply by inviting them to look at and touch my body.

They coexisted, my tender, shy reaching out to those two boys at Solebury who liked me, and this urge toward a bold display of my physical charms now to be followed by sex. In college these two different girls occupied parallel universes in me and struggled along in a grim, ongoing war. The one who still ached for some assurance of mutual tenderness would not be closeted, and sabotaged all my attempts to act as a sophisticated adult. In bed with a man she sometimes emerged and wrought a havoc of tears and confessed desperate needs I knew were not appropriate to that setting.

I refused to imagine that any of the men I slept with would think of me as "loose." But I picked up hints of how the people around me thought about sex. Their ideas haunted me. What I was doing was called "sleeping around." When I engaged in a "one-night stand" it meant I didn't "respect myself." The idea of "self-respect" remained a mystery to me. My mother could see I did not have it, since I was too ready to have sex. I could see that I did not have it, for I noticed that every time I slept with someone different, I felt ashamed. But why?

Before too long I did find a boyfriend. Because he fell in love with me instead of the other way around, I thought all my problems would be solved. He gave me an affectionate name, Moon-calf, from a line of Shakespeare, sometimes shortened to Mooney. He adored me and I knew it. He admired my intelligence and my looks, and when I wasn't driving him crazy with anxious or angry storms, he treated me much as he treated his younger sister, with a teasing affection.

He had a big heart and a decent soul. In sexual matters he was oblivious. Once we had begun to have sex together I knew I would never be in love with him. I might laugh with him, I might cry in rage or frustration, I might refuse to make love or tease him on to it, but he was never going to go out of his way to give me pleasure.

I considered that the problem might be with me. I'd been raped, after all. Maybe because I'd been so young it had somehow modified my anatomy and made me incapable of having an orgasm. I timidly confessed my worries to an older student I looked up to.

"What do you do when you masturbate?" she asked, tackling the subject head on.

"I've tried putting things in my vagina," I said. "But nothing seems to happen."

"Do you know where your clitoris is?"

"I think so."

"Well, just put your hand on your clitoris and keep rubbing it. Don't stop no matter what. If you keep doing it eventually you'll come. It's guaranteed."

I tried it at home in my own room, not daring such a venture in the relative lack of privacy of the dorm. It took an hour. When it finally worked and I felt pleasure creep slowly, suspensefully over my body and break over my sexual parts in a blissful, calm wave, I was overjoyed, as though a miracle had occurred. I really was capable of orgasm. I wasn't frigid. If I could do it myself surely I could learn to make it happen with him.

I announced my triumph to him as soon as I saw him again.

"Guess what! I had an orgasm," I said. "I found out what to do and I tried it and it worked."

"Oh," he said, vaguely. "Masturbation is fun for a while. But then you move on to other things."

His response discouraged me, but I hoped it might happen when we made love anyway, without any help from him. It didn't, though. Our lovemaking continued exactly as before, leaving me miserable and frustrated. Soon I began to worry again about frigidity. Psychologists had written that women who could not have vaginal orgasms were immature. To be a whole woman you had to be able to enjoy sex with a man, not just by yourself. You were supposed to get turned on by giving pleasure to another. I only felt angry, which must have meant that I was unable to connect, to care about others, in or out of bed. Maybe I was incapable of love.

When I broke up with him a year and a half later, I told him that I just wanted to be free again. It was true, I was beginning to feel trapped in a too-small space. Although he seemed bereft and mourned, I was not moved. For all his affection and support, I could not forget my anger at his selfishness in bed. I had never spoken of it directly to him.

During the summer between my sophomore and junior years, while I was living at home and working in a local restaurant to earn money for college, my mother came home from her shopping one day and told me that Frank Miller had now apparently committed a murder. She had bought the *Hunterdon County Democrat,* and gave it to me to read.

I read it quickly in the kitchen when no one else was around. I did not want to know anything more about Frank Miller, but I could not keep myself from reading it all. On August 13, 1973, two days into his first parole and five years, to the day, after my rape, he had approached a seventeen-year-old girl on her family's farm. He said he had seen an escaped heifer and suggested she get into his car to go and look for it. She happened to be wearing a bathing suit. He drove her to a concealed spot and brutally murdered her, cutting her throat and mutilating her breasts and genitals with a knife. Her father and brothers, assisting the police, found her body later in a gully. One of the brothers had recognized Miller's car. He was arrested within hours.

Now I ought to be convinced that he was the one who had raped me. The date of the murder was especially convincing, wasn't it? But it still felt impossible. Even if it had been him, and even though I did remember being raped, it did not feel now as though it had exactly been me who was raped. I told myself that he no longer had anything to do with me. I felt thankful that I was in college now, living far away from him.

My father saved this newspaper story in his files. It reveals things I must have tried not to see in 1973. In his picture Miller looks like a murderer: he has a thin, sunken face, a look of detached violence in his eyes. His victim, a student at Hunterdon Central, had excelled in her schoolwork. Like me she had brown eyes, brown hair worn with a simple part, and a serious look. She was seventeen, the same age as me. I must have wondered then, as I wonder now, whether he had attacked a girl who reminded him of me, the one who'd told on him five years before. It seemed as if the lurid vision I had in the clearing—of my body in a ditch, my father and brother finding it—had happened to her. In averting my own fate maybe I had transferred it to her.

I had jailed him, and in jail he had grown into a murderer. It was not just him I had destroyed, it was that other girl. She hadn't had a chance.

I did not speak to anyone about it, and tried to forget about it as quickly as I could.

The hidden truth about me in college was that I knew only one powerful, genuine desire—to be loved, saved, and repaired—and the agent of it would be a man. Now I thought I would know him by a foolproof sign: when I made love with him I would have an orgasm. His love would make him patient and anxious to give me pleasure. He would be not merely willing to help me but powerfully able to take me and release me from the prison of my so turgid body. To make me whole, to make me relaxed, sexual, and female. To *unrape* me.

When lying with someone after sex, aroused but still unsatisfied, sometimes I felt as though my predicament would drive me mad. I yearned for this one thing with a pathetic and consuming need. I could not act, I could only wait, and keep trying, allow every suitor his turn at my secret test.

In moments of near truthfulness, when my lover lay sated, I sometimes complained of my physical dissatisfaction, in obscure words intelligible only to myself. Sometimes I cried and then could be comforted, as if that would make up for my uncompleted lovemaking. It seemed that some men felt that I had misled them, while others imagined that it was just an off day for me and didn't bother themselves about it.

For several years I kept a list of the men I'd slept with. Writing their names made each encounter feel more real. I had known them, however briefly. That knowing was something I treasured and wanted to keep track of. Even if none of them had really loved me much, each of them had loved me a little and that was better than nothing.

Once, playing an anguished game with one of the nicer ones, I asked him to try and guess how many men I'd slept with. I finally confessed there had been seventeen.

"That's not too many," he said, consideringly. "You don't have to worry about being too promiscuous."

My hopes for sexual intimacy were now tremendously overburdened. Although I could not allow myself to know my own loneliness, sleeping with almost any man who asked me was becoming an unconscious bargain I was making with a bad situation.

I couldn't say to a man, asserting my heart's need, "Let's wait and get to know each other better." I could only assert, silently to myself, my sexual frustration, thinking, "Oh, God, he's just like all the other ones."

Memories of the rape were unavoidably and vividly evoked by the experience of being physically penetrated again. However, I did not at all think of the rape as having contributed to the yearning that led me into my sexual adventuring. I did not see the rape as a factor in my constant anxiety about whether I was really all right inside and all right in relation to the world. When I thought of the rape I thought of the man attacking me on the road. I did not remember the silence of everyone I might have received comfort from. I thought of the pain of him tearing my hymen, not of my shame when I'd found I could not talk about it with anyone.

Sometimes I thought, *Maybe if I tell him about the rape he'll get more interested in me* or *be more careful with me,* both sexually and emotionally. After I'd told him I said to myself, *How could you try to use the rape as a way to get attention? You ought to know better than that, you know it earns you nothing and is a cheap trick.*

Was I telling about the rape to try to get the love and support I still very much needed? Or was the rape a specific pain that was crying out for attention? Both were true. Mentioning the rape was both a device to get something else and an expression of a real need in and of itself. I was uncertain of my right to either.

Each time I told a man about the rape I half hoped that I might be able to really feel it as I told it, and that he might be able to really respond. In his embrace I might resolve the weeping that I had suspended when I sat on my mother's bed.

It must have confused my partners when I told them of my rape at the moment it became clear that intercourse was about to happen. Caught in their own struggles with sex, how could they know that I was using them partly to try to deal with the obscurity of what had happened to me? I didn't even know it myself. At any rate, we usually went ahead with sex. There were a couple of times when my partner, touched, said, "Let's not go on with this—it just doesn't feel right to me." When this happened, I simply felt rejected.

Almost ritually, what followed the frustrating sex for me was a sense of further violation that I could not name: the sense of being with a stranger, of having been taken from, the desperate stirred-up yearning for compassion and understanding, the certainty that I was not going to get that, and finally, a familiar, recurrent rage about it all.

My sexual experiences, taking place in an obscure, half-conscious realm, caused great upheaval. They threatened and disturbed my familiar habits of living and competed shamefully with my desire and love of learning. Latin and Greek excited me, even though I knew they seemed dry and narrow to many people. In reading the ancient classics I was seeking the meaning of life.

Part of my interest had to do with trying to understand what had happened to me at thirteen. It was a literature in which rape figured largely. Europa, Leda, Daphne, the Sabine women—many nymphs, maidens, wives, and even female animals had been raped by gods or men. I had dreamed of being adored by a divine male figure. I had got instead a low and gross man, a terrible parody of what I'd imagined. Yet I felt an affinity with the maiden raped by the god. In the myths the raped ones never spoke, except when they begged the gods to deliver them somehow. They simply were hurt, or they turned into something else—sometimes both. I recognized the way these girls had small parts in their own stories.

What had it been like for *them?* The myths were strangely silent on this. No narrator or character ever expressed horror or outrage at these rapes. They were simply part of the way of things. In this mythic world females were overpowered because they could be overpowered: it was that simple. This absence of useful insight disappointed me. But at least it was not a world in which no mention was made of rape at all.

I committed my yearning to understand life to the care of my male professors. But my once-cherished bonds with teachers had changed shape, and I was tied to them now in a tortured routine of striving and guilt. Whenever I lapsed from my assignments, distracted by my sexual longings, my hopes and rages, my excuses, powerful as their sway was within me, were unacceptable and could not be told.

I stayed torn between my intellectual pursuit of enlightenment and my following of my physical, sexual appetite as if it would lead me to the ultimate gratification of my deepest need. I needed to stay torn, swinging back and forth from one to the other; to keep leaving one for the imagined truer reward of the other. If I fully committed myself to one or the other I would discover, painfully, its incompleteness.

My brother, too, was having trouble growing up, staying with his studies, knowing how to go about living in the world. He had returned to Hiram to try again to finish out his senior year, and at the same time of year, around Thanksgiving vacation, had had another breakdown similar to the first. He was now living at home.

What could I have said to my professors?

I can't concentrate because my brother has had two breakdowns, and his lottery number is high, and my parents don't think he can be drafted because he's psychologically unstable, but they're not sure, and they are sure he couldn't be a convincing conscientious objector.

They don't know what to do to help him and they don't know what to do to help me.

I'm still wondering why I can't handle joining everyone socially, and a lot of what people do together seems stupid to me. I don't know what to talk about with people or how to just make friends.

It seems like I feel very lonely and cut off from everyone. I try to make connection by having sex, and I know it's not working, but I can't stop trying, and every time I try I get hurt again.

I still really just want someone to hold me, but I'm supposed to be beyond that now.

I'm supposed to be able to keep doing my work no matter what my "personal" troubles are. But why? And how do I do this?

I don't know what this word means: "self-respect."

Unlike my brother, through it all I managed to get all As and Bs.

It is impossible for me to pin down exactly what part the rape played in my confusions and struggles in these years. Certainly many young women go through similar difficulties at this time of life. It is clear to me, though, that the two men I became most deeply emotionally involved with as a young woman—at eighteen and at twenty-four—both evoked the rapist in powerful ways; and these involvements are especially disturbing to remember in this hindsight.

In the middle of my junior year the first one came. I thought he was my redeemer, the bringer of light and hope to my dark and hurting condition. My infatuation with him carried me out of college and into the world, not ending until the spring of 1976, when I was twenty-one.

This young man was obsessed with getting sex. He was a rapist: not the kind who attacks on a deserted street, but someone who would force himself on a woman after she has admitted him to her home. In a way different from anyone I had encountered before (or have since), he didn't seem to have any concept of "no" as a meant answer. I learned of this gradually and from what others told me of his actions.

I had embarked on a year at Dartmouth College in an exchange program designed, originally, to bring some women to that campus. Like Trinity, Dartmouth had been a men's school until just a few years earlier. There, among pine woods and snowy hills beside the Connecticut River, which runs strong, narrow, and deep in New Hampshire, I enjoyed the country, my natural habitat, but I was even lonelier than at Trinity. The misogynistic, alcoholic culture of the fraternities was stronger at Dartmouth. Women were few and far between. Not that I really wanted to be with women. I still invested all my hope in the man to come.

He came to me in the early dark of a winter afternoon, while I was studying under a lamp in the library of the English department. I was bent over a table, reading my Greek assignment for the next day.

He sat down opposite me, quietly. He had not come there to study. He was no longer, in fact, a student at Dartmouth, having graduated a year or so earlier. He was small and seemed shy. He watched me. His gaze urged me to look up and see him. When I first set eyes on him he appeared as if he had come in just to be near others in this warm and cosy room.

He looked back at me calmly, welcoming my attention, greeting me. A faint curiosity tickled me. I felt a mixture of interest, indifference, and a sense of his loneliness, that here was a person who was in some trouble. He had a hungry air, like a gaunt animal walking the woods in winter. In that moment he reminded me, fleetingly, of my brother, the blackbird trying to fly in the black night. He looked hungry not for a meal or companionship or sex but for something bigger, something unfindable. He looked hungry the way my mother did sometimes, in a manic mood. Something faraway would glint in her eye. She would look as if she were listening with one ear for the coming of some larger voice who would answer all her need, something that had abandoned her but she couldn't help still counting on.

He had me pegged, I'm sure, right off, for sex and a place to sleep that night. I sat bowed over my dictionary and text, quiet, studious. My straight brown hair hung down plainly. Under my brown blouse I wore no bra. He later told me it was that that had first attracted him. I'm sure my own loneliness was palpable to someone looking for it. But it was not quite so simple. He too was starved for something unnameable, and he was acting in the grip of a powerful compulsion.

He began a conversation with me, the first meaningful exchange I had had with anyone for days. He seemed interested in me—my studies, and my life—in a way I no longer expected the men I met to be. His talk was friendly and companionable. I did not feel any stirring of sexual interest either on his part or my own. I was glad. I was feeling sick of sex and sick of men.

The clock struck five, the dinner hour. He allowed as how he was hungry, and we walked over to the dining room together. We talked more over the dinner table. He paid serious attention to me, continuing to ask me questions about myself, exploring me, wanting to know. Readily I began to open up to him.

He said he had come to Hanover to begin a new job, working with a theater group that had just hired him. They had not paid him yet and he did not, he confessed, have a place to sleep. I had a roommate I never saw, who lived with her boyfriend in his dorm. I offered him her tiny room adjoining mine. He met me at the library when I finished my work that night. We walked together from the dining hall to my room across a long expanse of snow.

After more talk in my room he abruptly, but casually, mentioned the idea of our having sex—not as a proposition, more as a brief but hypnotic suggestion slipped into the conversation. I don't remember if I answered *no,* with equal casualness, or if I answered at all. It was like this: he quietly announced that he was going to do it, and I simply wasn't listening; heard it but didn't believe I'd heard it.

Later, years later, it came to seem as if he'd studied just how to *trick* me into having sex with him before I knew what was happening, that he pursued that goal with a single-mindedness that would have appalled me if I had not been thoroughly distracted by his apparent deep interest in me.

What he offered was not the kind of long talk leading to hot sensations, wavering, and capitulation that I was used to. Maybe he sensed that I was not at that moment open to such a scene. His approach was both more direct and more detached than anything I'd encountered.

He did not speak in any way that was threatening or denigrating, but simply kept applying a subtle, intense pressure. He disarmed each of my half-conscious hesitations quickly and deftly, by ignoring them or responding to them in a sideways, nonsensical way. He used mainly surprise. He behaved as if he *were* a little mad and wanted to share that with me. He seemed to be inviting me playfully in our talk to forget my usual scruples and leap into strangeness with him, where, if I chose, we might both discover something new.

As if in a dream, we got into my tiny bed together. It felt good being close to him. For some reason I still did not think we were going to have sex, thought we were simply going to sleep together. I thought it was obvious that I was totally uninterested. I did not think he could be interested if I were not.

The next thing I knew I woke up all the way: already jammed close to me in the tiny bed, he had begun pressing his hard penis against my thigh, urgently. Unnerved and startled, I burst out, "Stop it, will you, I'm not interested in your cock."

He seemed completely taken aback.

His body relaxed.

"What do you mean?" he demanded, to my surprise. He said it as if he really wanted to know.

I had wanted simply to make him stop. I had not expected him to revert to curiosity about what was going on in me. He seemed surprised to discover that I did not care to have sex with him, as if he had never thought of this possibility. His surprise seemed genuinely innocent. He wanted to understand why I had said his cock did not interest me, specifically. My statement seemed to have shocked him back into seeing that I was a person, as if he had forgotten.

He then became very tender toward me.

Aroused to an anger that had freed my tongue, I told him about having been raped. It was different from when I had told other men: I didn't care how he reacted. Suddenly, as he questioned me about it, I began to cry, not on purpose this time, not hoping to be consoled, but just in pain. As if my talking and crying had opened a door in him, he told me about something terrible that had happened to him. His younger brother had recently died of a terminal illness at seventeen. He had not been able to talk about it with anyone. Suddenly he too was crying, for his lost brother, and I was holding him in my arms.

Nothing like this had ever happened to me with a man.

I felt deeply consoled, in a way I had craved for years, for the first time. Then the sudden, still-unexpected arrival of his body within mine felt like a strange rape that was not rape, a surprise that turned out to be good.

Something about the heat of that moment, of being prodded to real anger and real tears, may have enabled me to let go. I decided, while he was still in me, to go ahead and stimulate myself.

"Do you mind if I touch myself?" I said to him, not caring whether he did or not.

"No," he answered, absently. "Why should I mind?"

So there, in the midst of being taken advantage of, for the first time I began to masturbate during intercourse. I felt an opening and a warmth I'd not experienced before. I did not have an orgasm but in that moment I felt sure that I could, with a man.

It was as if he'd torn away a thick drape, shattered a heavy window, and

I was left astonished in the warm, soft air. No matter that he'd sneaked his way in, that he had in mind only getting something he wanted. I was, afterward, like someone whose house is destroyed, who finds she can think only what a burden it had been to her. It was as though a burglar or a mugger had paused midtheft to say something astonishingly humane.

Clinging to each other like two limpets in my tiny bed, we slept.

The next morning we were cheerful together and left each other with an agreement to meet again that night. I walked out into the snow feeling as if I had just been born. At last the god, daimonic, wholly animal and wholly divine, had come to me and unlocked warmth and light in my limbs and my heart.

Whenever I looked back on it, it seemed to me that we had joined in a union that was completely pure, our two souls finding each other and embracing like two lost children, all games laid aside. I don't know whether he shared this feeling at all. But the fact was that I made for myself out of this random coupling an experience of transcendence—engendered, probably, as such moments often are, by the intensity of my need and longing.

He stayed with me another night, bringing his guitar. I drank up the lullaby of his songs as in a dream. The next day he took off, with a regretful but quick good-bye, promising like a fairy that he would come again, though he could not be sure when. I watched him walk off through the brilliant snow in his woolen hat from Norway. My heart sang.

As the days, and then weeks, went by, I began to understand that I was not going to see much of him. I pretended to myself that I didn't mind. He cared for me as deeply as I cared for him, but unavoidable demands of his rigorous new life as a dancer made it impossible for him to get away. I tried calling him several times, with no results. Months passed. I mourned, I obsessed, I raged; I was hopelessly enthralled. He was an angel, an intermediary to me of sexual revelation and the divine. The enthrallment was fed by a mere handful of meetings with him.

At one desperate moment I visited the house where he lived while he was away. One of the people he lived with invited me in. I looked in his room, I looked in his closet, and I looked at the letters he kept there in a box. Next to my own passionate ones lay one from a Bennington student that sounded just like mine. I began to understand that what he'd done with me he'd done with others. I began to wonder whether he'd simply been acting the part of the gifted, caring, special figure whose love might transform me and who would not be around very much. I even sensed vaguely that my own yearning had endowed him with this power. His pose had found in me a willing and gullible response.

A few months after our first encounter, I began to keep a diary out of my need to affirm that my liberator had finally come. He had left me with too much I still wanted to say to him, and about my love for him. Spring had come. I had to write my joy, to try to keep it alive, since it was so fleeting, like an illusion.

The topic of rape surfaced almost on the first page.

5/27/74

> *I felt like Leda or Europa which I have always wanted. . . . I have lost that virginity, I have been unraped. Forgive me for wanting to do it again and again and again. No, that would make you laugh—forgive me for strangeness in the night and familiarity in the day, for pouting and whining. I did not weep any of those tears on purpose. . . .*

I began to read Virginia Woolf's diary. I deduced that if I was truly a writer I would naturally want to write about characters, scenes, and the kinds of thoughts people cultivated who lived the life of the mind. I tried to write about these things in fits of resolve, but I kept relapsing guiltily into my own urgent questions about myself. The journal of those months at Dartmouth reveals a young woman in a sad state: lonely, moody, mired in gratuitous emotional battles she could not get a handle on, and lacking all sense of direction in life, except for the new certainty that she wanted to be a writer.

My diary was my first real, solid friend. Unlike my dream men or vague imagined gods, this book was square and tangible and did not change. I could take it with me when I needed it and leave it in my room when I did not. It made no demands on me but inexorably, implacably showed me myself. I could see in my sentences faint signs of power, and I could write my determination to be sane.

7/16/74

> Wrote my first story Sunday night. I feel different now. . . . I begin to see that to be a writer I do not need to have an independent imagination. I'm excited because I see it now as more being a collector, of scraps, odds and ends, and being the one who has the skill to put them together, patiently, into a quilt; cut them into different shapes, make patterns and designs. . . . I sat in the classroom with a bottle of grapefruit juice and the room seemed one of the most beautiful I have ever been in. For most of the time I was completely alone and undistracted. . . .

Making one of his rare appearances, my magical lover, to my delight, decided to join me one weekend when I went down to Trinity to visit a friend. She invited us to spend the night in her room, since her roommate was away. While I lay in her roommate's bed, he crept out of his sleeping bag on the floor, crawled into her bed, and tried to force sex on her there.

She told me about it the next day, enraged.

"He just came up into the bed and started trying to shove his penis into me," she said. "I had to pull the sheet up over my legs so he couldn't get in." He was strong; on stage he lifted other bodies. But she was strong too; she rowed crew.

"Didn't you hear us?"

I had heard them scuffling but had tried not to hear, thinking they were making love. I had persuaded myself that he was gifted in his strange mad way. I could tolerate it because we had a special closeness no one else would understand. Besides, she had invited it, hadn't she? She had been flirting with him all day long while the three of us walked around campus together.

About a year later, after I had graduated from college, he succeeded in raping another friend in New York, whose phone number I had once given him so that he could call me while I was visiting her. She told me that he had called her out of the blue, told her who he was, and begged to spend the night on her floor, saying that he had no place to crash in New York. Once there he had forced himself upon her. This time I listened with more sanity.

I called him, secretly glad to have an excuse to confront him.

"She wanted it," he said, not defensively but softly, confidingly in my ear, as if still inviting me to be the special one, the one who could handle his truth. I hung up the phone confused, unready to wholly let go of him, wanting to believe him more than her. At the same time I knew I would never talk to him again. I was able to understand, finally, that these women were my friends, and he had hurt them.

I've still not forgiven myself for my part in it. Surely I betrayed both my women friends, allowing myself to be made into a kind of pimp for him. My weakness and self-delusion brought great injury on the second friend. Why did I not warn her? Why did I refuse to know what nature of man I'd gotten myself entangled with?

I'm ashamed of how I rationalized his attempts at rape, secretly gratified at what I felt had been my ability to disarm him, imagining my friends had not been bold enough to do the same. To them he was a rapist, though we did not use that word then. To me he was a boy trying to force things, against the need of his heart. He had lain and wept upon my breast.

I don't see him that way now. I no longer feel indulgent of his trouble. I have to forgive the girl I was, though, even if she ought to have been old enough to know better, at eighteen, or twenty-one.

I graduated at twenty, not much wiser than when I had arrived at college. Near the end I asked my advisor if he thought it might be a good idea for me to continue my studies in graduate school.

"I don't think so," he said.

"Why?" I asked, startled. I had done well, I thought, winning a prize in Greek translation and earning a high grade in my final comprehensive examination. I had even enjoyed studying for this special exam, going over my Homer, savoring all I'd learned, reading summaries of Roman history under a tree.

"I don't think you're sufficiently engaged," he answered, drily.

I could not think of what to do after college. Deep down I wanted to go home and stay home. I could imagine no better life than my family's life in the woods with our garden, our meals, our music and books, the fireplace in the library, the clotheslines strung between the dogwood trees on the lawn. But that dream could not happen again.

In my last year of college my visits home had become more difficult. Loch's argument with our father, like our mother's, was unending, but his made a lot less sense. He carped at both parents' daily inconsistencies, carrying my mother's ideas of radical self-sufficiency to extremes.

"Fred, you didn't really need to use the car to make that trip to Stockton."

"Mom, why did you throw out this plastic bag? You said we're supposed to rinse them out and use them again."

At other times he kept to his room, dour and resentful. You could feel him moving restlessly behind his door like a trapped animal, locked in a private war with his daily medication.

Alida had gone to art school in Baltimore, leaving the three of them in a tormented triangle. When I visited we would sit together at the dinner table into the late evening, bewitched by wine and a longing to achieve our old togetherness. But it seemed our talk could only go round and round in a descending spiral of anger and despair. I began to notice there was a mood that came over me at home and nowhere else, a black paralysis. I could not understand it. I thought I loved coming home to Mom's food, the woods, my little old drop-leaf desk and four-poster bed.

One night I stood in the kitchen and saw it whole: what I was watching was a tragedy, something out of Eugene O'Neill. These people were hopelessly entangled in each other's pain. No wonder I felt so awful.

I could step out of it as an observer, though. Someday maybe I would write about it, I would become a great playwright.

My mother said to me firmly, "You're going to have to find a job, because we can't afford to put you up here without your paying for yourself." Taking a job at an obscure magazine in New York, I made writing the tenuous thread of my life. Riding the subway I made notes on what I saw around me. I typed up my poems on the office IBM after five o'clock.

After a few rough months I decided to move to Boston, where daily life was easier to manage than in New York. I found a job at a library and moved in with a group of graduate students in Cambridge. Twice there I picked up men in a bar and went to bed with them. But these instant sexual encounters felt different away from college. Going to a strange city apartment and taking my clothes off felt genuinely sordid and a little scary, and I didn't do it again. Living with a group helped. My roommates' sleeping presences near me soothed me at night. I began to learn how to get up every day and show up on time for my routine job, and how to set aside some of my earnings in a savings account. I began to have friends, both women and men.

When I was twenty-three, the news that my mother had cancer shattered my fledgling adult life. After an operation, she did not recover her strength. She became unable to eat, unable to cook, unable to keep the garden going. In a wild act of self-assertion she insisted to my father that he leave the house entirely. He went to stay with friends. She told me over the phone that she had reached a point where she just could not stand to have him around.

I knew that what had to happen next was for me to go home. She did not ask me to. But someone had to take care of her, and it seemed that I was the only one who could. Loch could not do it. He had gone to live in a halfway house. Alida was still in school. I moved back to New Jersey and stayed with her until the end, living in a continuous state of terror, rebellion, and grief.

I remember . . . myself: I am standing in the kitchen of our house holding a glass. I've just filled it with carrot juice, made from a carrot in our garden. I am working the garden under her intense direction every day. I am her hands, her legs, her servant. I prostrate myself to her will, I want to become her life so that she can live. I wonder how long this can go on. I wish for a man to come and save me. But then in the morning if she smiles at me when I bring her breakfast, hope for her life fills me like a great swallow of sunlight. I stand outside hanging up the wash and my heart beats its wings in hope of life. Our will can make her live.

In the room of her dying our talk became not deeper but more shallow. She could not speak aloud of what was happening to her. There could be no mention of anything that mattered, and certainly not the rape. The silence between us remained.

In the days after her death the four of us came together in the house. A strange intimacy came over us, an awareness and sharing of affection, a relief. During this time my father told Alida that our mother had been raped when she was twenty-three. I was too preoccupied with my grief to take in this revelation. I did not speak to him directly about it to ask him what he knew. It would have been too great an intimacy after the years of my sealing him off. Nor did it occur to me to ask him why she had never told me. I knew. I understood now that she had been unable to share much of herself with anyone. I knew that she had told herself that to tell me would only burden me.

Our moment of tenderness could not survive amidst the unresolved pain she had left among us and the grief we did not know how to share. There were angry outbursts. My father drank openly, whiskey in small glasses, and made no effort to rein in his wretchedness. I fled to New York, where I had been working off and on during the months of caring for my mother.

In the weeks following my mother's death I was not thinking about the rape. Yet her death brought about a change in me that soon led me into an involvement with a man who evoked the rapist more strongly than any lover before or since.

When she died I felt as though I had lost half of my very self. At the same time I felt a tremendous sense of liberation. I could walk the New York streets without thinking of how she would feel if I were hurt. If something was stolen from me I wouldn't have to endure her reproaches for my foolishness. I could go on being an impoverished young poet without being haunted by her concern for my stability and happiness. I rejoiced, guiltily, that her death had given me a large, universal, important subject to grapple with in my poems.

She was no longer around to worry or to judge. I would never again have to ask myself if what I was doing with men, or the particular man I was with, would meet with her approval. I had always agonized over her supposedly casual pronouncements about the men she had met. She had never shown enthusiasm about any of them, though she tried to disguise her reactions.

Now I experienced a powerful infusion of energy, what felt like a new self-love and passion. It was really up to me, now, to decide how I wanted to live and whom to love. I had never felt so lone, so reckless, or so invulnerable. I turned toward the first man I met who seemed out for adventure, too, and handed myself into his keeping.

He had come across the country from out West in a magical camper he had built himself. He had dark skin and hair, and dark smouldering eyes, and was well aware of their effect. He was heading up the New England coast to Canada, to see an old church he had bought for fifteen hundred dollars, sight unseen. He thought he might fix it up to live in. Would I like to come? I would.

He seemed amazed and honored by my choice. He seemed to adore me, even to worship me, and yet he represented another reincarnation of the rapist. I was quite conscious of it as I invested in him my still urgent hope of finding repair. I imagined that in the arms of this crude gypsy I might lie, white and delicate. I was not really in love with him. I saw him as an underworld god, a daimonic horse who would carry me away and give me the teaching of dark animal love. I did not imagine that he would help me, or lead me, to the full revelation of my own pleasure. Instead he would force me to it.

I did not really think rape was the same thing as rape fantasy, but I imagined that this man, because he evoked the rapist, would be able to reverse the happening of rape, by a kind of double negative. To black out a terrible blackness with a good blackness. To bring me into a darkness where I could live.

What also drew me, of course, was an urge to follow my mother into the night.

David hinted to me that he knew why I wanted to put myself under his spell. He was ready to compel me to the place I could not bring myself. He would turn me inside out. I could tell he could do it by the way he looked at me. He was forty, and introduced me to new sexual acts at twenty-three. Our first few times in bed felt messy and animal. I tried to give in to them with sheer physical abandon, not minding that I still wasn't relaxing enough to have an orgasm as part of it all.

The first jolt of reality came when we were crossing one of the big bridges out of New York. A large toolbox, which he had built of plywood and chained underneath his truck, came loose and fell, with a sharp, loud thud, on the bridge. It was a heavy chest that two small children could have fit inside. While traffic roared past us with inches to spare, we lifted it into the truck, and he crouched down to deal with the heavy chains that hung loose below. It could have been funny, had I not known, deep down, that it was the first sign of a disastrous way of life. Cursing and struggling, he did what needed to be done, while I helped. I did not like the way it felt to be around him then.

After we'd been together for a while David tried a couple of tentative sadistic gestures with me. I was willing to try letting him pinch me. Maybe that pain really could somehow draw me to a deeper pleasure. But what I felt was simply pain. His force was not erotic insistence that demanded my release. It was simply force. It might be exciting to fantasize being fucked with a certain cruelty by a mysterious lover, a way of imagining concentrated male sexual energy. I found out it was quite different to be invited to any actual performance of this kind.

We drove north to the island where his church was and camped in his truck while he worked on his new home. After a few weeks I had had enough of him. We camped on his new neighbors' land for too long, and they became furious. We were asked to watch a sailboat for new friends. David did not watch it. Things broke, and he did not fix them. It seemed an immense struggle for him to deal with the practical exigencies of life. I still understood very little of those exigencies, but I could see that he was not functioning well.

I did not want to leave the island, though. The tides in the bay swept in and out with great power, wrapped in fog and sun together. Our new friends took us out in their sailing dory; I had never sailed. Our neighbors were island people, made as strange as the people of Appalachia by poverty and isolation. David seemed able to relate to them in a way I felt I could not. It seemed that he might be leading me out of myself to join the human race.

As the summer drew to a close he wanted me to leave, to go back to New York and start earning money, since we were running out. Finally I announced to him that I did not want to live with him in New York. But he kept at me until I agreed to let him stay with me for a while when he returned. I felt sad as he waved good-bye to me through the window of the bus, a piteous figure of a man in trouble, someone who had won me and needed my help. For the last few days he had managed to sway me back into the magical atmosphere of the early days with him and persuaded me that our love was of desperate importance to both of us. This feeling lasted only a few hours longer. The bus ride from Bangor, Maine, to New York is quite a long one. By the time I reached New York, I was beginning to realize that I wanted to go on with my real life, and that that should have nothing to do with someone like him. But again he kept at me, over the phone. When he returned to New York I allowed him to move into my apartment.

Nan, the friend who had introduced me to David, started to tell me some stories. She had first met him when she had lived in the rural South. She and his then wife were pregnant at the same time. One day the wife came over to see Nan and told her that she was trying to leave David. When she had told him so, "He beat her up." After the child was born she did leave him, taking the child with her to her mother's house. Her parents had seen to it that he did not have access to his child. He had told me a sad story: his ex-wife's uptight southern family had taken his child from him. He grieved that his child would never know what it felt like to be free like him. When I asked him about Nan's story he said it wasn't true.

One night, determined to separate from him, I called Alida, who was living downtown, and asked for help to get out. She and her boyfriend picked me up and drove me to a friend's place, where I camped out for two nights while trying to affirm to David over the phone that he had to leave my apartment. The next few days were difficult. I traveled hours on the subway between my apartment on 181st Street, where I had to get clothes and other things I needed, my friend's place at the opposite end of town in SoHo, and my job in midtown. Soon I was physically exhausted. Over the phone David promised reform, a return to his best self. He hammered at my reluctance, howling out his pain, painting glorious pictures of the life we could share, now that he understood what I really wanted. I returned.

It never occurred to me that I could take a few days off work to deal with the problem, or that I might ask friends to help me get him out. I could not admit to anyone, especially myself, how much trouble I was really in.

Things got worse. One day I came home and found the door ajar; someone had stolen my flute. Years later I realized that it had probably been David's way of raising some extra cash. One day we had an argument, and he picked up a small iron skillet from the kitchen counter and threw it across the tiny room. It broke in half. Another day we had another argument, and he shoved me backward into a door. I noticed that he had done these things. When they happened, they frightened me. Yet I could not believe things like this could really happen to me, so I pretended that they had not.

It took only these two signals of violence to seal my captivity. It took very little to keep me stuck. I had tried once to break out and failed. I did not feel that I had anywhere else to go. I tried to continue with my life, imagining it as normal—going to work, the usual daily errands, working on poems sometimes in the evenings. He drove a cab at night and was rarely in the apartment.

In the spring, feeling a revival of energy, I made an appointment with a psychiatrist a friend recommended, a fatherly figure nearing retirement. He seemed kind and his office felt safe, with its two big wing chairs and a rug patterned with vines and flowers. I told him something of my situation, not even really knowing what it was I was describing.

He said, calmly and consideringly, "There are various forms of entrapment."

Entrapment. That was the word for my situation. I felt that this man understood exactly my position. And that was as far as my consciousness could go.

I left and sat awhile on a curved cement bench outside the building, a beautiful white apartment building on the Upper East Side, waiting for

David to meet me as we had arranged. Another man, a typical denizen of that part of town, wearing a dark, refined suit, sat down on the other end of the bench. David arrived and began to berate me about seeing the psychiatrist, swearing, shouting that I was making a very bad move. The man on the bench, shocked, interrupted us and asked me if I was all right, and if he could help me in any way. I said, no, it's all right. David swore at him. He got up, shrugging his shoulders, and walked away. I will always be grateful to this stranger whose action lodged a question in my mind, part of my slow, hidden accumulation of understanding.

In May, about a year after I had met David, a new friend, a painter, invited me to join her in a rented house in Vermont for the summer, where she could paint and I could write for a few weeks. I scraped together all the money I could, quit my job, and went.

In the house in Vermont I breathed freely again, in days of sun and rain and peace, hours of sitting at my desk looking out from our remote ridge at blue hills receding into the distance. I decided not to move back to New York, where I found life so difficult and wearing, but to return to Boston. I was barely conscious that what I was doing was getting away from David, that I could not face him. I simply noticed, in the back of my mind, that one advantage of going to Boston was that he would not come.

I abandoned to him not just my apartment but the whole city of New York.

A month after my mother died, not long before I met David, I joined my first poetry workshop and came under the influence of my first serious writing teacher. My one subject was my mother's death, and this teacher honored it. It began to seem as though that subject might make a poet of me.

A year later, in the fresh air and peace of my retreat with my painter friend in Vermont, I discovered joy in writing and studying poetry every day. Most of the poems I attempted there never fulfilled themselves, as is usual. The following vague sketch about the rape was among those. It was the first poem I tried to write about the rape after the one I wrote at thirteen.

Rape at Thirteen

In that time of life
before the dawn of real things
when we know some of the words

she could speak it: "rape"—
but it was really a conspiracy,
a dark, permitted "love."

I know better now.
I see the daydreaming girl,
long-legged, with her bike,

the dirt road. A sick, brawny man.
She was an easy reed to split.

And I see now the secret arms
reaching from earth, holding her firm

through the strange, innocent pain.

Tentatively, and half consciously, my work to understand what had happened to me had begun. I was twenty-five.

Writing was, for me, a first therapy. When I came home after being raped, I quickly jumped past my first impulse, to be comforted by my mother, to my second, most natural urge: to inform the world. Just as naturally, at twenty-five, the urge to share my pain was wholly bound up with my desire to perform—to justify myself, or do well, in the eyes of the world. It did not occur to me, *I might want to talk to a therapist about this rape thing.* I began to see a therapist when I moved back to Boston, but I did not talk with her about the rape.

Even when I wrote other poems asserting a connection between having been raped and having troubles with men, I felt I was working with the rape in a literary way. I was more interested in it as a metaphor than as a memory. I put these poems in a folder labeled "Rape Poems." They remained separate from my other work, unfinished. In the folder I also filed a dream precipitated by an encounter I'd had with David, who'd come to Boston to try to win me back.

December 30, 1980

> This is the second night in a row I've dreamed of rape. The night before, I was walking down a country road. . . . Young country men, two of them, surprised me somehow and attacked me. But I was not afraid, I jumped warmly into the arms of one who was tall, thin, blond, a very sinewy, tough body, named Don, and we made love in a series of very warm sexual scenes, the longest I've ever remembered from a dream. But last night, it was a young black teenager, who didn't look very threatening. But . . . I chased him and pinned him down behind a brick apartment building . . . and I broke his little finger. It was not an easy job, I had to really bear down on it like a tough stick, but I kept at it and finally it broke off, and I saw the finger broken, the bone in the center, a tan color, and bloody flesh in a ring around it, on both pieces, next to each other as the piece I'd broken hung there. He yelled in pain, and the yell was good to my ears.

The violence of this dream was rare and striking, so disturbing that I tried to make it into a poem. Something about David had brought my buried horror and rage to the surface. But I could not leave that horror and rage to stand by themselves in the poem; I had to affirm the survival of the child's innocence and the healing power of nature.

I continued to write about the rape not as memory, but more as if I were reinventing it. The poems spoke bravely about my rape but they were, at the same time, acts of denial. They required happy, hopeful endings in a way my other poems did not.

Three years later I decided to go to graduate school in New York to develop my writing. While there I began seeing a second therapist who gently led me further and further into the emotional truth of my parents' abandonments of me. I began to recognize and name in my family the patterns described by many psychologists as typical of alcoholism. Since my mother's death my father had gradually lapsed into a more or less continual stupor of drinking and forgetfulness. One Thanksgiving I attended, at the suggestion of a writer friend, an Al-Anon meeting for "adult children of alcoholics." It had dawned on me, at this family time, that my mother was literally gone, my father was gone in spirit, my brother was long lost to both alcohol and mental illness, and my sister and I, unable to empathize with each other in our mutual sense of abandonment, were estranged.

"I've just realized," I said to this roomful of sad strangers, "I don't have a family," and found myself in tears. Following the usual practice of Al-Anon meetings, others described similar feelings. Surprising myself, I felt recognized and understood. Sad as they were, these people were fit companions for my grief.

Attending Al-Anon meetings was a crucial step. Before I found them, I had friends, and I had a therapist. I had begun seeing a man who was caring and affectionate. But still I had not really felt as though anyone understood me. In the meetings I began to feel empathy for the first time, in barely known, veiled, and passing moments, and my inner sense of my relationship with the world began to evolve. Instead of feeling *Nobody knows how I'm hurting,* it became *We're all in this together.* Many people's pain sounded worse than my own. I found myself feeling a mixture of concern, powerlessness, and indifference toward them. I began to understand the failure of the people around me to help me in the past.

I began to know that I was all right, and I began to make up my mind to the idea that I was a worthy and adequate person, capable of love.

While working on my first book of poems for my graduate thesis, I pulled out "Rape at Thirteen" and looked at it again. I saw what I had been trying to say but could not, five years earlier at twenty-five, and finished the poem.

TESTIMONY

At thirteen I could use words
like *death, bankruptcy, making love.*
the doctor, the nurse, the two policemen needed
words from me, and I gave them. I told
a clear story: his stocking mask, the rock
in his hand, my dress—short, red, with yellow flowers—
the parts and the whole, what he said, what I said,
what we both did and did not do.

Preliminary hearing was a word
I did not know. *It's not a trial,*
the prosecutor said, choosing his words.
It's just to establish what happened.
I was as smart as he, so cool on the witness stand
he chose to startle me. *And what did he*
do then? the prosecutor asked.

Where I Stopped

He raped me. The word
jumped out of my throat, and the questions stopped.

For years I thought: *rape*—a conspiracy.
Only he and I knew
just how it had been between us
in the woods, where even the rabbits
lay without moving in the August heat.
No one knew, I thought, the ways
our act had mimicked
love. His clumsy
thumb on my nipple, his murmur, *Ever fooled around*
like this with anybody before?

But they did know. When they heard my story
grown-ups saw: the long-legged girl
pushing her beat-up bike on a steep road,
the short, husky man in white T-shirt walking
quickly up behind her as she turned
and stopped
like a stiff deer.
Grown-ups could not help seeing
her private parts in detail,
the little stream of semen and blood
that fell when she stood up after he left.

Grown-ups did not see the secret arms
that reached around me out of the earth,
which continually nurses the grass
like a mother. As I lay down for him
earth nursed me against its flat body

knobby with tiny stones and roots of grass.
As he slit me, earth twined around me
such a binding love
I was not destroyed
and years of healing began on the same day.

Somehow I was now able to communicate my experience in a work that contained its complexity in a complete whole. Was it a growth in self-knowing that made that possible, or was it the poem's own call on me that drew me to complete my understanding? It is impossible to say which movement was stronger, but it remained true that the healing I wrote about was still more a promise to myself than a reality.

The rape began to claim my full attention a few years later, after I had returned to Boston. A friend I was living with began to come to terms with her memories of childhood incest. I witnessed Liza's slow labor to uncover what had happened to her, and to learn how to live with this knowledge and share it with others. I was moved by her courage.

Uneasily I sometimes turned upon my own memory some of the same kind of attention I was giving hers. What if some of the same problems were operating in my experience? Mine had never been a secret—or had it? I had not been betrayed by my parents, abused by the ones who loved me—but perhaps had my injury been in a way swept under the rug? I was not eager to explore these questions, but I was glad that because I too had been sexually injured in childhood, I could be in some way a comrade of Liza's hard passage.

One day she told me excitedly about a training for women she'd found out about, called Model Mugging. "It's a self-defense course for women," she said. "But not like any other. A martial arts teacher found out that a lot of his women students, when they were actually attacked, became paralyzed and could not use the skills he'd taught them. So he developed a new way of teaching women how to fight. They have men who wear protective padding and actually mug you, and you learn to fight back full force. The instructors are all women. They help you get past whatever blocks you have. If you have abuse in your past, it can also be healing."

When I heard this news, something in me sat up and looked around. I had begun to sense that a large, solid, knobby feeling was constantly bulking inside me. I realized it was anger. It seemed it had been there for a long time, cutting off too much of my breath and my voice. I had begun to experiment with talking about it and expressing it. Now the idea of being able to fight with a man and win excited me greatly. It would be great to know that if I were ever attacked again I would know what to do and be able to do it.

I knew I was signing up not just to learn how to fight, but to face the rape in a new way. In the Model Mugging class, having been raped would be the central and most relevant aspect of my identity. I dreaded it but I had a feeling the time had come.

Sure enough, in our second class we met in our instructor's living room and were encouraged to share our experiences of sexual abuse, if we had any and felt we wanted to. If a real attack came it was likely to stir up the old terror. If we shared that memory with our companions now and took in their recognition and concern for us in this room, we would feel their support more strongly whenever we had to fight again.

I was glad to be able to tell my fighting companions about what had happened to me and to feel their caring. Their listening did give me a deepened feeling that they were firmly behind me each time I walked out onto the mat to fight. At the same time I noticed that I had remembered quite a lot about my experience in a way that no one else in the class seemed to remember theirs. It occurred to me that there might be some good in this. Maybe I should write it all down.

Each time I fought my "mugger" to the ground, delivering several kicks to his padded head that would disable a normally clothed assailant, I left the mat exhilarated and exalted by the focused exercise of rage. Sometimes powerful feelings of grief or even sexual feelings were released. Why had no one ever told us what fighting is really like?

During one class those of us who'd once been attacked or abused were invited to set up a reenactment of our experience, with the chance this time to fight back. For a split second, as my attacker approached me, I knew myself on Quarry Road, facing the rapist. Rage surged in my body, an absolute, physical certainty that what was about to happen was wrong. With my mouth and throat and every cell of my being I yelled *No*, and delivered blows that felt superhuman, releasing tremendous energies through the action of my body.

That fighting rage began to enter my poetry, bringing with it indigestible, unpalatable emotion: blame, self-pity. I blamed the people around me for not helping me to heal after the rape. I described it in more horrible terms. Now I could not see how to end the poems.

They could not end, because they were a beginning. A few months later I went upstairs to my study to begin a summer of writing. I had been caught up in the demands of my job, teaching writing at a small women's college in Boston, and did not remember my story as clearly when I told it to the women in the class. I sat down at my computer without a plan, and it all began to tell itself as if it had been waiting for the right opening.

The energy of my story ran strong and I knew it would not flag before

I had finished the whole telling. Suddenly it seemed I had become able to write in a way I never had before. I would write my story in sentences, paragraphs, longer pieces; maybe this was a book. I was launched on a big new project and a new phase of life, as prose author.

I was thirty-four.

I was now married. We had met a few years earlier on a blind date. A friend told me her husband had a friend who was a carpenter, who seemed very sweet, and who was looking to have a serious relationship. She had been touched by his willingness to fix something right away that had urgently needed fixing. Would I be interested? Yes.

Eric arrived at my apartment late on a hot Sunday morning in June. He came in the door and stood in my kitchen, wearing clean blue jeans and a flannel shirt. He was tall and slim and had large brown eyes, a mustache, and a mop of wild black curls. When we greeted each other, shaking hands, he gazed at me a moment with a look that was sweet, light, and serious all at once. The warmth of his presence relaxed me; it was as though he were meeting the sister of an old friend. As I looked back at him, finding it easy, I saw the qualities in his face: honesty, bravery, intelligence, kindness. His eyes shone with friendliness and a twinkle of humor at our mutual first inspection. His quality of being was different from any man I'd met before.

My heart turned over and then, as if everything was now settled, grew very still.

In that instant I experienced in my whole self a new feeling: that everything in my life was going to turn out okay. I thought to myself, *This guy's all right.*

We drove to a beach near Boston and spent the day there talking about our work, our lives, and our families. I found that he had a sister who was mentally ill, something we shared. He said that he was a Quaker, a member of the Cambridge Society of Friends, and told me how he had come to join them. I told him about my writing and its central importance in my life. When I grew chilly in the slanting sun, to warm me up he playfully heaped sand over me until I was completely encased.

On our next date he brought me a handful of purple irises and took me swimming at a pond he knew about. We swam together across the cool, deep water. At the far end of the pond he pulled himself up on some rock ledges shaded by overhanging trees. Gently pulling me up after him, inviting me to sit in front of him, he encircled me lightly with his arms. His embrace awakened in me a sweet, childlike trust. Finally had come what I had yearned for since I was eleven, the simple feeling of being safely held.

That evening he showed me his house, a big Victorian mansion he shared with two couples and their children who were also members of Quaker meeting. They welcomed me warmly for dinner. Later he proposed in a lighthearted way that we spend the night together. I hesitated. This man who I barely knew seemed to know exactly the kinds of gestures I could not resist. Was he really as caring toward me as he seemed?

"You're pretty smooth, you know," I blurted.

"Oh, I have to tell you, then," he said. "I'm really, really excited about meeting you. I haven't been this excited about anyone I've ever met. I'm completely serious. My intentions are completely honorable."

We laughed. We both knew that we were serious about each other. We retreated to his bedroom under the eaves.

As I got ready for bed I felt unusually calm, almost as if I were staying overnight with a woman friend. In his bed he waited for me, leaning back against the wall. I kneeled there and faced him. We took each other in.

I said, "There's something I think I should tell you before we make love. I was raped when I was thirteen, and I think it must have affected me somehow sexually, but I'm really not sure how, and I'm not sure how it might affect what it's like when we make love, but I just thought I should mention it, because I just want you to know."

He sat up, his eyes widening with surprise. There was a silence. Then he looked at me with a softness and concern such as I'd never seen in the eyes of anyone.

"This is serious," he said. "It seems like we should really talk about this and make sure we don't just run right over it."

"I guess so," I said, looking down. Inside I felt like a little band had struck up a tune.

"What do you want to do? Do you think maybe we should wait? Do you want to tell me about it?"

I did want to tell him about it. He listened. When my brief story was finished he took me in his arms, held me tight, and said, "I'm so sorry that happened to you."

I did not cry, as I might have wanted to, then. My heart was beating fast because I knew that finally I had found a person with whom I could feel that I belonged.

Soon afterward I moved in with him and took up my work in a beautiful front room of the big house. On weekends we explored the nature reserves around Boston, spending long afternoons walking in the woods or floating around a pond in a borrowed canoe. We often arrived late for dinner, sunburned, famished, and in love. Our housemates teased us.

Sometimes he took me to see houses he was working on and introduced me to their owners. I saw that he understood not only houses but people and their relationships with their houses and instinctively tended not the house as such but this relationship. Most of his clients had become his friends, and many of his friends had become his clients, an arrangement that seemed happy all around.

In the evenings he played with the children in the household—hide-and-seek with the younger girl; painting pictures, playing with wood, and silk-screening T-shirts with the older girl. On Sundays he packed into his truck all the elements of his shop that children could use and drove to Friends' Meeting to teach "first-day" or Sunday school.

I understood why the children were happy around him. When I was with Eric I was in sunshine.

When I came out of my study dazed from the hours absorbed in drawing up words from the inner well, he would say, "Let's go for a walk by the ocean." We walked along the harbor pier where the water of the bay lapped gently, while kids on bicycles, dogs on leashes, joggers in headphones, and elderly people in windbreakers paraded around us. As we crossed the bridge where a row of men and boys leaned over the rail and fished, or sat on the grassy slope overlooking the bay with cardboard plates of fried clams in our laps, I would come back to the world and him.

RECOGNITION

For the first few months I wrote my memories of the rape with what felt like an uncanny ease. Like a magician with words, I was transforming the intangible past into something fixed and reliable on a page. This activity gave me a reassuring sense of control over what I was remembering.

Gradually it stopped working. I kept on, though. I had fought with my experience before in similar ways—at thirteen when I insisted on right away telling the police what had happened to me, at fourteen when I proclaimed it in my poem in English class, and in my twenties when I tried simply to make out of it poems that would be good poems.

After more than a year of writing, reluctantly I paused. I had to face and admit to myself that something was going on. It felt as if my remembering had awakened a force inside me that was forbidding me to go any further. I had written down a lot of what happened. I had thought that in being able to see and describe all the details I would be able to tell the complete story. But the story was not coming together, and inside me it felt like things were beginning to come apart.

I knew now that there was a Martha who had been damaged and injured by rape. But I still had no sense of really knowing her or of being able to find her. I had evidence of her existence, a partial sense of her based on feelings that I remembered, but most of her remained hidden, and how she had cooperated with other developing selves of me, exactly what she had told them about the world and what they believed, was also still hidden. After my writing of all my recollections, my mind still held the rape in a sealed compartment.

Surely if I found this girl, in the inner landscape of myself, she would be standing frozen, staring straight ahead, afraid. Her lips would be closed, and her eyes would see only hurt coming to her—they were incapable of seeing help. In her universe, there was no help.

Something cut me off, as if she were immured inside me in the forbidden room of a fairy tale, its door coated with dust, fast shut. All the stories I'd told about the rape, especially to myself, had been invented outside that door. I had sealed it as a teenager, intending it never to be disturbed. If I heaved the door open, what would happen? The room of the rape—what was it like in there?

I decided to forget about telling my story to anyone else for a while and just use writing to explore emotional reverberations within myself—to seek the hidden, wordless memories of the heart.

I began with the question: *What is in the way?*

From inside, the answer came.

I wrote:

Anger. It's all inside me—
the silence—
the wordless need—
and because there was no help for me—
rage.

Who was I angry at?
I thought of my mother, the ways she had not helped me.

She did not see that my breasts were growing, she refused to buy me a bra. And when I was raped, we didn't talk about it.

> She acted as if nothing had happened.
>
> Years went by. She stood aside, watched me and hoped.
>
> And when I got a diaphragm and told her about it, proudly announcing the beginning of my sexual life, she wrote me a scathing letter.

I remembered that even at the time, at thirteen, and afterward, through the years, whenever I thought about these things, I forgave my mother whatever she had not done. Yet it remained true that as I lay on the bed next to her the night of the rape, I was not comforted. Underneath my numb acceptance of our separateness, the questions must have stirred.

> I know I did wonder:
>
> *Why aren't we talking?*

Why did she not at some point just take me in her arms? I asked myself, even as I remembered my awkwardness when she did try to reach out.

Why didn't she try harder?

> She should have said to me, "We love you, we will not let him take away your self-respect, your soul. We will stay with you. You can be mended."

As I imagined it I could see the impossibility of what I wanted her to have done. It would be hard to say how she could have preserved my soul, let alone promised to preserve it.

But what mattered here was what I'd felt and not let myself know:

I wanted my mother to heal me.

And what if she had believed of herself simply that she *could comfort* me? She would not have had to make that little speech, in words.

I realized that back further, before wondering why she was not talking to me, I wondered where she was.

He is coming up the road toward behind me
he is leading me back into the bushes
I am going with him
because I can't believe no one will come to save me.
Where is she?

Where was she? She was at home taking a nap. While I was being raped, she was sleeping.

Now I saw it like a myth: the mother sleeps while the daughter is raped. Only a half mile away she lies in her bedroom. It was a pastoral: I imagined her much younger, not forty-five about to turn forty-six but a young mother sleeping soundly and sweetly under a tree. An evil being comes and seduces her little girl at her play, and during this moment the little girl is irrevocably harmed. Then the mother wakes up, and is grief-stricken. She rails against the gods when she discovers what has happened. But it's too late. She roams the earth and will let nothing flourish.

> She was my mother. What are mothers for? They are to protect their young from predators, to fight the predator when the young cannot, are not strong enough. I let him come, bewildered and surprised like a chick whose mother just happens to be looking the other way for a moment.

I never really *thought* that she should have been there on the road to protect me. But a deeper, more childish part of me *knew* that she should have been.

> There on the road I am alone with him, she is not with me.
>
> How does this feel?
>
> *She must just not care about me.*

I remembered an earlier close call I'd had with death, at an afternoon party I'd gone to with my father when I was five. I was playing in the swimming pool, pulling myself around the edge of the pool by holding on to the ropes that were looped along the sides. Proud that I had gone all the way around to the deep end, I hung on the ropes just below where my father was sitting, hoping that he would see me. But then my hand slipped from the rope and I felt myself going down under the surface, my nose and mouth taking in water.

"Fred!" I tried to yell, but panic made my voice feeble.

Water caught in my nose and throat.

"Fred! Help!"

He sat gazing straight ahead, drink in hand, and did not see me. He was talking with the person next to him and was not watching. After a few seconds I grabbed the rope again and saved myself.

They must just not care about me.

I remembered again the night of the rape, myself staring into the darkness of my closet, my mother asking me how I was feeling, myself saying, "I feel very old." I asked myself *What was going on there, in me, deep down? Do I have any sense of it that I can recall?*

> I stand looking into the closet.
> Inside me there is a yearning, a terrible sadness.

I remembered myself putting my clothes away like an automaton, very slowly, unbelieving, my mind slowed to first gear as it tried to absorb and make sense of what had happened.

> She asks me how I feel and I can feel that something has drained away out of me, I remember his penis like a knife made out of shit hurting my vagina. I'm withdrawn into myself, distracted and taken over by this hurt. I am sinking down into a very dark place. Inside me is now a realm of darkness, of horror and no-hope.
>
> I am wondering why I am not crying. But the daze seems to have absorbed the need to cry, to have taken over the part of me that would cry.

I remembered again what it felt like to wake up the next morning.

I slept, and when I woke up in the daylight, I woke up into nightmare.

I must hold my eyes open and walk forward in this real world, the house, the kitchen, the library, with trees outside.

I was untouched, without help, I was in a void where nothing could reach me.

I go and sit down with the detectives. I answer them as clearly as I can. As I answer them I come back to everything. I can come back, and no one seems to notice that I am not all here.

I could do these things, I said the words, I returned to the world. But doing these things was not facing the darkness. They were not a fight against the darkness, they were distractions from fighting.

I asked myself, *What happened to the darkness?*

I forgot it.

Yet I did not ever really forget it.

And because my mother, my father, the detectives, my teachers, and my schoolmates did not know how it had been in this darkness, because I was alone, and because I was left there by everyone around me, who looked at me and decided that I was fine:

What dried up in me was love.

I understood: How could I believe that caring was a real thing, when those who supposedly cared about me had not tried to save me?

During the days of these discoveries I became unable to perform even simple ordinary tasks like hanging up my clothes or cooking a meal. I couldn't stand to be near the friends I lived with in my house.

Their voices are noise that hurts my mind.

Thinking it might help to be outdoors, I went for a walk at the ocean with Eric and Liza. Liza began to talk of the abuse she suffered as a child. I felt myself sinking into my own silence, my separateness. Yet something was struggling to the surface and I felt I must try to speak of how I was feeling. The words came out wrong and unclear: I heard myself asking her not to talk about her experiences right now.

I wanted to say, "I too am in pain."

I could not say it.

I felt I must help Liza, but now there was no helping in me. Instead, I realized, this sense of *I must help Liza* was stirring up a rage that was frightening me, leaving me inarticulate.

Thinking that action might help when I had no words, I climbed to the little attic room in our house where a punching bag hung that Liza used. Scrounging behind the bookshelf I pulled out the plastic bat and started whacking the bag. The impacts made a sharp crack that was strangely sweet to my ears.

Soon they surfaced, the words I needed to speak—not to Liza, but to my mother.

"Get out of my face."

"Give me some room."

Your problems are not more important than mine.

I've been raped, dammit—don't you see?

I pounded the bag lamely, speaking sullenly, not yelling. Tears started and I was crying. It was mine, this enraged despair. Wildly I hit and hit and hit until I was dazed and my arms began to sag, a matter of only a few minutes or even seconds. I let the bat drop into the old chair.

I walked around a little and felt the lightness of release.

Get out of my face, Mom. Fuck your nervous breakdown, and your alcoholic husband, and your problem son. Fuck your problems. Fuck your anger about having to take care of us. Fuck your sadness about my leaving home. You worried about me endlessly, but what did you do? *Fuck your pathos, fuck your heroism. Nice try, Mom, to take care of me after I was raped. You couldn't accept my sexuality, and you couldn't handle my pain, because you thought that if you really took care of me, you wouldn't be able to take care of yourself. You could have helped me but you let it go. So fuck you, Mom.*

I wrote:

> In this rage is my resurrection.

My anger both frightened and exhilarated me. I felt unwilling to leave it for the deeper emotions of hurt and grief. Yet the anger itself seemed to hold that gate open, refusing to give up the effort to connect with my own deeper self.

> The anger arises from my becoming conscious of my wound—of what the rapist did to me, and of how my mother taught me to think always, first, of her.

It felt like grasping the heart of what happened, to place my rage toward my mother at the center of the pain. I knew it would be untruthful to blame her wholly. But my rage was not fair to her. My rage was concerned not at all with what she needed but only with what I needed. At this juncture it was my best guide.

I asked myself, *Has any raped child ever been well served by the people around her?*

> What if there were some healer, an older woman who could embrace the hurt one and somehow affirm to her that even then, while in the infernal dark, she was accompanied, that she could be healed? (And is this true?)
>
> Would there be some incantation this woman could say, to sing away the sense of invasion? Could it be drawn out of the child, sung out, like pulling out a great psychic splinter?

For it did seem to me now as though I had been rent by a splinter—a great sharp thing that had penetrated my vagina and became fixed within me, sticking up into me with its point in my heart. Stiff, taking up a lot of room, aching, and working its way in further in response to certain experiences and actions of my own. A hard, interfering knowledge, there all the time, though I had tried to ignore it.

> A splinter made of pain, disgust, and a sense of being able to see no light in the morning, and no joy in the gift of life; a hardness dwelling inside me, and within that hardness a nothingness.

I read *Female Adolescence*, by Katherine Dalsimer, and found some words about the early adolescent struggle to separate from one's parents that helped me to understand myself.

> Those who, in the magical thinking of childhood, had been endowed with omniscience and omnipotence must now be reduced to human scale. . . . The suddenness and intensity with which childhood feelings toward the parents may be reversed is a measure of how urgent is the need to create distance where once there had been closeness. . . . It is not achieved without considerable sadness and pain, which have been likened to that of mourning. . . . The comparison is an evocative one, suggesting the intensity of the grief and the deep subjective sense of loss.

When I read this passage I began to wonder if my whole consciousness had got stuck on the point of making this separation. My mother had remained omniscient and all-powerful, magically godlike, to me until her death when I was twenty-three. I had felt rebellious at times. But I had never really let go of her and the magic world I remembered we had shared when I was a child.

> I cling to my memories of childhood and never can accept that it is gone. I have been in a sort of continual state of mourning.

I wondered how much this sense I had of having lost something crucial when childhood passed could be identified as a normal part of growing up:

the loss of the illusion of a safe world, the loss of the faith in the parents' ability to handle everything perfectly.

To what extent had my experience been like most people's? Did some of my mourning for my childhood perhaps have to do with having been raped?

> After the rape I wanted to go on believing that my parents knew everything about how to proceed. But inside, I knew they did not know what to do.

It occurred to me that my loss had been too sudden, and perhaps I had not been able to accept it in the way that others do, gradually, as the years of adolescence go by. Perhaps I had been unable to move on because my loss had been too extreme, too wrong a manifestation of the world's danger. The illusion of my parents' omnipotence and omniprotection had had too drastic an end.

> My mother knew that she had failed me, had not been able to sing the splinter out of me, even though we pretended that there was no splinter. It was impossible for me to feel I could rely on her; yet with both of us knowing how much I needed her, it was impossible for us to let each other go.
>
> I could neither come to her, nor go from her. Altogether, I was forced too early on my own resources, lacking a sense of security in them. I managed well with those resources, but my connections with others were exceedingly difficult and confused.

This, then, was one way I could understand what happened inside me at the time of the rape: it was an *exaggeration* of what occurs to everybody.

The grief I experienced, in having to give up my sense or myth of safety, was *like* the grief of everyone who has passed through adolescence. The virginity that I lost *was*, in some sense, like everyone's virginity.

To what extent my losses were normal, and to what extent my trauma isolated me from a common experience, I could not sort out at thirteen, and could not now.

I looked again at the memory of myself rising from bed, walking into the library, and meeting with the detectives. There was something about me doing those things that was not all wrong.

> How did I handle the inner oppression, and the demands that were being made on me?
>
> I acted.

I had done it the day before, too, from the first moment of telling my mother. This had all been for me a kind of command performance.

I had been seeing this performance as a terrible moment when I had given up the "truth" of my suffering. Now it came to me that being an actress had also meant devising my own part, from my own resources, as I went along.

> There was strength in my acting. I was not a character whom things were only done to.
>
> What the police and the courtroom required of me went against my instinctive sense of how I needed to play the drama. I did not

> accept that fact, though. I adapted to it by *pretending to myself,* secretly, that I was in charge of the drama. It was I who commanded that the police be called, I who knew that a trial must happen. I was deciding where everyone belonged, telling them when to come on and off stage, what to say.

This realization affirmed once more my resilience, the resilience I'd always been so proud of. Yes, the silencing had been terrible, but I had not completely given in.

I remembered now:

> I did imagine, faintly, that after I had done my performance I would take off my mask.

I did have a sense that I was *deferring* something so that I could get through the immediacies of the situation. In a deeply hidden place in my consciousness, I anticipated that at some point I would return to the pain.

> I had a vague hope that I would sit with some kind person and talk about it, and maybe cry.
>
> I wished I had been able to do it with Mom when I'd first come home. I told her that I had done it with Allen. I tried to do it with Nora. I tried to do it each time I told a man about the rape half hoping that I might be able to really feel it as I told it. *I knew that I needed to take the mask off.* But the more time went by, the further away that possibility seemed.

As I wrote this it came to me that I had never really given this wish up. I still had it, a longing to go back, to cry with someone, to let it all come out.

> And this is now impossible, and has been impossible for many years. Whatever crying I can do now, and feeling of the pain, it is an old pain, and an old moment, and my crying will have more to do with memory than with the reality.

On August 13, the anniversary of the day I had been raped twenty-two years earlier, the event felt much closer in time to me than that. I felt a need to sit down and make some sort of reckoning. Where had I come to in my exploration? What was I really about here?

The answer came:

> I'm telling a story—a story I don't know yet.

In my story, what did I want to say the rape really had meant?

> If this tale is a moral one, I can't decide what I want the moral to be. I keep going back and forth about how I want to see myself. One day I'm the hero, girl martyred but still able to respond to rape with an imaginative power of her own. The next day I'm the victim, the girl is sentenced to a stunted, damaged life.

I know I need something more down-to-earth. I am myself, not these images. I am not a character in a book.

I am looking for some sense of truth, or reality, that is not—moral? To transcend my preoccupation with these opposites.

And not to forget it (the rape). Not to "move on." Not to "have healed myself."

I think of just being. Not being obsessed with how badly I was hurt, or the need to contradict that by affirming how brave and resourceful I was. Just the act of trying to write these things makes them sound somehow pretentious. I think what I need is to reach a lower level, where it simply doesn't matter. Not that I was raped—but how I should present myself to myself.

To think of walking away—to remember the injury of that moment, of him ripping into me, and to walk away, now, from that, saying *it doesn't matter*—it might sound like the most callous thing, or a return to the denial with which I had suppressed admitting, for so many years, that I had really been hurt. But I knew that wasn't the gesture I was making.

I was hurt.

It took twenty years to acknowledge this to myself. And it does not matter.

The compassionate one, the nurse, might say, "You do not need to trouble your *mind* over what happened to you. You were hurt—and at the same time, you lived—you live, and the difficulties presented by life to you are not so very different from what everyone else faces. You will not be a hero, but only one of many who have, in their own ways, lived, after great hurt, and chosen, in their own way, what their lives will mean to them."

> It doesn't matter, to choose victim feeling or hero feeling. What matters is that it happened.

I felt there was something special about this realization, having to do with the way others had told their own stories about my being raped, or told no stories about it, which had led me to become confused about whether, in a sense, it had actually happened at all.

What was coming to me now was not a sense of ownership, it was just a sense of having been there at the time. Which, at the time, I did not have.

> Now, I know that *I* was there. It was I who was there lying on that ground, and it was my body. The child I was then no longer exists. But I was there. I saw, I heard, I was touched. I lay down, I stood up, I walked, I felt the sun on my skin and the dust on my bare feet.
>
> Lying there, having yielded almost all my power to him, how could I endure to be me while he was hurting? I could not; instead I told a story about it to myself.
>
> Now, I do believe it.

My long debate with myself over whether I had been badly or not so badly damaged had dissolved, in this simple coming to know that rape had really happened, and to me.

Feeling that I had come to an important stage of seeing, I asked myself, *What would I want to pass on to others?*

I might say, You may have to go over and over it in your mind and your memory, because they don't know how to help you. (And only you can really know what happened.)

One day it may dawn on you that it really did happen, and it happened to you, and you really were hurt. You will no longer need to decide whether to see yourself as victim, or hero, or both. Then your own pain will not matter to you in quite the same way.

You will not be "healed"—cured.

But your consciousness can embrace the whole of your hurt self.

When starting work on the book, I had obtained, through interlibrary loan at the college where I worked, a microfilm of the trial transcript from the archives of the state of New Jersey. I had copied all five hundred pages of it onto paper and stored it in a box in a closet.

For years—since I was twenty-five—I had thought now and then of obtaining this transcript, wondering what it might reveal. Might it fill gaps in my memory? Might it restore to me a clearer sense of who I had been in the courtroom and what I had done? What speech had I used, at fourteen, to talk about what had happened to me?

I felt a strong curiosity to read this document, yet a certain dread held me back. Opening this box of gray photocopies, like the closed room within myself, could also release something of *her,* the Martha who had been raped, whose hurt I now was beginning to better know and understand. I had a feeling I was going to find out more about that hurt and I didn't want to.

Finally I opened it.

Mr. Rittenhouse began his questioning by asking me to tell about the trip I had taken on August 13, 1968—my visit with Betsy Retivov and my setting out for home. Under his direction, I drew a map and marked the route I had traveled, and answered many questions about it, leading up to the place on Quarry Road where I had stopped.

I described the man who had come out of the woods behind me.

Now, what happened then?

He ran up to me, told me not to drop my bike, and lay the bike down for me, and he grabbed me around the waist and started to drag me to the other side of the road.

Did he say anything at this time, Martha?

He didn't. He said, "Don't drop your bike," as if he didn't want me to make any noise.

MR. BERNHARD: Repeat the answer?

"Don't drop your bike," he said, and he didn't say anything else, just mumbled and signaled—

Speak a little louder, Martha.

He signaled for me to go to the other side of the road and started to drag me across.

Now, how far did he drag you?

Back into the woods for a few feet, about twenty feet.

And at this time did he say anything? . . .

Yes.

What did he say?

He asked me if I was a virgin several times.

What did you say?

I said no, and that I was only thirteen years old.

Now, did you say "no" the first time he asked you?

Yes.

Then what happened?

Then he made me take off my clothes, blindfolded me, tied my hands, and he began to rape me.

Now, did you say anything at this point?

Yes, since he asked me several times whether I was a virgin, I thought maybe if I weren't a virgin he wouldn't commit the act, so I told him that I wasn't a virgin, but it didn't make any difference.

Well now, Martha, did you tell him you were a virgin or you were not a virgin the first time he asked?

The first time I said I was, the first time I said I was.

And then after he continued to ask you that you say you changed your answer?

Yes, sir.

Why did you say you did that?

Because I thought maybe a virgin would have a special attraction to him.

And what happened then?

Then he raped me.

Did you say anything at all to him, Martha, with respect to whether he would take your life or not take your life?

Yes, I asked him several times not to kill me.

Why did you say, do that?

Because I believed he was going to kill me.

I told how I had put on my sweater and walked home with my bike.

And when you got home who was there?

My parents.

What did you do?

I put my bike away underneath the overhang of the house, and asked my father if my mother was home and he said, he said she was taking a nap in her bedroom. So I went into her bedroom and told her that I had been raped.

And what did she do at that time?

She reacted and I can't remember what she said.

What did she do, or did she or your father do anything?

She comforted me, comforted me, and I said that I wanted to tell, tell them, my parents, everything I knew right away, everything before I forgot.

Here, I noticed, my speech had faltered most—not when I told about the rape, but when I told about coming home to my mother.

Mr. Rittenhouse asked me to look at Frank Miller.

> I want you, Martha, to look at the man that is seated at the defense table, and I want you to tell me whether or not you can say at this point that man does or does not look like the man you saw on August 13 that performed this deed.
>
> *No, I can't.*
>
> You cannot say.
>
> *No.*

I was shown the clothes I'd worn that day and asked to identify them.

> Now, do you or do you not recognize that as the brassiere you were wearing on August 13?
>
> *I do.*
>
> Now, I show you, Martha, a red dress, cotton in material, and ask whether you recognize that item of clothing.
>
> *Yes.*
>
> How do you recognize it, Martha?
>
> *By the pattern.*
>
> Would you care to examine it, please?

Yes, it is the same dress.

I show you a cotton item of clothing and ask whether that item of clothing is familiar to you, Martha.

Yes, sir, that is a pair of underpants.

Would you care to examine them, please?

Underpants, yes.

Martha, do you recognize this pair of pants as your own?

Yes, sir.

And is it similar to or is it the pair of pants that you were wearing on August 13, 1968?

Yes, it is.

It is similar to it?

Yes.

There was trouble about my underpants.

MR. BERNHARD: My only questions, Your Honor, it may be a technical question, but Mr. Rittenhouse asked the question: Is it similar to it? That's not the point we are concerned with. There could have been four million cotton underpants in that particular size in that particular area that looked like them in a soiled condition.

THE COURT: Can she positively say they were hers, her size?

Could you give a description as best you can, Martha, of the pants that you were wearing on August 13, 1968?

White cotton and elastic waistband, this brand, Carter, and this size.

This is the brand of the pants that you were wearing that day?

Yes, sir.

Is that the size you were wearing that day?

Yes, sir.

MR. RITTENHOUSE: Your Honor, if there is objection—

THE COURT: Do you believe they are your pants, cotton, underpants?

Yes, sir.

MR. BERNHARD: No objection.

THE COURT: No objection, S-14 in evidence.

As I read I was surprised to see how simply I spoke. I had remembered myself telling a great, long tale of my ordeal and my journey back to the world with my responsible message. What appeared on the page was strangely small and limited.

My words revealed little of the turmoil going on within me. I was even capable of affirming minutiae about my underpants in front of an audience of strangers, as if I felt no embarrassment. As an adult I could see that this matter violated my privacy. Reading it, I felt embarrassed and angry.

At thirteen I knew, rightly, that the people in the courtroom saw my bravery, both in helping to catch Miller and in publicly telling what I had undergone. But now I saw that my appearance must have also been full of pathos. They must have seen and known it better than I did.

Yet as I imagined the girl, or remembered her—I wasn't quite sure which—I felt her short clear words as a frail banner of her personhood; with them she managed to affirm her own presence amidst the fray of the courtroom, the pitched battle being fought there.

Was this feeling about her a truth of her time, or was it just my natural sympathy now for the child whose words I was reading, a child I had long ago ceased to be and whose way of being I could never experience again? Did this child in this text really have anything to do with me?

Something in me knew that she had been me. I knew it not by feeling connected with her now, but by how I shrank from her and her experience. I did not like reading the trial. After reading it I felt as if I had been in a kind of dingy machine room where no human warmth was likely to come—the raw, dreary reality of crime.

Next Mr. Bernhard cross-examined me.

> Miss Ramsey, you realize, of course, that I have an obligation to ask you some questions, and when I ask you these questions if there is some question that you are not certain of, will you ask me to please rephrase it?
>
> *Yes.*
>
> Did you ride beyond those houses?
>
> *I was still within sight of them, probably, when I probably stopped.*

Where I Stopped

When you say you stopped, you got off your bike and proceeded to walk?

Yes.

Now, do you know what time, Charlotte—

Martha.

I am sorry. Martha, do you remember what time that was?

No.

You didn't have a watch?

No.

Now, at that point, X-2, you stopped.

No, I stopped at X-1 and X-2 would be—

Just a second. You stopped at X-1.

Yes.

And looked to the rear?

Yes.

And at that point you saw something below you?

Yes, just about where X-2 is.

I think you indicated how many feet that was.

About one hundred feet.

The road was straight as far as you can see back, it may have curves, but straight back?

Yes, sir, until it did curve.

That would be back in here [indicating]?

Yes.

At that point, Martha, you were walking your bicycle?

When I stopped, yes.

Immediately prior to your stopping?

Yes.

And you saw a man?

Yes.

Now, this man came towards you?

Yes.

Would you tell us specifically, Martha, how this man was dressed?

He was wearing navy blue pants.

I don't mean to interrupt you, but would these be characterized as blue jeans or overalls?

No.

They would not?

No.

You are familiar with blue jeans?

Yes.

They were dark blue?

Yes.

What else?

A "T" undershirt with straps, a white undershirt.

White?

Yes.

Now, can you describe this undershirt to me in more detail?

What do you mean?

Well, you say a T-shirt with straps. I am not sure I understand you.

Undershirt with straps.

Would it be helpful at all if you were to make a little diagram of this type of garment?

Something like this, drops off like this, like that. That is the general idea.

Arms come out here?

Yes.

Martha, you are sure that the undershirt did not have sleeves?

Fairly sure, yes.

Well, you recall, you recall testifying earlier at the hearing as to probable cause on September 17. That is your description of the shirt, isn't it?

Yes.

And you saw this shirt very close to you, did you not?

Yes.

Reading, I remembered that I had thought maybe Mr. Bernhard was stupid. He seemed to be acting as though he simply had not heard what I had already told about that afternoon. Even when I told him again, he seemed not to take in what I was saying.

I remembered that I could not tell, at thirteen, if he really was as dense, or even as sloppy in his thinking, as he sounded. I sensed that he was trying to make me sound less sure about things than I was. He knew I had a clearer memory than he wanted the jury to think I did. Or did he? Maybe he really didn't know that I was smarter than he wanted me to be.

Now, Martha, on direct examination you indicated that the man who stepped out of the woods and proceeded up the roadway to you was muscular. I wonder if you can describe that to a better degree.

I suppose I mean not flabby. You could see his muscles but not, you know, not prominent, muscular.

Would you say he was a heavy man?

What do you mean by heavy?

Would you say he was obese or extremely fat?

No.

Would you be able to say how much he weighed?

No.

Martha, when you looked at this face on the afternoon of August 13 under the mask, was that face, as best you can recall, distorted? Follow my question, Martha?

I assume it was distorted, but since I'd never seen it, without, to my knowledge I['d] never seen it without a stocking mask, I can't definitely say it was distorted. I assume that it was.

Now, do you remember, Martha, Mr. Rittenhouse asking you a question on that afternoon of September 17, a question by Mr. Rittenhouse, "Now, if I may, Miss Ramsay, was the face beneath the nylon stocking which you observed that afternoon distorted? . . ." Remember your answer to that question?

No.

You heard the questions, did you not? I'll repeat it.

No, you don't have to.

Remember your answering, saying, "No"?

Yes, I said no.

So—

I said that it was not distorted.

Let me read the question and your answer, starting on line 2 on page 27. Mr. Rittenhouse asked the question. "Question: Now, if I may, Miss Ramsey, was the face beneath the nylon stocking which you observed that afternoon distorted?" Your answer, "No." Next question, "Have you ever seen a face beneath a nylon stocking—" Your answer, "Yes." [Continuing] "—before?" Answer: "Yes, sir." Question: "Would you say you could recognize a face that was concealed beneath a nylon stocking, could you see beneath the stocking?" Answer: "I could see through it. I don't think I could recognize it." Remember those answers?

As far as to asking me it was distorted, I can't remember saying no. I don't remember that. I do remember saying that I couldn't recognize the face again.

Just what you said here, correct?

Yes.

And, Martha, if the person that attacked you on that day wore glasses under the nylon stocking, would you have been able to observe or see the glasses?

Probably, I probably would have been able to.

And did the person in fact have glasses on that attacked you?

Not to my knowledge.

In other words, you could not see them, correct?

No.

Martha, did you observe the man run away from you or leave you when you were back in the woods or brush?

I heard him.

You heard him?

I didn't see him.

So you don't of your own knowledge know which direction he proceeded?

To me it sounded as if he ran toward the road.

Then you heard a car start?

Yes.

Then you had not seen any cars, is that correct?

Yes.

Now, I think on direct testimony, Martha, you said that the car went towards Federal Twist Road, is that correct?

Yes.

Are you sure that is where it went?

I was never positive, I was never positive.

I remembered that Mr. Rittenhouse had told me to stick to the truth as I knew it, and then whatever came up, I would get through it all right. Surely he had felt that coaching could only make me seem self-conscious. He knew I already wanted only to tell the truth and my sincerity would come through no matter what Bernhard did.

Giving my answers to Bernhard, I had tried to hold to Rittenhouse's instructions. And this girl, the record showed, was able to stick to her story, to affirm what she knew and, what is trickier, to affirm what she didn't know. She astonished me.

In the transcript I discovered a part of my testimony that I had forgotten or suppressed. The record showed that at one point the courtroom had been cleared, leaving only Judge Beetel, the court stenographer, Mr. Rittenhouse, Mr. Bernhard, Frank Miller, and me. Were my parents allowed to stay with me then? The transcript did not say.

MR. RITTENHOUSE: Miss Ramsey, you testified that on August 17, I am sorry, the 13th when you observed the person who perpetrated this attack upon you, he wore what you described as a stocking mask, is that correct?

Yes.

And you testified in response to Mr. Bernhard's question on cross-examination that you got quite close to that man whose face was beneath the mask, is that correct?

Yes.

And you also testified that that man's face was somewhat distorted by this mask, is that correct?

Yes.

Now, you also indicated on cross-examination in answer to Mr. Bernhard's questions that the man whose face you saw at counsel table yesterday and who sits here with his attorney today, Mr. Miller, the defendant in this case, that his face was, I believe you said, "Still not very similar to the face under the mask," is that correct?

Yes.

Now, have you since the time of the attack on August 13, Martha, seen the mask which you saw on the face of the person who you saw that day?

Could you repeat that?

Have you seen the mask that you would know was the same mask that was on his face?

I don't believe so.

If you saw a mask today, a stocking today, and I show you a woman's silk stocking with a knot in the top and ask you to examine that, please.

Knot on the top.

Would you say whether that is similar to the device or mask that was over the head of your assailant on August 13?

Yes.

It is similar to that?

Yes.

Does it—is it similar in color?

Yes.

Is it similar in texture?

Yes.

Now, how close to the man's face at that time were you on August 13?

Two or three feet, I believe.

MR. BERNHARD: Now, Martha, in answer to Mr. Rittenhouse's question you indicated that the face of the man was distorted under the mask.

I assume it was distorted, yes.

You assume it was distorted.

Yes.

Martha, I am not familiar with women's stockings, but they come in various textures, do they not? You are familiar with them, I am sure, through use.

Yes.

Now, this is called a gauge, or denier, or something, if I quoted the word correctly.

THE COURT: Denier.

Are you familiar with the word denier?

No.

Are you familiar with gauge?

No.

Stockings come in certain thicknesses?

I suppose so.

Some stockings are thinner than others?

Yes.

And do you know how thick the stocking was that the man wore?

MR. RITTENHOUSE: Your Honor, I think that question, how thick it was, is not proper.

MR. BERNHARD: Maybe I used the wrong word. But some ladies' stockings are more thick, if that is the right word? Maybe the word is "sheer." I am not familiar with the word. I am groping, to be frank.

Well, I don't know what you mean.

There are stockings that are thinner in texture than others, correct?

Yes.

Is "sheer" the right word? I might add that the county clerk is nodding her head. If it is significant, I don't want to have any extrajudicial comment, and I submit I am groping as far as this is concerned. So some are thin and some are thick?

Yes.

Now, had you an opportunity to observe the thickness of the stocking mask on August 13?

I don't understand.

Let's go back.

You mean could I see through it or do you want me to say how thick it was?

I'd like you to say how thick it was.

I can't say.

THE COURT: Would it be better, Mr. Bernhard, if you put it over your head?

MR. BERNHARD: No, I am not about to do that.

As far as I am concerned, it wouldn't make any difference how thick it was. It wasn't extremely thick.

Was it thicker than this?

I can't say.

You don't know?

No.

Now, stockings also come in various colors, do they not, and degrees of colors?

Yes.

There are some that are black, dark black, some that shade into a gray area, and there are some that have various colors of brown, is that correct?

Yes.

Now, was this the exact color of the stocking mask that you observed on August 13?

I can't say.

So you don't know whether this is the color. Would that be a fair answer, Martha?

I can say that it is pretty close to the color.

You don't know exactly, do you? This is not the stocking. Am I correct, I think Mr. Rittenhouse started with that basic proposition?

Yes.

Now, this is about the same color?

Yes.

Now—

[Continuing] *But go ahead.*

Would it be fair to say—and, again, I am not sure I am using the right words, and I call upon you to indicate if you don't know—that stockings vary in size, and I would assume to the size of a person or a lady's leg, is that correct?

Yes.

In other words, a smaller stocking would be tighter?

Yes.

Consequently a larger stocking would be looser?

Yes.

More loose?

Yes.

Now, do you know if this is the same size stocking?

I don't know what the size was.

If you know, is this the same size stocking, yes or no?

I don't know.

Therefore, if this is significantly a smaller stocking, it would be extremely tight around the face, would it not?

Yes.

On the other hand, if this was an extremely larger stocking, it would be significantly loose around the face?

Yes.

Was there a knot in the stocking, the mask of the stocking?

I can't remember.

Did the stocking hang over the man's head on August 13 in a tassel type fashion I am demonstrating or was it snug around the top of his head?

I can't remember. It didn't hang down noticeably.

It did not hang down?

Yes, but it could have been a small knot on the top.

My description of holding part of the stocking, letting it fall down, does that demonstrate it to you? I don't know how I can better do it.

Yes.

You don't remember if that happened?

No.

If you can remember, Martha, and referring to this particular stocking, whatever number it is, did you see on August 13 this heavy, or fold or hem part of the stocking?

I don't believe. To me at that time it looked as if it had been cut off or there was no darker part of the stocking.

This stocking would not appear similar to the stocking, to the one you observed on August 13 in the sense that this has a hem?

Yes, but the top part of that appears to be the same.

In other words, it appears to be the same in what respect?

It seems to be the same texture. It is a nylon stocking.

As to the texture, this is nylon?

Nylon.

Do you know the material of the stocking mask on August 13?

No.

Do you know the texture of this stocking?

It is a nylon stocking.

I don't know what it is. That is why I am asking the question. Do you know what part of the stocking, with relation to the fitting at one end, was over the face?

No. I assume it would be—

The answer is yes or no. You don't know, is that correct?

I couldn't say definitely.

If you can't say definitely, Martha, I'd appreciate your answer. Have you had an opportunity to feel this stocking?

Yes.

Did you have an opportunity to touch the stocking on August 13?

No.

Do various types of stockings have different feelings?

What do you mean?

Well, I don't know. In other words, I am not that familiar with the texture of nylon or rayon or silk or whatever stockings are made from.

I can't say.

All right.

Reading the record, I laughed at the awkwardness of the debate over the size and thickness of the stocking. The judge himself was wryly amused. Yet when Bernhard questioned me, it was torture. The only time I had seen the rapist's head, and the stocking mask over it, had been in the seconds when I had turned and watched him run up to me, and then when he came close to me, embraced me, and put his hand over my mouth. I had tried, in that moment, to remember what I had glimpsed of the face underneath the stocking. I was still trying to remember it, in the room with the men of the law. Meanwhile, they were having their way with me without anyone looking on; a bit of fun to break up the monotony.

Did the men in the courtroom see anything of me besides my quick responses, besides the smart kid who dared to show some impatience with their groping? Did they sense at all the growing girl, the raped one caught already in her own special yearnings and resistances toward becoming sexual?

I had heard it said more than once that in America a rape trial is also the victim's trial and that there she is violated a second time. For years I had reassured myself that fortunately for me, I had not had to endure that kind of trial, because I had been underage and the fact of intercourse was proven. I was a child, and no one ever questioned that rape was what happened to me.

Reading the transcript I was forced to accept that even that assumption had been mistaken. I found that Rittenhouse had felt it necessary to state, twice, that I had tried to resist Miller, and this was not fact. Bernhard, in his summation, had felt compelled to bring out the old warhorse:

> The crime basically is a crime called rape. Because of Martha's tender age it is couched in a more technical frame called carnal abuse. This is merely because of her age but essentially we are all talking about a word that we all understand, "rape."
>
> Now as a preface to my talking about this crime, this defendant and these facts, I would like to just recount for a moment what an

> aged student said about this particular crime. It is true that rape is a most detestable crime and, therefore, to be severely punished, but it must be remembered that is an accusation easily made and hard to be proved and harder to be defended by the party accused though so ever so innocent he may be.

It had been easy for me to understand that in any woman's rape trial her truthfulness may be open to question, but to discover that my own truthfulness had been open to question was acutely painful. I had sensed it but not let myself know it, then. Now as I read the transcript it was as fresh as yesterday. I was that child, as I read, and I felt the pain of it, as a child.

I was still working with the therapist I had started with in New York; we conducted our sessions by phone. I told Janet that I felt while reading the transcript that loneliness was the strongest and clearest sensation; after the anger, of course, which made me speak fast and loudly to her about the absurdity of the business about the stocking.

Janet asked me if I could say what my feelings were, any other feelings, besides the loneliness.

"I am noticing again," I said, "How hard it is for me to believe that you really want to know what my feelings were or that you could understand. Even though you are the person I'm most likely to believe that of. I just can't imagine that you could *get* what it was like for me, being raped."

Finally I was crying. "I just can't imagine that anyone could get it. I couldn't imagine it then and I still can't."

"What would you wish could have been different?" she asked, when we talked again. "What would have helped?"

"If I could have just sat down with someone, instead of those detectives, and that person had said, 'Now we're just going to sit for a while and talk about what happened. There's no rush. Ask me any questions you want to.'

"I had questions about everything. Why was he carrying that rock in his hand when he came running up to me? Would he have used it if I had resisted? Why did he put his mouth on my nipples? It was as if he thought I would enjoy it, or as if he thought he was enjoying it, but his movements were so mechanical."

She said, "You already knew not to expect your father or your mother to be able to help you . . . you were already very alone with most things that troubled or challenged you."

"Yes," I said. I just wanted Janet to be there for me now, to be my mother now, and to ask her all the questions I could not ask my mother.

"One of the things that really bothered me was when they found his semen inside me. I knew that the man ejaculated, I knew that word, and I had felt no change in his movements. I could not imagine that he could have ejaculated inside me without my being able to feel it."

I was crying. "How was it that I could not feel it? There was so much that I didn't understand, about sex, that I didn't know.

"It is very hard for me to talk to you about these details, the actual act of intercourse."

"Why is it so hard?" she asked.

"It just feels so uncomfortable to say those words, as if I were trying to say them to my mother."

"How do you imagine I will react to them?" she said.

I was still crying. "I'm sure you'll just laugh," I answered. "You'll just laugh and say, Oh, that's not important, that doesn't matter, don't worry about that."

The day after this exchange, I wrote:

> I feel as though I am softening, loosening inside. I can't choose, anymore—don't want, anymore—to cling to some sense of strength. It is no specific memory, it's simply all the years of loneliness gathered within me, all the weight of my childhood anxiety overwhelming me.

After months of being wrapped in a depressive fog while working as hard as I could to sustain my writing, I had to sit and cry.

I could feel now that I had been living as if I were behind glass, even when walking in the woods or by the ocean, or spending evenings with Eric. Neither the person closest to me nor the trees and sea I loved had felt real or had touched me for a long time.

> I'm not sorry, at last, to be able to feel pain. The fog has begun to lift, and I see that I am alone. I was not helped. No one can make it any different.
>
> I cannot make it different, not with any labor of my pen or mind.
>
> The frozen girl turns to me, sees me, and does not begin to speak. She simply begins to cry—quietly, and for a long time.

My therapist helped me. In the other hours of the week, it was just me. At moments, when I recovered a kind of normal self, who felt strangely open, I was glad simply to be near Eric, and we would go for a walk. He would laugh and I would find I was laughing. We made love and I found I knew he was with me.

> I don't care what we do. It is a quiet ecstasy, simply to have understood that someone is near me.

I decided then that I must give myself the opportunity to talk about my rape with those who would understand in a way no one else could—people who had been raped themselves. I found out that the health maintenance organization I belonged to through my job offered rape-survivor therapy groups every so often. I joined the next one.

There were six of us in the room, a mixture of races, ages, and occupations. The leader suggested we begin by telling briefly what happened to us—as little as we would like—and what we hoped to get out of the group.

As they spoke, I realized that I was raped younger than any of them, closest to childhood. I wondered how common it is for a child to be raped by a stranger rather than by a known person.

Each person's story was too vivid. I closed my eyes, only to see it more starkly. Their voices came to me like radios, both intimate and disembodied, as if they were whispering unspeakable happenings right in my ear. I felt smothered as rage gathered in me—rage for the others, not for myself.

Two speakers began to cry. Their tears disturbed and frightened me.

They swamped the therapist with impossible questions—tough urban girls, ready to let out their anger. Surely when I talked they would not understand me. I would be a talking head, my voice high and faint, carrying a restrained hysteria.

When my turn came I told my story briefly, clearly, dry eyed.

Our therapist talked about posttraumatic stress syndrome. She said that generally people do go completely numb during and after a rape. Very often the powerful emotions surface about six to eight weeks later.

I listened closely. I did not remember this happening with me. Six to eight weeks later: I didn't remember anything.

As we closed, she asked us each to say how we felt. I sat, staring down at my hands, playing with two loose threads at the bottom of my sweater. She said, "Martha, how are you feeling?"

I didn't want to say it. "I feel stirred up—angry, and nauseated."

"Can you connect any of these feelings with how you remember feeling at the time?"

I didn't want to. "The nausea, I guess, I can connect that with what I felt then."

As I walked out the door I felt amazed at what a difference this meeting seemed to have made: I felt relieved, and grateful for the group, now that I was away from it.

When I arrived at home everyone was sitting down to dinner, and I joined them. After a minute I had to leave the table. Their voices buzzed around me like flies, and I felt sick, overtired, an invalid. I needed to get away from all stimulation. I went up to my room and ate alone in relieved silence. I crawled into bed without even taking off my shirt. I picked up a mystery novel and read for a while, thinking I would sink into sleep. But within an hour I was up, no longer exhausted but open and quiet. I pursued a normal sort of evening from then on, surprised at how quickly the oppression had passed off.

The rape therapy group went on for twelve weeks. During each session I experienced the same constellation of sensations and emotions as in the first. They became more familiar and less frightening.

It was hard to know how to speak because I had already written so much. I felt like I knew too much; so much that I couldn't really know what I knew. It felt like a nearly endless amount of talking was in me trying to get out. I felt like a child who is too articulate at some times, inarticulate at others.

In fact my essential experience in the therapy group was the experience of myself as a child. I could not, in that room, pretend that being able to act like an adult was the same thing as being an adult.

One day in the group someone asked me, "Are you writing a book?"

"Yes," I answered.

Someone else turned to me: "Can I ask you a question?"

"Sure."

"Why? Why do you want to do that to yourself?"

I could not find words to explain it to her. It was too huge in me to be put in one answer.

Suddenly, I was not sure I really knew.

Someone else answered for me, as if to defend me.

"Can't you see?" she said. "It's clear that she has to."

RETURN

I decided to go to New Jersey and talk with people about how they remembered the rape and the trial. As I prepared myself for the trip, I came to see that it was not just a way to find out more about the past; it was an important action in the present. I felt an urge to speak aloud with those who had been involved in a way we could not speak aloud then.

In the therapy group, in the common way of such groups, what we did and said among ourselves remained in a twilight realm. When the hours of our dozen meetings were finished we would return to strangerhood, like people getting off a train and going in different directions. I felt an urge to meet my quarrel with the world in the world, not only in a safe remembering room.

In the picture we all were separate, frozen, and silent in our urgent poses. But I had the power now to bring the figures to life, to sit with them, to ask them to attend to me—to awaken their attention not just to Miller or the trial but to Martha as a living human being. I felt an urge to affirm to them that the child they'd been concerned about, and didn't know what to do with, had grown up and gone away but was still in the world and still experiencing what happened as her history.

I would go to New Jersey alone. Eric was not able to accompany me. I knew I could call him every night if I needed to. But we both knew also that this was my own exploration of my own past. No matter how close he was to me, or whether he was physically at my side or not, he could not really travel the paths I was traveling.

The smell of hay and alfalfa came in my window on soft air as the October morning dawned, warm and clear. I was waking up in Flemington, where I had spent the night at an inn.

I was home.

I was in the Delaware Valley, surrounded by the hayfields and cornfields I remembered, sprinkled with neat white houses, barns, and sprawling chicken coops. As I walked the quarter mile out of Flemington to the Avis office on the highway, the smell of the hay was intoxicating. The wild grasses, now thick and abundant right up to the edges of the main highway, made the road itself seem just a narrow path through one spreading, fertile field.

I drove to my father's house along familiar roads. Of those now living, he had been the adult most involved in my life at the time of the rape.

I had not seen him for over two years. As far as I now knew he spent his days drinking himself into a quiet stupor, alone in the house in the woods where I'd spent my childhood. Visiting him, which I had always found difficult, had become a matter of simply witnessing his disintegration. I had finally told him, about two years earlier, over the telephone, that I could no longer stand to visit him and watch him destroy himself with liquor. It was the first time in our lives that I had named his alcoholism aloud to him.

He had replied nonsensically, "Well, then, I guess this is good-bye," and hung up. Since then I had found it impossible to call him.

Before coming to New Jersey I had called to let him know I was coming and why.

"I'm writing a book about—the rape," I told him. "I think that this could be helpful to other people who have been through the experience."

"Yes," he said. "Doctors and psychologists say that it is good to go back over it."

It was strange, almost shocking, to hear his immediate and lucid response—almost as if he had been waiting for me for years to mention the rape to him.

"So anyway, as part of what I'm doing," I went on, "I'd like to ask for your help. I'm trying to remember as best I can what happened, and I was wondering if I could come and talk, first, to you."

"Anything," he answered, making his voice louder, clearer. "Of course. Anything I can do. After all—" He broke off.

He could not bring himself to say it: *I am your father.*

"After all—" I repeated, trapped in a nervous, conflicted smile. I could not, either, say the words. *You are my father.*

You were my father.

"Thanks, Fred," I continued. "I really appreciate it. I was thinking of coming down on October fourth, if that's all right with you."

"October fourth?" he said, his voice becoming uncertain. He was afraid he would forget.

As the days went by and the time of my visit approached, my hopes and fears gathered momentum together. I began to confuse my aims; I began to suspect that this "interview" was simply one more tactic to try to get my father to father me. I tried to stay clear with myself: *This was over twenty years ago. He is seventy-five now. His mind is clouded.* But in secret recesses of my heart the hope had been stirred up that he finally would. At the same time I dreaded the familiar disappointment I was sure would come.

After ten miles the stately old iron bridge over the Lockitong Creek rose ahead of me like a revelation. There it stood, quiet and grand on its rise, my old creek bridge, a web of iron shafts amidst leaves that glowed disembodied and pale like fairy coins or slowly drifted down in the dappled air. There it was, the bridge I loved, its upper spans so elegant, fine and high, the creek running sleepily around leafy banks and stones below.

So I did not imagine it, I thought. *This place is magic.*

My father's mailbox was rustier than the bridge. Because no one had cleared the leaves from the culvert beneath it, the rain had run across the entrance of the driveway many times and made a gully I had to drive over with care. The old gravel driveway itself was so overgrown with grass that I could barely discern its tracks. The quince and privet bushes my mother had planted beside the terrace had grown so tall and wild that I could not see the house behind them.

He came out and waited for me on her walk.

A tall, large-boned man, he was somewhat stooped now but still seemed substantial. He wore the overalls and shirt that had been his uniform for as long as I could remember, an outfit the old farmers in the area have always worn. His hair was completely white and so was his beard, and he had acquired some dark red spots on his temple and brow, but he seemed otherwise not changed at all since my last visit four years earlier. Looking at him I found it hard to believe he was seventy-five and still walking around with no sign of ill health. A doctor he had seen a few years earlier had told my sister that his liver was enlarged, as alcoholics' generally are, and that had been his only indication of bodily trouble—except, of course, for the premature softening of his mind.

He was wearing a chamois-cloth shirt on this warm day. I thought he must feel the cold more than younger people. We embraced. I smelled a pleasing combination of mold, from the dampness of our house in the humid New Jersey summers, and clean clothes hung up to dry outdoors. This cleanliness surprised me; I was glad he had not grown sloppy or dirty in his drunken old age, as I had feared he might.

Our greetings were not hard to get through. He didn't fuss; after our hug, we smiled.

He said, with his familiar air of grave openness, "It's good to see you."

I said, "Same here."

The sun shone on us, and I felt my old affection for him.

I asked him if we could do the interview first and then do whatever else we wanted to do. I was anxious to interview him before he began drinking, if he had not already begun. We decided to do it on the porch because the day was warm. He made himself comfortable on our old rattan settee covered by an old mattress, and I pulled up a chair facing him.

"I don't really want to ask you a lot of questions," I began. "If it's all right with you, I'd like you to just—start talking, about what you remember."

"Of what?" he asked.

"About the rape," I answered quietly, not showing my surprise. I had not expected him to forget even that, the subject of our interview.

"Oh. Sure," he said, and paused.

"That is very strange," he began. "It's almost ghostly. I was seated exactly here when the rape took place. I had just finished some kind of job, and decided it would be nice to sit out here and have a beer. And something happened that really drew my attention, because it didn't happen often. It was a pickup truck, and it was going up the hill like crazy, I mean at a speed that was absolutely insane. At that time I didn't know it, but what had happened was that you had been raped, down on that other road, and this guy was getting as far away from that place as he possibly could. I forget whether I testified to that or not. The guy who handled the case, if you remember, was a very, very persistent and intelligent and sensitive lawyer.

"The other thing is—"

He paused.

I felt contented, in an animal way, to be sitting on the porch where I used to lie on the sun-fried boards, resting my cheek on them and peeking through the cracks at the deep shadow underneath, the ground twelve feet below striated with sunlight. I felt as though I would hardly mind, now, if he remembered very little or if he remembered wrong. Maybe there would even be some relief in his forgetfulness. Here we sat together on this porch that I loved, and he was willing to talk about what had happened to me, something that had also happened to him and to others; that was enough.

"Did you come home with your bicycle? Did you walk home with it?"

I nodded.

"Yeah," he continued. "I remember that. And then I remember the next thing—Amelia saying, 'Fred, Martha's been raped,' and I said, 'Oh, my God.' "

His voice lowered and shrank to a thread as he spoke these words, nearly mumbling them, their thin stream drawing him too quickly into a dark valley he had forgotten about. He instantly recovered himself, and then began to say words that I sensed he must have said more than once to neighbors and friends.

"We decided that we should report this immediately to the police.

"And then the other thing that came out later was that—word got around—I think it was published in the paper, perhaps—without your name being mentioned."

He spoke as though talking to a child, as if this suppression of my name had been very important, to him, or, he thought, to me.

"There had been other rapes in the vicinity by the same person. He had quite a record behind him." His voice took on an edge of hard disgust. "Obviously a dreadfully sick person."

"Of course, eventually—I don't—you know—there was a trial. And you, you—testified, as I recall."

I nodded.

"And I remember the lawyer who was handling this thing did every possible thing, got every possible bit of evidence that could pin this man to this spot at this time. This is probably everything that you remember. I feel that maybe I'm repeating a little bit—"

"No, it's great," I said.

"Beyond that, I don't know as I have much to flesh it out with. It all happened in an almost unbelievable—it was unbelievable to all of us that—"

His voice became light and caressing, as if he were an English actor or were reading a delicate poem aloud. As if he were telling a young woman some terrible news, trying to soften the blow.

"—this could have happened to *you.*"

As if what had surprised them was that I—*Martha*—had been attacked. As if they, too, and not just I, had been living in a dream world.

"And the sharp, sudden realization that it had happened made us all feel as though we were hardly alive or hardly real."

He paused, searching for words, and then made a small noise of exasperation.

"You know, everybody knows about rape, I suppose, the crime is fairly common and everything, but"—wrily—"there's a difference when it happens to you, or your immediate friends or relatives, an enormous difference."

He paused.

Two crickets sang in the dying grass below.

He sighed.

"Now at this point I'd have to say, do you have any questions, because I've given you just about all I can off the top of my head. But then, interviews usually aren't one-sided."

He took a swallow from the can of beer he had brought with him onto the porch. I had not had the courage to try to talk him out of it.

"I think one of the more interesting things was the reaction of the women of the entire community, who were outraged, and sort of gathered together. I remember hearing some of them talk, or they would meet me in the store, and say, 'Oh, we heard about Martha. They oughta'—his voice grew very faint, as if reluctant to repeat that women had said this—'kill that guy.' "

He stopped.

"Everything that you said is really helpful, Fred," I said. "I don't remember, really, much at all." I thought that if I pretended to remember very little he might be more likely to mention something that I had truly forgotten or had never known.

"Well, that is to be expected, it's the most normal thing in the world to block out on a thing like that happening to you. That I fully understand. I guess maybe the reason I remember it so is that I was so shocked and so enraged that something inside me just set something going to remember all of this.

"The thing that really got to me most of all was that I heard this, this wagon go charging up the Twist making a sound I had never heard from any wagon going up the Twist. And that pinned it for me. This guy was exceeding the limit in every possible way.

"Oh, and the other thing is—this is really trivia. I had somehow cut my left thumb, and it was a pretty nasty cut. The best thing to do was to make up an antiseptic solution, and I was sitting there with my thumb in this mug, trying to get the poison out of my system."

He laughed ruefully.

"Come to think of it, it's a rather, almost fictional thing. Here I am trying to get poison out of my thumb and there you are"—

He paused, and when he spoke again it was with disgust.

—"just having been raped.

"I can remember that first evening when so many people came, to show that they cared. I was very moved by that."

"That's amazing to me, that people actually came," I said. I had not remembered anyone visiting us that evening.

"Oh, yes, the kitchen was full of people. I mean there were maybe eight or a dozen people. How the word got around, with the speed it got around —of course a thing like that, in a community like this—you have all kinds of people with children. It was quite a thing.

"And then of course there had to be the examination, and you were declared to be not pregnant. That was a source of relief. Then I think when you went to Solebury some of the kids started making remarks about it, and there was a female teacher there—she told me that she told them all to get the hell off, and if they ever made any remarks in her class they would really go to the bottom of the class and be penalized.

"I mean, there was a definite feeling from everybody who knew about this, everyone had a heavy reaction. I think it changed, maybe forever, the feeling of people in this region. I think it took a long, long time for many people to get it out of their mind. I suspect that all the people who knew about this right away still remember it and are horrified by the recall."

"After all, this is a community. We know each other's names. We may not be on the best of terms, but, you know, this is a neighborhood. And when a thing like this hits a neighborhood, it stays. It makes a deep impression. It's not a thing that people like to think of as having been anywhere near possible in the neighborhood they live in, I mean it's a horrendous shock. I think everybody's concept of rape is something that takes place in a big city, or the back of a dance hall, or a couple out in a car and the girl won't deliver so the guy makes her deliver"—disgust shadowed his voice—"you know. And those are things that happen.

"I don't think that people in this community had ever even entertained the possibility that anybody could be doing rape. Except for those people who knew that this guy had already raped somebody. People would come up to me and say, 'He did it to so-and-so, and to so-and-so,' that kind of thing. He'd been doing it for a good long time."

"So you were letting anyone know, who you thought should know about it," I repeated, to make sure I understood.

"Yes, precisely, because—you see, we'd never known about this."

His voice rose. "This is the thing that really gets me mad. The very first time he did it he should have been put off—put out. And nobody around here made one single move. I suppose it was to protect the old American system, or the old system, of the woman having to be pure and untouched when she marries."

He stopped.

I prodded him: "So some people knew that this guy had actually raped—"

"Absolutely. And none of them had done a damn thing about it."

"That's amazing," I said.

"All I can remember is the feeling of absolute outrage, and despair, and getting on the phone and raising hell. I mean, reaching out to anybody that I thought should know about it. And with a sense of forcing a reality on this community. These people were lying back and letting their daughters be raped and doing nothing about it.

"This was the outrage of it, to me. That people are such clucks and cowards, that they would attempt to cover up—it was all selfishness on the part of these people. The only way to handle this is to bring the culprit to bear. To punish him. And to make it a long stretch in a nasty jail. That's almost too much for them. I mean, too little for them.

"I do remember what one man said. It's pretty rough stuff, what he said was done to a rapist. He said they got him and they tied him to an anvil and they put his balls on the anvil and let the hammer come down on them. If you want violence, that's it.

"Certainly, many people were outspoken in their feelings. They told me the old-fashioned thing was they got him out in the woods and cut his balls off. I learned things that I wasn't too happy to learn that night. I'd already had the thing of your being raped."

"It must have been a real overload to take in," I prompted.

"Well, I think it was for everyone—including you, for God's sake!" He laughed gently as if to chide me, almost, at my restraint about my own experience.

He drank a couple of long draughts and was silent for a long moment. Then he said, "I'd like to ask you a question."

"Mmm?"

"Your adjustment has been, I'm certain, perhaps long and difficult, but —you don't seem to have let it wound you permanently. There's always a wound, but—I'm wondering about a lot of women, young women, around here, who may or may not have been raped, that somehow the possibility of it doesn't seem to be real to them. There's something wrong about this that I don't quite understand. I'm being vague, I'm trying to grasp something. I'm not going to make it; it's not going to come to me."

My father sounded to me as though he was constantly trying to sound as he should sound, and was almost bringing it off; but behind the facade of his civilized manner and his verbal acuity, I felt, the rest of his mind hung like a dark, holey fabric of chaos, burned largely away by alcohol—what I could only call a kind of madness.

My father as I had known him had always been darkened in this way. I had never been able to find any way to the person in him; yet other adults who knew us never seemed to see anything strange about him. We had never openly named it, except when my mother in our teen years complained about his general incompetence and—once—his drinking.

"Do you remember where I was, when all the neighbors came over, that night?" I asked him. "Was I with everybody, or was I—not?"

"That's a tough one. Thinking of our family and the attitude we have about a thing like this, I think that you were there. But I couldn't swear to it. Do you remember being hugged or kissed by any of the women?"

"No," I answered.

"Hmm. That's interesting; that's very interesting. That would be the first thing I would expect every woman who appeared to do. I mean, there's this whole thing about women supporting each other. And it's true. But—what did take place if none of the women spoke with you, or embraced you, or commiserated? Probably a great many of the women there had had a history of having been raped—maybe that's one thing that made them afraid to come forward with their story, who knows. I'm really surmising, I'm out on a limb here."

Running through his mind, I guessed, were some confused memories of my mother's worry about not having properly comforted me, her own experience of having been raped, his knowledge of other women who had been raped, and perhaps some long-withheld anxiety about whether I was going to be all right. I had a strange feeling, also, that along with his horror and rage at what had happened to me, he had been able to see what I needed, but had never felt able to offer me any sympathy or comfort of his own.

At the same time, his courage in prosecuting the rapist, his absolute disregard for the general opinion in doing so, this affirmation of the reality of the wrong, must have been of real value for me as a girl.

"What do you remember about how Mom reacted?" I asked.

"Well, obviously she was very—upset. But you know how Amelia confronted reality. I mean, she had a protective thing, when she was threatened by something. And this was one of the most terrible things that could ever happen to any mother, or any parent. And yes, the way—she came out, and I can remember now the firmness of her voice, and the implication of that voice—'How could you possibly be peacefully sitting out here when Martha has been raped?' I mean she was feeling it really hard, Martha."

His voice became lighter, childlike, wandering.

"Of course I didn't know until she came and told me that you had been raped. So then I got up and asked her when and how, and everything. And then—who was the other person who heard about it right away and went down to check—was that Loch? I think it was! Yes, Loch went down there. And of course the guy had left. It was probably just as well for Loch, the guy could have killed Loch. You know, he was a real sicko, that guy.

"Quarry Road, I will never forget the name of the road, because somebody said, 'Martha was on Quarry Road and she's been raped.' "

He was becoming more and more disoriented and began to repeat himself.

"Loch went down right away, then I went down right away. No, I went down by foot, he went by bike. I wanted to be sure, to see if there was any evidence that perhaps would help in the trial. As a matter of fact there wasn't."

He became unable, finally, to take in my questions and respond to them directly, and wandered on in a ramble that turned over and over on itself and revealed no new information. His understanding of my presence began to fade, as well, and he seemed less and less to know me as an actual person; his inflections and thoughts became meandering and childlike, though his vocabulary remained sophisticated. He did not ask me to stop the interview but kept on trying to talk, less and less connectedly, as if I were some vaguely tormenting authority for whom he would continue to produce speech as long as he was asked to, though it no longer made any sense. His talk began to remind me of the long senseless stories that very small children tell you if they can get you to listen, the major function of which seems to be try to engage your full attention upon them. Indeed, my father did not want me to go away from him.

I left him, though, taking with me the tape I had made.

He remembered inaccurately. He did not remember me coming home, putting my bike away under the porch where he stood at his workbench and asking him where my mother was. He did not remember that Loch did encounter Miller when he rode his bike down to Quarry Road and that they spoke with each other. Oddest of all, he seemed completely unable to speak coherently about my mother or to remember much of anything about her.

I could not know if he spoke accurately about the neighbors visiting that night, the other rapes, the punishments the men had told him about. But all that he told me revealed his own anguish, and I was glad I had spoken with him.

His old voice had sounded good to my ears. The remnants of his manners, his cultivated welcome, his vocabulary, and even his interest in my writing all worked on me. While he talked I had found myself whispering to myself that perhaps I had even come to forgive him.

After I left I found that my mind and heart were not in as good order as I had thought when I was with him. His wanderings, seemingly harmless in these late years, had disturbed me greatly. For all my pride in my detachment, after I returned home I spent several days as if inside the darkness of his world. The attention he had given me had been again like fairy gold—love and concern made apparent in words but without the capacity to abide firmly. For all the beauty of the place, it had been as draining as a visit to the dead.

Four months after my talk with my father his mind became impaired to the point where it was no longer safe for him to live alone. He was admitted to treatment for alcohol addiction. Ceasing to drink had no discernible effect on the condition of his mind. He was diagnosed, after treatment, as having dementia—possibly Alzheimer's disease, possibly a result of alcoholism, possibly both.

When I heard the diagnosis I knew that I would now be easier about my father. I would never know exactly how long ago his faculties had begun to fail, or if there had always been something wrong. But now it was at least clear that I had no father left. I would not have to try anymore to connect. Along with the sadness of it I felt an obscure relief.

I had not seen Loch for several years. Not knowing how to respond to his continuing mental illness, I had found it too painful to try to stay in touch with him. For many years he had been unable to take any action to stay in connection with me.

It took some time for me to track him down; he had moved since I had last been in touch. I finally got hold of his number and called him from the inn where I was staying.

"Oh, hi, Martha," he said, sounding cheerful for a moment, surprising me.

I asked him how he was.

"I, I've quit drinking," he said in his halting, raw voice. "I'm trying to stay off the booze. I'm living in a, ah, subsidized apartment that's not bad. I, I get a check from the state welfare system, and I get food stamps. But, you know, it's not really enough to have a decent life."

I asked him if we might get together, since I was in the area.

"Ah, no, Martha," he said. "I don't want to do that."

His no was strong, and I guessed it might be that he did not want me to see him as he is now.

I told him that I was writing a book about the rape and asked him if he would be willing to talk to me about it in any way.

"No," he answered. "I can't talk about it. I always was very upset about that."

It seemed clear that Loch would never be able to speak to me about his feelings of that time, something that might have helped both of us had it been possible. But his refusal spoke worlds. I had not known that he had "always been very upset" about the rape. I had never understood his silence. Now I glimpsed a personality so sensitive to the disturbances of the world that it could not allow itself any memory or speech of what happened. I had survived the rape better than he.

I was reminded of his action at the time, his mad ride down to Quarry Road, and how I could not stand knowing how upset he really was. Now his refusal touched me, because it did recognize the awfulness of what had happened to me. The forgotten feeling of an unspoken kinship between us stirred in me, as it had then.

I felt I had an intimation of a thread of connection between us that, amidst the shreds of our vanished family, remained. I knew that I would have a lot to work out if I were to try to have much contact with Loch. I hoped that at least I would not let myself fall so far out of touch with him again.

Alida and I had been able to mend somewhat the mutual estrangement we had felt in our twenties, when we were struggling to emerge from the isolation of our family's world and define ourselves as distinct adults. She had established a knitting-design business, and was now married and living in New York. We were not close, but our relations were cordial.

In the course of one of our occasional telephone conversations, I told her about my book and asked her if she remembered anything at all about the time of the rape.

"You know what," she said. "What I remember most strongly is that I was very angry. Because nobody would tell me what was going on. I wanted to participate and they wouldn't let me. I remember those two detectives came and Mom and Fred took you into the library with them. I wanted to come in too. But Fred closed the doors in my face. I was furious. I stood outside the doors and tried to hear what everybody was saying, but I couldn't hear anything.

"I could tell that something terrible had happened to you. They would not tell me what it was, they just kept telling me, 'Martha has been attacked,' like they were talking to a child who didn't know anything. But I was eleven, I thought I was old enough to know. I thought I could do something too. I wanted to be with you and they wouldn't let me. I thought I could help.

"I wanted to hold your hand, or something."

My father pursued justice and raged against the community that had allowed the rapist to operate freely. My mother had tried to stay by me, but we had not been able to reach out to each other. Alida, my playmate, who laughed with me over our Barbie dolls, had known exactly what to do. After talking with her I felt a great sadness. Not only had my parents' fear kept them apart from me, it had made them act to keep her apart from me. And she was the one person who might have been able to help me feel less alone.

I wanted to talk with Edith Kawano, our neighbor, because she had probably seen more of my mother, when she was alive, than anyone else outside our family.

My mother had told me that when Edith and her husband, Yosh, had built a house and moved in, in the early fifties, only two neighboring households welcomed them, because they were Japanese. When we were growing up their family had been the friendliest with ours of all our near neighbors, and they were probably the most liberal minded. Edith and my mother had raised children of the same age, and Yosh and my father had spent many evenings drinking, talking, and arguing with each other while their wives looked on.

Yosh had died and the children had moved away, but Edith Kawano still lived down the road from our place in a small white house on the edge of a field.

While I talked with her at her kitchen table she worked on some fabric she was piecing into a quilt. She seemed far more peaceful than I remembered her, standing on her tiny porch and calling out to her three kids that they had to come inside and get ready for dinner right this minute.

"What do you remember about that day?" I asked.

"What I remembered most clearly about that afternoon," she said, "was that I had run out of ketchup, and one of the boys was going to go down to Lumberville on his bicycle and get some for me at the little store there. Instead, I put them in the car and went to Errico's. It was that very afternoon."

If she had let her boy go, he would have been riding his bike down Quarry Road.

"I always had a rule that they couldn't go alone on the roads on their bikes, but always with each other or someone else."

I wondered if Edith had felt my mother should have had the same rule.

"Do you remember how the children reacted?" I asked.

"I don't think the kids really knew what rape was. But they knew something terrible had happened to you," she said.

"I asked your mother whether you were all right—had been hurt. She said you were all right but that you were—of course you had been affected by that experience. She said she had taken you to a psychiatrist and that it was best to let you talk it out."

I had no memory of being taken to a psychiatrist at the time of the rape or at any time in high school. I remembered only my mother telling me that she and my father had talked to a psychiatrist. I felt sure of this; yet my memory of the last two weeks of that August, after the rape and before I went back to school, was nearly a blank. Could I have been taken to see someone and been observed without knowing it? Could I have been so out of it that I repressed a memory of being helped?

If only my mother were alive! I thought. *She would remember.*

"Later that evening I went to see you. I cannot even remember what we talked about, but I think we talked about your rape, and I think you talked about it. I thought you were quite calm."

"Surprisingly so?"

"Yeah. I don't think you were crying. Somebody being raped, you would think they would be hysterical."

"Was it hard for you, seeing me?"

"I wasn't embarrassed—it was a difficulty thinking of the right thing to say to you. I was trying to think of something to reassure you that we were there to support you. I was thinking the way you react is going to make her react—depending on your reaction the victim will be affected. All I knew was I had to be very careful."

While I remembered so much of that day, I had no memory of being near anyone but my mother that night. Was it possible, as my father had also said, that between coming home from the hospital and going to bed there was dinner, Edith, others? If I did forget this, was it because I just could not take it in, could not handle any more input, interaction? I might even have talked a lot but without allowing anything to register in my mind.

"Your mother was shaken by it of course," Edith continued. "She was really upset."

"Was she crying?"

"Not when I saw her. We talked about it. I didn't have much to contribute because it was so new to me too.

"Fred must have been there, that night. I don't remember him. I don't remember Loch and Alida, either. It was in the kitchen. Everybody was upset, your mother was upset, and she said Loch was very upset. It was your mother that called me and told me. It must have been after dinner, because Yosh stayed with the kids.

"With Amelia—all I could think of was to reassure her that she was doing the right thing and support her wherever I could. I told her to call me if there was anything I could do. She wanted to know whether I knew the guy. I said No, I didn't. She said to let her know if I heard anything about him. Later I saw a woman at Errico's and she told me that that guy Miller had been up near your place. I called your mother and told her. I don't know if your mother called her. It was Stan's wife who told me that, of Stan's Auto Body."

Her speech still retained an accent; she seemed to be struggling to find the right words in English. As a child I had never quite realized how little at home she must have always felt in our language.

"Your mother wondered whether the psychiatrist was doing you any good or not. I don't know how often you were seeing him."

I wondered if Edith might be mixing up my mother's concerns about Loch's psychiatric treatment, later, with my experience.

I told her that I did not remember seeing a therapist.

"I always assumed that she had taken you to a psychiatrist," she said, "because that was my impression of the kind of person she was, someone who would not try to shove something under the rug. I admired that. Our relationship was very warm and open. She thought the trial would be a catharsis for you, and that's why she persuaded you to participate in it."

How could I tell if this was accurate? I didn't think my mother had had to persuade me to participate in the trial, but maybe my parents had been much more zealous in pursuing the rapist and insisting on a trial than I had remembered or ever known.

There had been intimations in my father's account that they had been trying to carry on their own investigation, had been very active in suggesting lines of inquiry to the prosecutor and in insisting on the investigation going forward. I had always thought that Rittenhouse had managed everything, but now I was getting a picture of my parents calling everyone they could think of to ask for help in finding out who had raped their child.

"I remember people saying, *It's a terrible thing for a girl to have to go through it.*"

I imagined people clucking over my parents' decision to allow me to testify.

"But it had to be told, and people had to be aware of what can happen to girls when there's a guy like Miller around. Up to then we had all been so innocent, we never thought that something like that would happen.

"Your mother and I did talk about the guy, Miller, and your mother told me that you were so scared you just told him *Don't kill me, don't kill me,* and you did whatever he said, because you thought he might kill you—he had a big rock. She was very upset.

"I think she thought you had recovered quite well. She was very concerned but she thought you handled it beautifully. Both your parents had so much confidence in you. They were relieved to think you didn't suffer—no, I wouldn't say that—they thought you took it much better than they expected. They were worried.

"Years later when you had a boyfriend, your mother said to me, 'I wonder if that rape had a lasting effect on Martha'—more than she had realized."

"Did she say what she was worried about?"

"Something about the boyfriend. I surmised that you had broken off with this fellow, and she was wondering whether it was because of your experience."

I thought it might have been my first boyfriend in college. Was she concerned that I'd been unable to make a happy relationship with him? But how could she tell what was just adolescence and what was rape? She and I had both wondered and been uncertain of me.

I asked Edith how she had thought of my parents. "Did you ever think they were just living in a world of their own?"

"Yeah, sometimes I did think they were living in their own world. They had their own philosophy. Most liberal people would like to live like that —don't pay any taxes, live an independent life."

My father had always been very proud, I remembered, of keeping his income so low that he never had to pay a penny to the government to support the business of war.

"Amelia felt that she and Fred were much more true to their philosophy by not falling for that way of life that everyone succumbed to. It kind of annoyed me. It was like they just didn't understand that we had to survive, Yosh had to work, and we also felt that we should give back some of what we earned, to cooperate with everyone else. They really thought that everyone should just stop going along with the whole system."

"What did you think about their relationship?" I asked.

"They sort of complemented each other," she said. "Your mother sometimes said to me that she wished that Fred had a job outside the home, because it drove her crazy him being around all the time, and also that it was so hard never knowing if they were going to have any money."

"Did she ever complain about his drinking?"

"I don't think he was drinking. I thought he was drinking just two or three drinks. Amelia never mentioned that. Fred, I didn't have that close relationship as with Amelia. I think he was more bookish, and couldn't really relax with people the way she could."

"Do you remember what I was like as a kid?"

"You were very independent. I think you had a mind of your own."

Her words reminded me of my father's voice as he had spoken of how surprised he and my mother were that "this could have happened to you." Had I seemed so sure of myself, as though I felt very much in command of my surroundings?

"Did you think my mother had a superior attitude?" I asked.

"Your mother wasn't so much superior, as—she wasn't interested in the people around here—whereas I think neighbors are important.

"I liked Amelia as a person. I think there was trust between us. We *were* very close friends. There were some blind spots, but we went around those.

"The day before she died she thanked me for being such a good friend, and I think that was true—that we were."

Edith did not cry, but I could tell she was moved. Other friends far away had perhaps felt closer, but Edith alone had come to visit my mother on the day she was taken to the hospital to die. There had been no one else visiting for a long time.

"I still miss her," she said. "We could always talk about things."

My eyes filled with tears. I missed her, too.

Later, in the rape therapy group, we would devote an entire session to talking about our mothers in relation to our rapes.

Some of us were still furious. Their mothers had not taken what had happened seriously, or denied it altogether, or were unable to support them during the ordeal of a trial.

One said she had no anger toward her mother, whom she had recently lost. Alone among us, she had never told her mother that she had been raped. I imagined that whatever anger she felt was being repressed because she could feel nothing but yearning for her mother just now gone.

For all I now knew of my own rage toward my mother, though, I felt the strongest identification with this young woman, while the others told stories of confrontation and conflict.

Finally our therapist said, gently, "Now, Martha."

I burst into tears—messy, sudden weeping that I couldn't control.

The therapist asked me to try and say what I was feeling. "I just wish so much that I could talk with my mother," I got out. "I wish I could have things out with her the way some of you are trying to. I'm grown up and am strong enough to face her. I know what I want to talk about. But what's the point of knowing that now? She's gone."

That day I left the room crying.

I thought that if she were still alive I'd probably be carrying on a struggle more like theirs. I would be having to learn not how to accept my mother's absence, but how to try to speak with her about the rape in some way we could both manage, and how to live with however she continued to disappoint me. Still, I envied them with an animosity that surprised me, and with a child's furious longing I wanted her back.

After I left Edith's house I drove across the river to see Judy Clarke, who had been the librarian and taught ancient history at Solebury when I was there. Her husband, Robert, was the son of my father's closest boyhood friend, and they had been friends of our family. She had had a solidity and practicality that had contrasted with my mother's intensity of inspiration about our different way of life, and with the tendency at Solebury at that time toward a free-spirit attitude. I had chosen her as my advisor early on, when I arrived at the school in seventh grade, because I already knew and felt safe with her.

Arriving at the Clarkes' place and finding no space in their crowded lane, I parked on the edge of their lawn where it bordered the road. Judy came running out, arms akimbo, shouting; I had parked on her herb garden. I was instantly filled with shame of a quality I had not remembered experiencing for years.

I moved my car to a spot Robert showed me, and Judy and I inspected the place I'd driven my car over, as I apologized with chagrin. Since it was fall, there were no living plants there to be damaged, so no harm had been done. She instantly calmed down and warmly invited me to join her in her kitchen, where we sat down together.

"Why don't you just start telling me whatever you remember about the rape," I said. "From the beginning, or whatever you remember first."

"I don't remember whether Amelia called us or whether we happened by the house," she said. "But it was definitely Amelia who told us, not Fred. Her reaction was just—disbelief. Horror is the wrong word. She looked as though someone had just drained the life out of her; she was white. She had a bad feeling—*I should have gone to pick her up that day,* the feeling of prescience. When you came in the door, you almost didn't have to say anything, she knew something was wrong, even what it was.

"Of course, any parent would want to lock the guy up and throw away the key. You really want vengeance. I think they did realize the man was sick. They thought he needed psychiatric help, not a jail term, that would only aggravate it.

"I remember a feeling about Fred, later: disbelief, and just confusion—*How do you handle something like this?*"

"I didn't know how to react. I was angry, shocked. Bob was too. It was the kind of thing you read about in the papers, but it doesn't happen to you. It was just—*How do you deal with a child who's been raped?*"

"Do you remember any conversations you had with my mother about it?"

"I think Amelia was fairly astute and fairly direct. I think after the fact she realized what effects this kind of experience of brutality could have. She didn't strike me as the sort that would shove this under the rug, but would have got counseling for you."

"I never received any counseling," I volunteered.

"I'm really surprised," she said. "I just assumed she might have followed through with getting some kind of psychiatric help. The way she talked, it seemed as though she was confronting it directly. Maybe this one specific thing she couldn't deal with. For example, with Loch's problems, with the drugs and the physical and emotional problems, they could be more objective."

"Do you remember speaking with other teachers at Solebury about the rape?" I asked.

She answered as readily as if her words had been waiting to be said for twenty years: as if something in her was jumping at the chance to explain herself to the girl she had worried about. "I think everybody knew, because it was a small school, but it was the kind of thing, at that time, that you just wouldn't talk about. And that was probably not a good thing at all. It was probably very hard on you, that we didn't. I remember that I was very upset, but I just didn't know how to talk about it with anyone."

"Was it traumatic for you?"

"Oh, yeah. My first reaction, like anybody's, was shock and disorientation. Then, I think as you went through Solebury, the one thing I really saw was that you became withdrawn, socially, and became concentrated on things of the mind.

"It was the school's fault. They skipped you. You were not ready. You needed time to develop socially, and being put in with a bunch of kids a year ahead of you was not going to help, was going to be very hard for you. I thought we should give you advanced courses but keep you in eighth grade. Your entire thrust was to be as academically perfect as possible—to excel. You were never part of the scene. You never relaxed.

"When you were a little kid, you were a lot more open."

"Would you use the word obsessed?"

"No, that's not the right word. You were good at both academics and music. They were safe, a lot safer than trying at something you might fail at, like a relationship. You had friends—you kept the same friends all the way through. You didn't reach out to others. I think you wanted to be safe.

"The school was at fault. It didn't say, *Back off a little, it's okay to try something and not be good at it, instead of just doing what you're good at.*"

"Did you think of this as being associated with the rape at the time?"

"It was part of it. It was deep, inside you. I think if you hadn't been raped, this wouldn't have happened. Especially with the boys—you didn't have much to do with them. You didn't have the puppy love things with boys."

Judy had not guessed, apparently, how I had longed for Allen, and later Chris and Andy, to touch me and take me in their arms. But she had noticed that a relationship had not happened with anyone.

"You would still have excelled academically. I don't think you could relax. You were more—rigid, standoffish, perhaps. All of your drive and energy had been put into things of the mind."

"It sounds like you were concerned about me," I said.

"Oh, yeah," she answered. "I can remember when you got married, or engaged to be married." I had sent Bob and Judy a wedding announcement. "I can remember Bob saying, 'I guess Martha has finally come to grips with the rape, learned to deal with the fact that she had been raped.'

"What you had done was taken this and put it way down, and focused all of your energies, just erased it, *Go away, go away.*"

"Did you ever talk to my parents about that?"

"Even though I was concerned, it wasn't until later that I could see why it happened. You were doing the really cerebral things—you wanted to take pride in the fact that you were doing something as of the mind as the classics. You were involved with the 'eggheads,' you know, the ones who were studying Latin, and—medieval madrigals, for God's sake. It was as if you had chosen the things that were as removed as possible from real life and emotions."

I remembered how I loved singing the madrigals and learning those languages. They might have been my hiding place, but they were also my affirmations of the worthwhileness, the glory, of life.

"But at no time did I feel that you were part of your generation," she said. "Whether or not this would have happened if you hadn't been raped, you couldn't say—but not with such fervor. You came in to school, you had been raped, then you jumped a grade," she said, reversing the order of events. "It was a big jump—you were with kids you didn't know as well. It was an uncomfortable situation in any case, coupled with this recent trauma. It probably just shattered your personal life. Thirteen and fourteen is always confused, even if you have had the most serene and untraumatic upbringing.

"On the surface, being skipped was worse, but probably a lot of it was the basis of the rape. Somewhere at the back of my spine I knew part of the problem was the rape.

"I think you got a hell of a bum break."

"Do you remember how Fred and Amelia felt about me being skipped?" I asked.

"I don't really know. They might have had a little bit of trepidation about it, but I don't think they realized the emotional impact of skipping. It seemed as though you were doing everything that was expected. The reaction was probably a sigh of relief. All the outside signs were that you had recovered. She's into her music, her appetite is good. And since you seemed to have picked up the pieces beautifully—

"It was sort of a *don't touch*—you didn't really want anyone to get too close. Before, you had a lot of exuberance, you would be chasing Alida, and so forth. You still laughed, still talked to people, but it wasn't as spontaneous.

"I think actually, you probably would have been better off if you had just simply fallen apart. Then everyone would have said, *My God, we really have to do something.* But you didn't, you just simply withdrew. You probably would have been better off if you had screwed up. You sailed through with flying colors.

"I had the impression that while you were still not as relaxed as others, you did ease up some over time. At Solebury, nobody was going to think you were strange. Sometimes you were considered a snob, but really you were just closed in, you just shut up tight.

"The more I thought about it later, I thought it would have been painful, but it would have been better if I could have said to you that I knew, and it was okay to talk about.

"When you were in college—but then it was too late."

My talks with my father, Loch, and Alida, and with Edith and Judy, revived my memory of just how troubled as a family we had been. Somehow I had never looked at the rape as one important source of that trouble. How could I, as long as I had not looked at it even as a source of trouble for myself?

Perhaps also I had not wanted to know how badly my rape had disturbed my parents, and Loch and Alida, because I felt responsible.

Clearly it had contributed to Loch's mental anguish and his difficulties in college, which had culminated in his first breakdown. The persistence of his mental illness as the years passed had aggravated in my parents the despair that found its outlet in drinking and bitterness. Their radical ways had already isolated them from the people around them. Their helpless rage over what had been done to me, their rage at the community that had not acted to protect me, got turned inward. They were never able to communicate to me how deeply they cared about me and my hurt, how precious I really was to them.

It was too late to mend things, if they ever could have been mended. At least I now grasped the totality of what had happened. I could see that for them it had been impossible to face the depth of their feelings for me, and for themselves, when the rape happened. And I could see that this was not my fault.

I thought I might visit the county offices and see if I could unearth any documents that would shed light on what happened. If there were records of the investigation, of what Goreski, Rocco, and Rittenhouse had found out and thought about Frank Miller, I might find out how they came to see him as their prime suspect.

When I read the trial transcript I had discovered that Rittenhouse had made a clear and straightforward argument for Miller's guilt.

> We know that Martha Ramsey was ravaged, raped on Quarry Road on August 13th between 3:30 and 4:00. The testimony is clear to that effect and not disputed by Mr. Bernhard. We know that she could never identify her assailant and she has been honest about that. We know that she did say certain things, however, about this attack. . . . We know that Quarry Road . . . was a lonely and remote spot . . . there are no houses on either side . . . and the

pictures . . . show that it was heavy foliage, trees, and so on, and from that you know then that this is not the kind of a spot where any kind of sex deviate would just lie incriminately and wait. You know that whoever was there and attacked Martha Ramsey that day knew she was going to be there and had time to make arrangements to perpetrate the act. . . . You know, also, that no one who testified here knew that Martha Ramsey was going to be at that particular spot at that time. . . . So whoever perpetrated that act—and this isn't conjecture or just mere theory or surmising—you can deduce and know whoever perpetrated that act at some point had to see Martha Ramsey start up that road. . . . We know by tracing back the times that . . . the assailant had to be at the location of the intersection of this road at approximately 3:25 P.M., on August 13th. . . . We also know that that assailant had to be familiar enough with this scene to know that Quarry Road was remote enough to let an attack like this take place. That just follows logically. . . .

Frank Miller, the defendant in this case, seated here at this table, he knew this quarry area. He had been there before. He talked with Charlotte Tritt. He said he used the dump area. He was going to rent a house in the area. He knew all about it. He knew the trees, the grass, the ravine, he knew the triangular route which could easily be traversed by anyone knowing the area to know how to intercept Martha on that particular day. We know that Frank Miller was there on the corner that day, ladies and gentlemen. I want you to look at the photographs carefully . . . to notice how it is so clear that observation could be made right from that house that he was renting . . . to see that little girl start across the road at 3:15 that day. No one else is placed at that scene at this particular time but Mr. Miller, who by his own testimony places himself at that particular scene at that time.

We know Frank Miller watched that little girl walk up that

lonely road that day and start there, and he says and he admitted to the police, "Why would I do this if I was a guilty man?"

Ladies and gentlemen, the truth of the matter is that Frank Miller was parked at that particular house that day, his truck was there. Martha Ramsey didn't see him. . . . She might have but she said she didn't. But Frank Miller doesn't know whether she saw him or not. When he talked to Detective Goreski he had no idea that little girl would say she saw him at the bottom of the hill and wouldn't [he] have been in a fine fix if that little girl had said she saw him and then he said to the police, "I wasn't there and I didn't see a little girl"? . . .

Frank Miller knew where the clothes that were taken from the scene that day were. How do we know he knew? Is there any reason that any of you can think of that Mr. Anthony Capizzi would come here and testify about a conversation in the bar that night and lie or fabricate in any way at all? . . . We know that he told Mr. Capizzi where he threw an item of clothing, and when the police went there they found those items of clothing exactly where Mr. Miller said it would be. Now, who else would have known about it?

Mr. Miller said he was driving down the road with his wife and he came upon an item of clothing that looked like a teenage brassiere on the other side of the road at forty miles an hour, and we are expected to believe from the testimony that he slammed his car to a stop because he just had to see what that item was and went out and picked it up and threw it out between the bridges and later on he and his wife looked all over for it and couldn't find it. . . .

There is another thing that we know from the facts. . . . when Frank Miller was approached by . . . one of his best friends on August 22nd alone in that bedroom, that man looked at him and said, "Frank, did you do it? Did you rape that little girl?" He nodded his head and you saw Mr. Schavemaker explain how he

> nodded his head in the affirmative. "Why, Frank, why?" He shrugged his shoulders. Now, shrugging isn't going to do it.
>
> Ladies and gentlemen, Mr. and Mrs. Schavemaker took this stand and told me the story. They have been honest and straightforward about what happened. They have indicated there was trouble between them and the Millers after this but you can't believe after hearing them testify that anyone would be that vindictive that they would lie about a thing like that.

These arguments, when I read them as an adult, were far more convincing to me than anything I ever actually heard Rittenhouse say. I had not heard him make his summation; my mother had reported his argument to me as best she could.

I had always remembered learning, during the trial, that Miller said he had seen me walk up the road, and that Rittenhouse argued that he had driven his truck around a triangle of roads to park ahead of me and crouch in the gully waiting for me to pass. But I had always imagined that someone else, coming from some other location, could have driven his truck there and waited in the gully to pounce on me. It had never occurred to me, and no one had ever explained to me, that that person would have had to see me entering Quarry Road; that before that moment no one could have predicted which way I would turn when I came to the crossroads from which Quarry Road led.

Even at this late date, when it felt strange that it still mattered so much, when I read the trial transcript my discovery of this argument reassured me. It brought a refreshing sense of conviction.

All my life I'd been haunted by the thought that perhaps I was responsible for jailing an innocent man. I'd been haunted too by the figure of the unknown rapist, the one who had gotten away with it and was out there somewhere, in the rapists' realm, despising me for my lies to him in the clearing and ready, if he should ever run across me again, to wipe me out. No matter that as a girl I tried to convince myself that these were figments, or that in adult life I relegated them to the furthest possible recesses of my mind. They had lived. I could tell, by how it felt as they finally began to dissolve.

When I read Rittenhouse's argument a late movement stirred in my heart—the girl's heart—of gratitude to him. He was smart enough to figure out the problem; he didn't give up. He had enough faith in his small-town jury to challenge them with an intricate reconstruction. He hadn't been content to build his argument on what other people said Miller had said. I felt regret that he was no longer alive and I could not thank him for his work.

My mind now accepted Frank Miller as rapist, but another part of me still refused to know that the rapist really existed as a man. I wanted to gain a picture of Miller as a real person that I could hold in my mind as an adult. I hoped that further interviews and other documents might reveal more to me of who he was, whether he was someone people had found it easy to imagine raping an adolescent girl. If as an adult I could handle finding out what he was, the girl within me might now come to know it too without fear.

Another woman in my rape therapy group decided to try to talk with some of the people who were in her life when she was raped at sixteen. Like me, she said, she thought they might help her understand better what she could not understand then. Some of the people she asked were willing to help her and talk; others seemed unable to handle it. The man who had been her boyfriend at the time of her rape agreed to meet with her and talk but then did not show up.

She called me. "How do you ask people about this?" she asked. "I have such a strong urge to talk to them, but I don't know exactly what I want from them, really."

We didn't say it but we both knew we wanted something big and undefinable that no one could give. Yet we also were willing to take whatever we could get. The act of trying seemed the main thing.

"Do you know how to get the trial records?" she said. "It just occurred to me that I could do that."

"Yes," I told her. "I already got mine."

I wondered if anyone who had not been raped could understand our urge to recover these things.

As I planned further travel to New Jersey to talk to people I knew less well, I found myself not thinking very clearly. Each step forward was slow and difficult. Finally I had to admit that I did not really feel like doing it. I was afraid.

I wondered whether, if I were not writing a book, had not committed myself to this exploration as a project, I would be able to go forward with these actions at all. I couldn't pretend to myself now that my interest in the rape could be in any way detached. I couldn't pretend that I wasn't very nervous about speaking out loud about the rape to people who also remembered it.

I tried to let the nature of the fear be a guide for me. Afraid, I was thirteen again. Now, I reminded myself, a part of me was fully adult and could keep perspective on what was frightening.

The girl had dreamed of rescue. I knew she was gone but I couldn't help myself: I wanted to ride in and save her.

Neil Cooper, the current county prosecutor of Hunterdon County, had already sent me a couple of documents from his files. Now I hoped to find out what else they might contain.

Over the phone he had told me that he had not been in the county at the time of the rape in 1968 and remembered nothing about it. But he had been working in Rittenhouse's office when Miller was tried for murder in 1973, and that case had interested him greatly.

"Miller's appeal of that conviction went all the way to the Supreme Court," he told me proudly. "And it was upheld. The appeal was based on the circumstances of his questioning and confession, given at the police station the day of his arrest. The entire questioning was taped. Everybody at the police station wanted a piece of him. Lou Rocco did all he could to preserve the integrity of it. After Miller gave the statement he went comatose. He just passed out cold in his chair, and they had to take him to the hospital. This did not look good for the police."

He had sent me an excerpt from a textbook that described the questioning of Miller. Miller admitted that he had approached his victim at her family's farm. He said she had followed him in her car to the place where he had seen a cow that was loose. While they were walking through the fields he had turned and seen her being attacked by another man with a knife. He tried to help her and the man ran away. He then "put her in his car, but panicked because he thought she was dead," and " 'dropped her off' the bridge into the stream."

> "I'm telling you the truth. Sure, that's her blood in the car because when I seen the way she was cut I wanted to help her, and then when she fell over I got scared to even be involved in something like this, being on parole. . . ."
>
> The officer persisted that truth was the issue, and truth would prevail in the end. . . .
>
> "That's the most important thing, not, not what has happened, Frank. The fact that you were truthful, you came forward and you said, Look, I have a problem."

Miller finally confessed. He admitted that the girl had gotten into his car with him.

> They drove down by the bridge where defendant took a penknife from his pocket and started cutting the girl . . . he had no real recollection of just what he did to the girl or why, although he remembered throwing her body off the bridge. . . . he drove home and, using a hose, washed the blood from the seat of the car. . . .
>
> Shortly after the questioning was terminated, defendant ap-

peared to go into a state of shock. He slid off the chair onto the floor and had a blank stare on his face. When he did not respond to questions, he was taken to the Hunterdon Medical Center.

"The people of Hunterdon County were so outraged by that murder that Miller had to be tried next door in Mercer County," Neil Cooper told me. "He could not have received a fair trial here."

"Where is he now?" I asked.

"He is currently serving a life sentence in Rahway State Prison," he said. "This office will see to it that Miller is never paroled again."

When I met with Neil Cooper, I asked to see the files of the case, which he agreed to. Then I asked if I could visit the courthouse. He offered to take me there.

As he led me into the courthouse I did not see what I had expected. In my memory the courtroom had been grand, dim, and imposing. The room I was standing in reminded me of the assembly room at my elementary school. It had the atmosphere peculiar to municipal buildings furnished in the 1950s. The chairs and tables were pale, highly varnished wood. The walls, above the wooden wainscotting, which was painted white, were a sickeningly sweet pale blue, a color you would expect to see in a second-grade classroom.

The room was smaller, more intimate than I had remembered. I had felt alone, marooned, surrounded by scary space. The room then had been both too large and too small. It had contained no one who could help me; it had contained too many who could not help me.

"It was probably white when you were here," Neil Cooper said.

He noticed that I had become abstracted and he stayed quiet, making small remarks, commenting that little had changed since he had first come to work here in the early seventies. We walked up the aisle between rows of benches like pews and stopped at the two tables the lawyers for prosecution and defense used. He asked me if I would like to try sitting in the witness box. I knew then that he understood something of why I was there.

When I sat in the box my view was lower and I got a better sense of the courtroom I remembered. The judge's bench was very close to me. I remembered now the terrible closeness of the judge. The jury's chairs, too, were close to me. They began right at the left edge of the witness box.

He walked toward me and stood with his hands on the edge of the box. He looked down at me and, in a way, through me, just as he would when prosecuting a case, not really engaged in the interaction with the witness but performing it in interaction with the jury, as Rittenhouse had done when questioning me.

He began talking in a legalistic manner about the preliminary hearing procedures that would have been followed at the time of Miller's trial. As he talked and I looked up at him, I began to feel as though I were much smaller. His gray suit turned into a wall, like the side of a military ship, and his face lost its friendly quality. He loomed over me, and his voice spoke of powers and methods I could not comprehend. I found myself looking at him, for a second, with eyes filled with fear. I had to ask him to repeat himself, for his words had become lost in a haze of terror.

It seemed to me that he saw that look on my face. Perhaps he had even deliberately put his hands on the box and leaned over me, talking as any prosecutor would, knowing that this behavior would prompt my remembering, to make my return to the witness box feel real.

Like Neil Cooper, Judge Thomas Beetel remembered Miller mainly for the murder he had committed upon being paroled in 1973.

"Oh, yes, I remember your case," he said. "I sentenced him to the full term. We did not have parole disqualifiers then. I wrote, in light of his tremendous responses, he not be allowed out. They released him. It was a tremendous disappointment to Bill Rittenhouse and to me."

I spoke with him in his law office, the ground floor of a small two-story house, with bay windows and an aluminum screen door, on Main Street near the courthouse. He was not especially tall but seemed dapper, round, and quick, and so sharp I felt I would have to concentrate hard to keep up and even then would probably not be able to. His manner made it clear that he was a busy man.

"I'd like you to tell me whatever you remember about the case," I said.

"I can recall the jury panel," he said. "I was the sole judge in the county. There was the usual reluctance to serve, and the usual reluctance on my part to allow excuses. There were eleven challenges from the prosecutor. It came close to not being able to have a panel.

"The trial was quite contested."

"What do you mean by 'contested'?"

"Bitterly fought. No conceding of anything.

"I remember you testifying."

"What was I like?"

"You were a tall, lanky teenager—weren't you? With long hair. I remember you saying you got on your bicycle and went home."

"What do you remember about my parents?"

"They were very sincere. They gave you great support and realized what you were going through—great empathy—this affected the jury. The sincerity of the family unit was very apparent in the courtroom."

"Do you remember how I behaved on the stand?"

"It was clear that you were very anxious."

"What were the signs of my anxiety?"

"You were closest to me. I was watching you relive it. I saw the usual things—twisting of the hands in the clothes—moving around in the witness box, tension in the voice, twitching in the face."

"Were you surprised at all by the verdict?"

"I thought the verdict was totally commensurate with the evidence."

"What did you think of the identification of Miller?"

"It seemed to me the description had some open edges but pretty much fit the defendant. The prosecution requested the jury be taken by bus to understand the terrain. The loneliness of the area played a factor in the conviction. Miller did not make a very good appearance. His manner and demeanor made an issue for the jury."

"What did you think of the prosecution?"

"Bill Rittenhouse was a wonderful man; I considered him to be a personal friend. I trained him. He had almost a James Stewart approach to the jury. He wasn't quick—at times there were definite pauses in his delivery—but it worked.

"I respected Ed Bernhard. He was a scrappy defense counsel—took no nonsense, insisted the proofs be properly carried out. If he didn't object he would have lost the grounds for appeal."

"So would you say that Miller hired one of the best, if not the best?"

"Yes."

So Bernhard, with his endless questions that had seemed idiotic to me when I was fourteen, had known exactly what he was doing.

Judge Beetel described me as "a tall, lanky teenager," a term that made no reference to my sex. I remembered how tall and lanky I had been. In the courtroom I had tried to dress and present myself as a woman; he had not noted that. Still, I welcomed his three words, the way he described this rape victim without referring to her victimhood. Of all those who remembered me at the trial, only he would use such terms.

I was able to locate and talk with five members of the jury. I was curious to know what had stood out for these people who had been most detached from the entire affair. I was also curious to know how they had arrived at a conviction, the certainty of Miller's guilt that had evaded me.

Edward Busher had been the bartender at the Wunderbar in White House, a small town about ten miles north of Flemington, at the time of the trial. I called on him at his home, a small, comfortable house of suburban design on a country road near White House. He introduced his wife to me; she busied herself in the kitchen while we talked but would not miss a thing, I suspected. We sat down awkwardly together at a table, and I asked him what he remembered.

"When we went in the jury room we took a vote; six voted guilty, and six were undecided," he said. "About halfway through we took another vote, and nine or ten voted guilty. The next time, it was all but one. We all brought out our ideas on why he was guilty, and he finally gave in."

"Do you remember what I was like?"

"You were nervous. You were good with your answers. When one of the lawyers asked a question you came right out with the answer."

"How did you feel about the conviction?"

"I felt good about finding him guilty. Right away on the evidence I thought he was guilty. When he was paroled, I said they let that SOB out, and he's gonna rape somebody again. I always knew he had done it.

"The thing that was most convincing about Miller was his prior history. He had been arrested for stealing women's underwear from neighbors' clotheslines when he was a teenager. This was really strange, it made a big impression on all of us."

John Ericson's occupation, on the list of jurors, was listed as "estimator."

"Would you be willing to talk to me about what you remember about the trial?" I asked him over the phone.

"Yes," he answered. Then he burst out: "You were great!" Clearly, what had stood out for him at the trial had been me.

The Ericsons' door opened directly into a small living room crammed with old furniture and objects that seemed treasured for their personal appeal and interest. An old upright piano, a worn patterned rug, three chairs that did not match, piles of magazines. It reminded me of the house where I'd grown up.

Patience Ericson made me a cup of tea and brought it to me in a mug. I sat down facing John, and we began to talk.

"Before the trial started I thought, this is going to be awful, a tearjerker. With a young girl being raped, you know, I thought it would be very emotional. But I soon found that the lawyers were proceeding in a very rational manner, and I was relieved—there was no problem.

"You were exceptional. He led you through it. I thought there would be breaking down on the stand, a disaster. But you were extremely well composed. For a person your age it was extraordinary."

He spoke so eagerly, it sounded as if he had been waiting for twenty years to praise this girl.

John continued, "You were just young enough. It left little doubt that we should be believing this—it convinced us—it made us look beyond if there was a question about your validity—and you held up through it."

I asked John what he remembered of Bernhard.

"He was all right. I know there was some humor involved about the stockings—it didn't work."

"How did you become convinced that Miller was guilty?" I asked.

"I was not totally convinced until we went over it. It was really the timetable. You had to go through it to make it work. They took us there on the bus. Most of the people did not understand the timetable business. It was a lot of long, hard talking. In my mind there was no doubt at all."

They invited me to sit down with them at their kitchen table, and we ate some pumpkin pie. As they asked me about my life now, they seemed comfortable with me and able to treat me as an adult without denying the fact of the hurt that had brought me there.

Dorothy Haman had been a checker at the A & P at the time of the trial; now she worked in a bank and lived with her son's family in White House. She had discouraged me from coming; she said she remembered very little of the trial. Her memory was in fact the least detailed of any of the jurors I talked with.

But when I saw her I remembered her sitting in the jury box, her face looking beaky and closed to me, her dark sculpted hair. I began to have a sense that I could remember how some of the others in the jury box had looked as well.

The interview was quickly over, as we mutually acknowledged that nothing much had turned up. Then, unlike the other jurors, Mrs. Haman then began to tell me about her own life. She showed me a picture she had painted of the farm where she had spent her girlhood. She pointed to a painting resting on an easel and another hanging beside the bed. "These are all my paintings," she said. I could see in them an urgency of her having to paint the landscapes she had loved as a girl. I complimented them, and she accepted my compliments with quiet graciousness.

William Sassaman, whose occupation had been given as "paper maker" on the jury list, had sounded like a fairly old man on the phone and had been so interested in having me come that I had kept the appointment, even though it didn't sound like he had much to offer.

I drove in the dark to his house at the top of a hill, and he came outside to meet me. He took my hand as if to lead me through the darkness toward the house. I instantly felt uncomfortable and pulled my hand away.

We sat in his living room.

"If you could just tell me what you remember," I said.

"The one thing the prosecutor brought up—and they got so mad at him—he brought up about the clothesline, just started onto it—right away the other lawyer jumped up and stopped it. The judge said strike that but of course you remember it."

I was beginning to understand, from this conversation and from my talk with Dorothy Haman, that Rittenhouse had mentioned something about Miller stealing women's clothes, and now I knew why I had read nothing about it in the transcript.

"Do you remember me?" I asked.

"I can still picture you in my mind," William Sassaman said. "At first I thought, *That's probably some girl that was pretty good-lookin', and brought it on herself.* Then when I saw you I thought, *No way,* because you were pretty small then. I expected to see a girl more well developed. If they'd have told me you were eleven I would have believed it. That sort of made up my mind.

"If you'd have been a bigger girl—

"When I saw you, and he was sitting there so smug, cocky like he could get away with it—"

It was not a new discovery to me at this point that I, like so many women who have to testify to rape, had also been on trial, vulnerable even at thirteen to the question of whether I had somehow "asked for it." William Sassaman had assessed my readiness for sex on the basis of my physical maturity. Because I looked like a child, there could be no doubt of the fact of the rape or of the perversity of the man who had desired sex with her.

I now knew that at least one man on the jury, and probably others, had been ready to try me. I was not surprised by Sassaman's attitude so much as by his readiness to tell me about it, his failure to see anything wrong in it or to wonder how it might affect me. Along with my disgust and anger, I felt perversely pleased simply to have unearthed such clear evidence that the kind of prejudice I had sensed in the atmosphere at the time, and deduced from reading the transcript, had really been at work.

Hazel Ott was a stout grandmother with white curls cropped in a practical style and a straightforward manner. I stepped into her house and we sat down in two easy chairs in her living room. She looked me over.

"You're an attractive girl," she said.

Even though we were sitting at opposite ends of the room, there was no feeling of stiffness or distance. Most of what she remembered was a repetition of what others had said. When I asked her what she had felt toward Miller, she said, "I didn't think he got as much as he should have. He wanted to 'get me a virgin'—that came out in the trial. A married man with kids—he should be put away and throw away the keys."

More than any other juror, Hazel Ott said she clearly remembered my mother.

"Your mother had dark hair—she wore it back like this. I remembered her because I was watching her and I felt like I knew exactly what she was going through. She just sat there, and she had some knitting, or crocheting, in her hands, that she kept doing. I knew she was doing it because she had to have something to keep her from going nuts. I imagine she was knitting but wasn't missing a thing."

"What did you think was going through her mind?"

"She just wanted to jump up and kill him!" she exclaimed, as if she was surprised that I had to ask.

Over and over the jurors and others pointed out to me that, at least after they'd seen and heard me testify, they had viewed me simply as a girl, a "little girl," not someone who could in any way be perceived as capable of inviting sexual advances. It was strange to discover this, since I myself had been enjoying showing off my newly forming curves in a short dress, excited about the idea of my new breasts and long slender legs as objects of admiration. My secret guilt that perhaps I had wanted to invite some kind of sexual attention—they had not seen it.

Their perception of the wrongness of the act had been clearer than mine, I was also discovering. To them it had been monstrous, inconceivable, deserving of the most severe punishment. To me, though, it had always been something that had actually happened, not something that never should or, one told oneself, never would happen.

I began to see my thirteen-year-old self with their eyes—innocent, young, and badly hurt.

As I spoke with each of them, I remembered their faces looking closed and detached within a row of other faces. Their individual personalities and expressions were submerged in the unity of their duty: to hear the evidence without drawing conclusions, to preserve a demeanor that would neither encourage nor discourage anything.

This impassivity, I now realized, as the memory stirred again, had frightened me. Just as now I was surprised by their matter-of-factness, I had been frightened by it then. They had sat there in a row like still birds, eagles with keen eyes, sharp beaks. Mercy was not their assignment. At thirteen I thought I understood that very well.

When I returned to the prosecutor's office two brown accordion files, bound with brown string, one much thicker than the other, awaited me on the table in the back room.

In the bulky file I discovered Rittenhouse's handwritten drafts of his opening and closing statements. I could see how he had revised them when he had spoken at the trial, bringing his language down to earth and making his points more simply.

On another page I found his timetable.

MARTHA:

2:50	Left Retivov	35 min.
3:26	Route 29	6 min.
3:32	Scene	21 min.

3:53	Left scene	5 min.
3:58	Saw Michel	7 min.
4:05	Arrived home	

MILLER:

3:00	Left home
3:20	Arrived at Tusche home
3:25	At rented residence
3:30	At scene
3:49	Left scene to Sergeantsville Bridge
4:09	Back past Tritt home

TRITT:

4:09	Left home
4:14	At Quarry

LOCH:

4:20	At Quarry
5:00	At work

This list had been erased and repenciled many times.

I found the reports that had been filed almost daily by Detective Frank Goreski, the state trooper whom I had remembered as being unusually sensitive, who was later removed from the case.

August 14, 1968

> Det. Rocco and I returned to the scene and began a detailed search of the area. . . . We then entered the woods, following the trampled grass approximately 100 ft. in, where the attack had occurred. This spot was completely flattened out in the tall grass, an area of 4 ft. by 8 ft.
>
> The undersigned was able to find the victim's sunglasses, only by clearing out the grass with the aid of a sickle. A thorough search for the victim's clothing or any other evidence proved negative. It is the opinion of this investigator that this spot in the grass had been prepared prior to the crime.

The reports told how Goreski questioned all the residents nearest the scene. No one had seen or heard anything strange.

August 17, 1968

> . . . Douglas McMichael, age 14, approached the undersigned and stated that he was fishing in the quarry and saw a woman's silk stocking in the water. Douglas . . . was taken . . . to the spot. Found the nylon stocking hanging over a small branch in the water. . . . This stocking was of a skin shade and had been cut off, so, if

worn, would come short of the knee. It was believed that this stocking could be the one used in perpetration of this crime.

August 20, 1968
Suspect: Frank Melvin Miller Jr., Box 17,
Sergeantsville, NJ

. . . received information . . . that one Charlotte Tritt of Federal Twist Rd. may have information connected with this case.

Located Charlotte Tritt, age 20, working at the Hunterdon Medical Center and interviewed her there. She stated she had met a man, a couple of days prior to the crime, who was driving a blue pick-up truck. He stopped to talk to her at the cut out area off Quarry Rd. which is approximately 150 ft. east of where this crime occurred. This meeting was brief and he left saying he would be seeing her. The following day he saw her again at the same place, at approximately the same time, between 4:00 and 5:00 P.M. Their conversation came to sex and he asked her if she was a virgin and proceeded to tell her about the pains experienced by a woman losing her virginity and about loose women that he knew. He further told her that she should save the bottom half of herself for her husband.

On the date of the crime at approximately 4:00 P.M. she saw his vehicle pass her house. She was pulling out of her driveway. He saw her, turned around and followed her down to the same meeting place. Charlotte pulled her car into the cut out and he parked on the left side of the road facing west. They again talked about sex. She recalled Loch Ramsey whom she knew, stop his bicycle near the truck. When the man she was with asked Loch what he wanted, Loch said never mind and rode away.

Charlotte recalled that on the second meeting, he had given her

> his name, but that on the next visit he told her that that name was the name of his foreman. She could not remember that name, but believed he lived in Sergeantsville and worked in Belle Meade, N.J. A physical description was obtained from her. He was a white male, 28 years of age, 5′7″, 165 lbs, brown hair, blue eyes, slightly heavy but muscular and wore glasses. He wore dark blue pants, a T-shirt and on one occasion were a matching blue long-sleeved shirt. . . .
>
> I asked Charlotte Tritt whether this man did or tried to molest her in any way. She stated he had not.

I couldn't quite picture the meetings of Charlotte Tritt and Frank Miller. It didn't seem to make sense, that he simply sat with her and talked about sex, and she simply listened and allowed it to continue, more than once, and that was all. I hoped I might find out more.

> In checking the Sergeantsville area, located and questioned Frank Melvin Miller . . . learned he is married, has 4 children and is employed by the . . . 3M . . . Co. . . . as a forklift operator. He admitted knowing Charlotte Tritt and talking with her at the Quarry Rd. location, on several occasions and on the day of the crime.
>
> Miller was asked to explain his whereabouts during the entire day. At this point he asked me if this was in regard to the rape. I told him it was and he said he had nothing to hide. He stated he did not go to work that day, due to being sick with the virus. He visited Dr. Fuhrman's Office, Flemington, but was not able to see the doctor because he did not have an appointment. This was about 11:30 A.M. He then stopped at Jenning's Ford and returned

home to have a cup of coffee with his wife, at between 1:30 and 2:30 P.M. He asked his wife for the key to the apartment which they intend to move into, located on Rt. #29, Raven Rock. She gave him the key and he left the house.

When he arrived at the Raven Rock Apt., he found that the key would not open the door. He then went to the property owner, Mr. Tusche, and obtained another key. Returning to his Apt., he checked the place over, staying about 20 minutes, locked up and then left. He then met Charlotte Tritt.

It takes approximately 5–10 minutes to get from Miller's present home to the Raven Rock Apt. Subject was asked to explain his whereabouts between 2:40 and 4:00 P.M. He became confused. . . .

What happened next was described by Miller himself when he talked with his lawyer, recorded in a transcript that was also in the file.

BERNHARD: O.K., now tell me what happened when you went to the police station.

MILLER: You don't want to know anything about what they done when they came down—

BERNHARD: Yup. Tell me everything.

MILLER: Well this girl had gotten raped. So he [Detective Goreski] wanted to know if I'd mind if he went out and looked through the house. I said no sir I do not. So he said will you go with me. I said yes sir. I went into the house, got the keys from my wife. I took him in, he looked all through the house and everything and he couldn't find anything.

He asked me, he says, you was down through here that day. He said did you see anything? Yes sir I said that there was a girl on a bicycle. She was pushing a bicycle up the hill as I was going down the hill with my pickup. What colored clothes did she have on? I said really I don't know. It was a red top, now whether it was a dress, or just a blouse or not I don't know. He said describe the bicycle. Well it was an English type bicycle, a racer. What color? I said I believe it had chrome wheels, but the color, I couldn't be sure. It was a dark colored bike.

So he went out the very road where this all happened. . . . He showed me approximately where this was supposed to take place. And, then he asked me where did you see the girl on the bicycle? I pointed that out to him. . . . He wanted to know how I knew the color of the girl's clothes and what they were looking for. Well, Saturday night we were up to this Forge and Anvil, it used to be Farmers Inn in Barbertown. People from Raven Rock that was there at this place, I was talking to this woman because they live in the area, about this. I said I was a little leery about moving out there now that this had happened, being that I have two daughters of my own. She said that there are so many cops and detectives around there that there was nothing to worry about and she would tell me what they were looking for. They were looking for a red dress, a pair of white cotton pants and a white bra with some kind of designs in it. So this is what I told the detective. And, he said how did you find that out, we never gave that information out. I told him, I said I don't know the woman's name but I know she lives in Raven Rock. Well, he says we never gave that information out. Well, I was told yesterday that the same date this happened, this girl's mother called everybody in that surrounding area giving a description of the girl's clothing, and told them that her daughter had been raped. . . .

He gave my the [polygraph] test and he mentioned the girl's

name four or five times, this area, four or five times. After this was all over and everything, he says to me . . . either you're holding something back or you're very nervous about this. I said why? He said as soon as I mention this area and this girl, he says you're nervous. He says, watch. . . . I says if you was in my shoes you'd be nervous too wouldn't you. He said yes I would. I said well my reasons are that I have two daughters of my own, I rented a house as of September 1st to move in that very area. . . . I think that's a pretty good reason to be nervous. He said yes, it is. So that was it with him.

I stayed in that room by myself for quite awhile. Well, oh, and I told this detective on Tuesday when he was down there, I said I'm going to meet this girl face to face and talk to her. Well they arranged for her to be up there on Wednesday. She was there and they had me stand on one side of the wall and she was on the other. And they had me read off some sentences which were on a pad they had put down. Now I take for granted that this is what was said to this girl when this all took place. And I said them and they went into the other room and come back and say say them over again louder, like you know the sentences but you don't need the pad to say them. Well I done my best. Well this girl claims, the detective claims that this girl says it was my voice. So I said look, you've got the girl here, I'd like to talk to her. I said I sure can't pull anything I said if I was the guilty one, I couldn't pull anything in this barracks, because you'd have me so fast that my head would spin. Yeah, he said I guess you're right. So they took the girl outside and had me run up to her alongside the barracks. Her mother, her and the detectives was up at the other end, this Rocco. So, he told me, he says now, run up to her. So I ran up to her. And, then he gave me this paper, I was supposed to be face to face with this girl and talk to her, at least I asked to. But he gave me this paper and pad again and said repeat all this. I had to talk through this Rocco because he stood right between us. I didn't even get the sentences finished or anything when Rocco grabbed me spun me around and said back in the barracks, that's enough. . . .

This one detective was Frank Goreski. He was very nice, I got no complaints on the way he talked to me or questioned me or anything. But this Rocco, he was slam, banging things around, slammed the door, throwin' things around and I told him right out. I said if you're going to be like a wild man, I said and not like a human being, slam, bang scream at me, I said I'm going to shut up like a clam and you're not going to get a damn word out of me. . . . Rocco wouldn't tell me anything. Goreski was the one who told me the girl said that it was my voice, the girl said it was my run, the girl said it was my features, then this Rocco comes back in and tries to tell me how tall I am, how much I weigh and how I've done it. . . . Rocco said I know you done it, I want to know what you've done with the clothes. I said I don't know what you're talking about. He said you know, we've got the rock that was used to threaten this girl or something like that I said alright then where's your fingerprints. He said you can't get fingerprints off a rock same as you can't get blood out of a rock. Now is this so?

Bernhard asked Miller what he was doing during the time the rape had occurred.

These detectives claimed that they was going to hang me with my times. . . . I'm not one for keeping times as you probably already noticed, I've turned to my wife a few times for times. . . . I stopped at the house because the keys the landlord had given us for

> the house we were supposed to move into in Raven Rock, didn't fit. . . . Now, this is where the, where I am really in trouble because of the time. Anyway I got the key and went out, it wouldn't work in the house. I walked around the outside of the house, at daylight, because when I did look at it with the landlord, it was at night and I couldn't see that much, it was that dark.

At the exact time the rape had occurred, Miller's account became confused.

> So, then I went out and got the key and I came back and this girl I had met at different times, I had seen her and I had talked to her along the road and I stopped talking to her. This same after, after I had gotten the key for the house I went back to the house and looked better inside the house because the landlord, he zooms, zooms, you know, just to see what the house is and to see what you got, and if you want it, alright, and if you don't alright. So I stopped, well I came right up back this road where this was all supposed to take place and instead of going home the way I went I went right on up over the Federal Twist Road because there is another road up in there somewheres. I have been on that road once or twice because one night the fire company had a bad fire up there, a barn burned. . . .

Bernhard tasked Miller what had happened when he had met Charlotte Tritt a few minutes later at the quarry.

> BERNHARD: Well, did you do anything?

MILLER: No sir, I never laid a hand on this girl. She is 20 years old and the first time I met her she was laying out in this quarry area. She had all her clothes on but she was laying there in a pair of shorts and a blouse sunning herself is what it amounts to. She was completely dressed and she was doing nothing wrong and I've done nothing wrong. . . .

BERNHARD: How long a time did you spend with her on the 13th?

MILLER: The 13th. I must have been there maybe an hour or so talking to her, but this was along the road, sitting in her car. . . . One detective claimed that this is going to hang me too, because of what her and I was talking about, which was sex. Now, she told me she was a virgin . . . and I told her I'm glad to hear that, because I said anymore around this area or around any other area, it's damn hard to find a virgin, I said, when you get married. Which is true. At least from what I've been told, and from what I gathered from guys I've talked to, my buddies. And, I made no passes whatsoever at this girl, and the main subject was sex. She, you know, she said that her parents had never explained anything to her and this and that. And, somehow we got into this subject of sex and I started talking to her, well, some of my friends will tell you, I guess you would call me bold. I could walk up to a stranger and start talking about just about anything. . . . This is my nature, it always has been like this.

BERNHARD: Well it sounds pretty good Frank, what we do is, we have a hearing as to probable cause. . . . Have you ever had any problems with the law before?

MILLER: Outside of moving violations with a vehicle, no. I've been in jail once and that was a month or so ago and this was for refusing to pay a fine in motor vehicle court.

BERNHARD: How about as a juvenile? Did you ever have any problems?

MILLER: Yes, but I was never convicted on anything. As far as problems, yes. I was roughly 13, 14 or 15 years old, I was stealing women's underwear. I went to a psychiatrist over here at the Hunterdon Medical Center. I don't know what his name is, for treatment. My parents, my mother always took me. I had no choice in the matter.

BERNHARD: What would you do with these things?

MILLER: I had them folded up over the top of the garage where I lived.

BERNHARD: And what did you do with them, play with them?

MILLER: Myself. And otherwise than this—and I never went to court on any of this or anything, but I did go—

BERNHARD: The police came up to your house—

MILLER: That's right. They came out and talked to me and what not. I did have to go to the doctor's.

BERNHARD: And everything worked out all right.

MILLER: And I never had any problems as far as that goes.

BERNHARD: O.K. I think we've gone over enough. I think we've gone along pretty good. I know a little about you Frank, your background and what you've told me.

Opening the thinner file, I found photographs—of the road, of the woods where the rape had happened as seen from the road, of Miller's house, and of the entire area taken from the air. It was strange to see these places through the detectives' and photographers' eyes. All the color and sensuality of the scene were missing: the heat, the dusty road, the shade of the trees that was always too scant on such hot August days, the sound of the cicadas monotonous in the heavy air.

These black-and-white images, with their fixed, harsh quality, both aroused and tormented my memory.

There were several pictures of Lou Rocco, a large, fleshy man in a white undershirt with straps, with very dark straight hair. I felt again the feeling of being afraid of him mixed with the understanding that he meant me no harm. Standing near the covered bridge near where he had found my clothes, posing in front of the open trunk of his car, he held up my dress, limp and muddy. I felt a pang as I recognized the drape of it as it hung there, the shape of it and the pattern on the cloth. My bra and panties were arranged next to him on the car. His expression was impassive as he posed for a photograph that might be used as evidence. But there was also an air of success to his look and his way of holding my dress aloft. *Now I've got him.*

Soon after this picture was taken, I remembered now, Rocco stopped by our house and showed them to me, and I had said, "Yes, those were the clothes I was wearing that day."

There was a photograph of the place in the grass where I had lain. My sunglasses, which had fallen off and been forgotten, lay on the bright, flattened grass like an afterimage, a Hitchcockian touch.

There was a photograph of the rock the rapist had dropped on the road after he grabbed me; it looked huge and ominous lying in the pebbles along the roadside.

There was a photo of Frank Miller taken a month before the rape, when he had spent a night in jail as punishment for a driving charge he had refused to pay. When I looked at that photograph something strange and powerful occurred. I was flooded with the sensation that this was the face I had seen under the stocking mask in the few seconds when it had come close to me.

This was not the same man who had sat in the courtroom next to Bernhard, the stuffed man in a dark suit. Nor was it the emaciated, haunted face pictured in the newspaper five years later just after the murder of Deborah Margolin. By comparison in this picture he was "fat and happy," his expression suggesting stubbornness and stupidity.

I remembered his air of determination to be master, combined with what I had felt was a sad limitation of ability and awareness.

Looking at his face, I remembered being with him.

I felt certain now that he had been the one.

I met with Frank Goreski, the detective whom I had rememberd for his gentle, understanding presence, in the Union County prosecutor's office in Elizabeth, New Jersey. Union County is urban, encompassing the most heavily populated parts of New Jersey around New York City, and this prosecutor's office was a hulking six-story office building.

He was a little under six feet tall, and slim, and he looked about sixty. His grey hair was carefully combed straight back from the V at his brow, and he wore a blue three-piece suit with a striped shirt. He had a slight stoop. I recognized that stoop and remembered how I had felt that he was bending down toward me, to hear me better or to try and become less tall and threatening to me. Looking at him and imagining him with dark hair, I could vividly see that this face had belonged to the man whose quiet attention I had never forgotten.

He greeted me. We sat at a bare plastic table in a tiny cubicle with cinder-block walls that I guessed was normally used for questioning witnesses. I asked him to tell me whatever he remembered from that time.

"It was hard for me to set aside my work duties and my personal life," he said. "So when I went home I was always thinking of, gee, I should do this and I should do that. I remember your father—I think he was a writer, wasn't he?"

"Yes."

"And still is?"

"Yes." It was his habit to be the one asking questions.

"I could not, probably, identify him, but I remember him coming in with you, on occasion, especially the time that we had attempted a voice identification with the defendant. I don't know whether—I don't think I even had you—face him—did I? I can't recall. Because I know there was a mask or a stocking or something involved so that you could not visually identify him."

His voice suggested another question, and I found myself explaining.

"Right. I couldn't identify his face. But I think it was my father's idea that perhaps I could identify his gait and overall appearance. So there was a confrontation outside the barracks."

"Mm-hmm. Yes, I think we did it inside and outside also. To try to simulate outdoor voices."

"I don't think I could be positive."

"That's right. After you left we continued talking to the suspect, and I remember receiving a telephone call from your father an hour or so later stating that yes, you did identify his voice. And from then on in we felt that we probably had sufficient grounds for complaint."

"So my being able to identify his voice was a crucial step in the process."

"Definitely."

I had not remembered telling my father after we got home that I thought it was Miller's voice. I had remembered only that I remained doubtful of Miller's guilt.

"I can't recall whether he ever outwardly admitted it," he said. "He did make some, as I recall, statements from which we could have inferred that he did know more than what he was saying."

"So you were pretty convinced, very early on. Do you remember at what point you really became sure that it was him?" I asked.

"Well, I had interviewed a woman who worked in the Medical Center." Charlotte Tritt. "She had been speaking to a young man in that general area. And at the interview I was assured that he had seemed to be proper. But I pursued it a little further and went to interview him. And there was something about keys, that I saw him either jingle them in his pocket, or maybe he wore them on the outside, I can't recall."

"Why was that significant?" I asked. "Everybody carries keys."

"I believe in your statement you said something about keys, keys jingling. It wasn't really the clincher, but it was a good piece of circumstantial evidence. Everybody carries keys, but not everybody jingles them.

"It's difficult to talk to a youngster about a crime that is, and at that time was, well, something that not too many people spoke about. Police were not really schooled in any way to be able to handle and question people in that sort of crime. So that you had to just play it by ear."

"I remember—you, and Lou," I told him.

"Besides the gray hair, have I changed any?" he asked.

"You have changed very little," I said. "It's very interesting, your voice—I have had the same experience with Judge Beetel—I couldn't have told you, before seeing you, what you were like, but now that I see you and hear you, the memory is definitely there."

I asked him if he had been reassigned out of the Flemington barracks because working on my case had been too much for him.

"It wasn't this particular case, it was all of them combined, and I became kind of, well, what would you say. I couldn't relax, and it seemed like I got very involved personally in every specific job, and that was probably what affected my health.

"The irregular hours, poor eating habits, and then the load of—doing all the work, investigating—we took responsibility for half the county, Clinton Barracks took the other half."

"You wouldn't say that it was particularly the emotional factor of having to deal with so many rapes, that wasn't a factor," I persisted.

"Well, I don't think it—it was a contributing factor—that I could say.

"I am retired, by the way, from the state police. I retired in 1974, and upon retirement, I became an investigator here in this office. So I've been active in police work just about all of my adult life."

"That pretty much comes to the end of the questions I had," I said. But the interview did not feel finished. He was still listening. I heard myself say, "I could tell you a couple of things, if you'd like."

"Sure," he answered.

"I do remember you, and I remember you as being very sensitive to me, and very—gentle, and the way that you dealt with me—it's—the exchange with you was probably one of my most positive memories—of the whole experience."

Suddenly I was crying.

"Excuse me," I said, struggling for control.

His response seemed in character.

"I guess we could both sit here and cry," he said.

For a moment I gave in to my tears.

"Sure," he said soothingly, as if to say, *Of course you're crying.* He sounded as though he was holding back tears of his own.

We talked about Lou Rocco, and then turned to Miller.

"Do you think it's at all likely that he could actually have molested other girls, and that this could have been kept completely away from the police?"

"No doubt about it. No doubt about it. You know, in that time era, I don't think many girls were—they weren't willing to talk about it. They were ashamed if they were even involved, whether they could help it or not, they still didn't want to talk about it, because—they probably felt that somebody would accuse them of starting it or encouraging it."

"If they felt that, it probably wasn't totally unjustified."

"Maybe in some cases, but—" He changed the subject. "Every case is different. And that's what intrigued me, and still does, in police work. They're all the same crimes, but the individuals and their motives, and their thinking, of why they did it, were all different."

"Yeah," I said. "It came to me to tell the story of this particular one, because each one is a story, and I think there's a lot that's been written about rape and rapists that's very much generalized, making categories and types and all that, but to me there's also a use in being specific."

"Yeah," he said. "You know—my impression—as I think back, I said to myself, I know, many times—that—*it coulda been my daughter.*"

He began to cry.

"You were about the same age—"

After a pause, we smiled at each other.

"This is worse than talking to hardened criminals," he said.

I realized later that what had drawn me back to Frank Goreski was his own capacity for compassion. It was no accident that it was with him that I had found myself speaking suddenly from the heart. He had understood that the thirteen-year-old was alive at that moment in me. He had responded to me with simple, human empathy as someone who had been hurt.

I had felt the urge to thank him for the sensitivity he had shown me years ago, for brief as it was it had made an important difference. I realized that there was no one else I had ever felt an urge to thank, from all that time. I wondered—had anyone thanked *me* for my contribution to the work of the law?

After our talk he led me through a warren of offices and introduced me to the two detectives who ran Union County's child sexual abuse unit. They showed me the special playroom they used to question children who reported being abused. While the children played and talked with a trained examiner their statements were filmed with a hidden video camera, and were then used in the trial so that the children might never have to directly face a judge or lawyer. The two detectives said they had a high rate of guilty pleas—which make it unnecessary for a child to testify—because the videos were so convincing. They added that when perpetrators were shown the videos of their own children describing what they had done, their sense of guilt could be touched again, and they often then confessed. The detectives also told me that the other detectives regarded their work as the lowest branch of investigative work, because of the sordid nature of the crimes. They offered guidance to others faced with having to ask children to describe what exactly had been done to them, trying to help them understand how to communicate with children. They seemed dedicated and intelligent, and Frank Goreski, it appeared, had been involved in their work from its inception.

In the hall we shook hands and said good-bye. I thanked him warmly. His last words were, "I'm sorry I wasn't more there for you then."

"No," I told him. "You were great."

Charlotte Tritt had had to testify that Miller had approached her at the quarry and sat with her in her car within a half hour of the rape. At that time she was twenty years old.

On that day Frank Miller had come to her driveway in his truck as she emerged and had gone ahead of her down to the quarry.

DIRECT EXAMINATION BY MR. RITTENHOUSE:

And when you pulled in . . . was the blue truck . . . still in sight?

Yes, it had stopped and parked on the left-hand side of the road.

By this time you knew who the occupant of that vehicle was?

Yes.

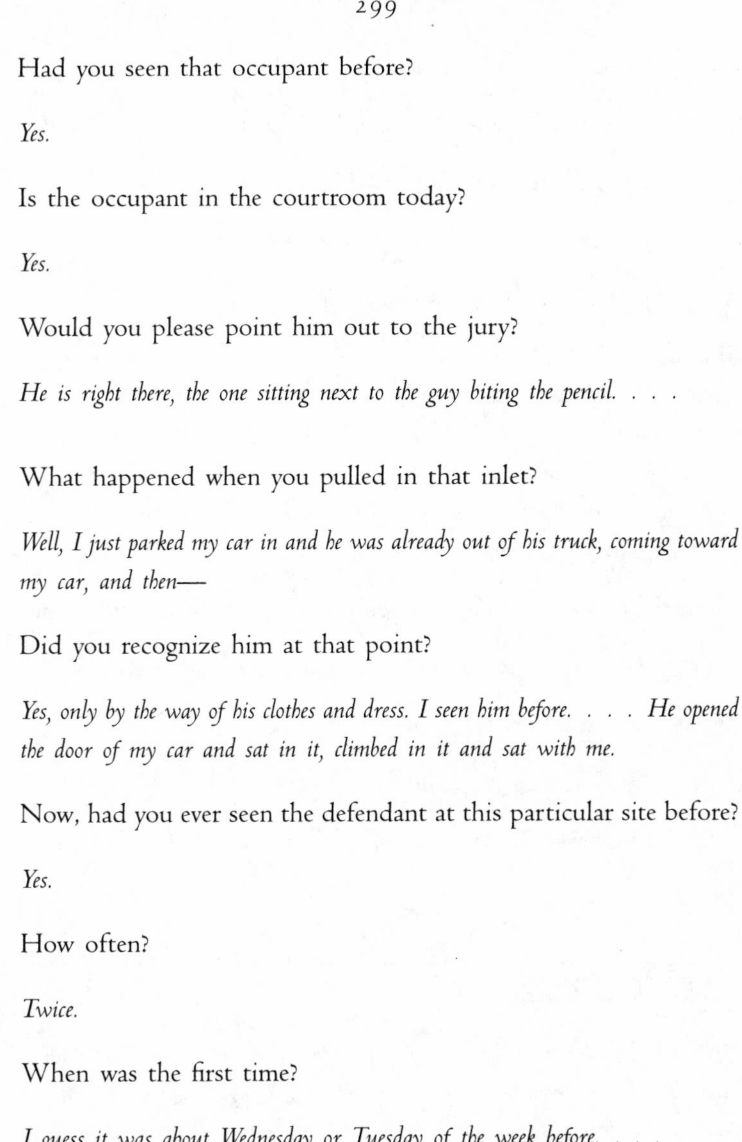

Had you seen that occupant before?

Yes.

Is the occupant in the courtroom today?

Yes.

Would you please point him out to the jury?

He is right there, the one sitting next to the guy biting the pencil. . . .

What happened when you pulled in that inlet?

Well, I just parked my car in and he was already out of his truck, coming toward my car, and then—

Did you recognize him at that point?

Yes, only by the way of his clothes and dress. I seen him before. . . . He opened the door of my car and sat in it, climbed in it and sat with me.

Now, had you ever seen the defendant at this particular site before?

Yes.

How often?

Twice.

When was the first time?

I guess it was about Wednesday or Tuesday of the week before. . . .

About the same time?

Yes . . .

And did you have any conversation with him at that time?

Only he inquired if there was a swimming hole down there. . . . That was it.

When was the next time you saw him?

Sunday afternoon.

What Sunday afternoon do you mean?

Well, it was the Sunday before the raping. . . . It was about the same time, again. . . . He had a couple of boys with him, and then they got in the truck and they were leaving. . . . They went on and so I pulled my car in there. The next thing I knew, he had come back. He made a circle down, he went down 29 and came up the Quarry Road. . . . He circled around and dropped the boys off at the bottom of the quarry.

Now, in those few minutes he pulled back and where did he go?

He stopped his truck. . . . He . . . climbed out and came over to my car.

What did you do at that time?

I was sitting there smoking cigarettes.

And did he have any conversation with you then?

Yes.

All right. I want you to tell us about this conversation, if you would, please, Charlotte?

Well, it had to deal with sex. . . . It was on the subject of sex and being a virgin, the hardships you have to go through of being a virgin, I guess the pain that would be involved in having intercourse with a young boy and it would be better to have an older man go through it once instead of having all these young kids, because more or less they'd be rough with a girl who never had it before and—

Charlotte—Go ahead.

He told me you had to do it three times to get any satisfaction for both parties; to have satisfaction out of it you had to do it three times, you have to do it three times.

Now, did he ask you whether you were a virgin?

Yes, he did.

And how long did this conversation last?

About three quarters of an hour.

Were you talking to him?

No, he was talking to me all that time.

During the course of this conversation did Mr. Miller make any advances to you?

No.

Physical advances to you?

No, none.

Now, Charlotte, when you talked to Mr. Miller the first time, did he tell you his name?

No.

Did you ask him who he was?

No.

When you talked to him the second time, did he tell you his name?

He didn't give his correct name. He gave his foreman's name.

How do you know it was his foreman's name?

Police told me.

And while you were at that location above the dump on the 13th, how long were you there?

Good hour . . .

During that whole time were you discussing matters with Mr. Miller?

Yes, sir.

And did you observe anyone else go by on Quarry Road during that period?

Loch had come down on his bicycle past us.

Now, you say Loch, you mean Loch Ramsey?

Yes.

All right. Now, did you know him prior to this time?

Yes.

How long did you know him?

Only that his name was Loch Ramsey. I mean we rode on the same schoolbus.

Had you ever dated him?

Loch Ramsey?

Yes.

No . . .

What happened when Loch Ramsey came by?

He passed us and he stopped at the back of Mr. Miller's pickup.

What, if anything, did Mr. Miller do?

He got out of the car and asked the boy if there is anything he could do for him.

What happened then?

He came back in the car. He says the kid said, I don't know. He said, "You wouldn't understand."

Then what happened?

He sat there and talked a couple of minutes. He kept saying, "Why is the kid staring at my truck?" So he got out of the car again, my car, went over and asked the boy again.

How many times did this happen?

I guess about two or three times.

Two or three times?

Yes.

Now, while he was seated in your car . . . what were you told by Mr. Miller that day?

Well, he told me that, he said, making an apology, but he didn't come out and say, "I am sorry that we had this talk on Sunday." He just sort of beat around the bush that he was kind of sorry about it, and he asked me, he did ask me would I possibly go out with him. I told him, "Well, maybe, I don't know, I don't think so." But then he came out and told me he wouldn't have to rape me because he has a wife and three kids at home, I think it was two or three kids at home, and that she would lay out any time for him. She was good that way.

CROSS-EXAMINATION BY MR. BERNHARD:

[On the 13th] You came home from Flemington to your home, which is located on Federal Twist Road, you changed your clothes. . . . When you left your house you were going to the quarry?

Yes.

To go swimming or—

No, go up there and sit around.

Is that where you had met Frank Miller on the two previous occasions?

I didn't meet him there.

Well, I don't mean in the sense that it was a rendezvous, but you and he had perchance met?

Yes.

I don't mean any date or meetings with you there. He came there, right?

Yes.

Did there come a time last week when representatives of the prosecutor's office instructed you not to talk to me?

He didn't instruct me not to talk to you. He said I didn't have to. I don't know whether I had to talk to you because you are a lawyer. I didn't want to get in trouble.

Did he tell you it would be better if you didn't talk to me?

No, he said I had to make up my own mind. I said I'd rather not.

You said you'd rather not. He didn't suggest you'd rather not?

No.

I was prepared to accept that Charlotte Tritt might refuse to see me and say she did not want to revive her experience. But when I called her she said in a friendly voice, "Yes, I'll do whatever I can to help you."

She was living in a small, neat suburban house with her second husband. She was now around forty, without children. She seemed cheerful and relaxed as I clipped the tiny microphone to her collar. With dark hair and large dark eyes, her face held an expression that was both startled and strangely candid.

"Do you remember how you felt about testifying, about having to be in the trial?" I asked.

"Scared," she said. "I am basically a quiet person. Even in high school I had trouble getting up in front of fifteen, twenty kids in the classroom to talk openly about a book report or something, it was just nerve-racking to me, and it was even worse, with all, I mean, the court was full. And you'd never been in court, you didn't know how the judicial system worked, you didn't know what they were going to ask you, so you were very apprehensive. And you didn't want people to think you were a—a hussy! you know, like you were a hussy just looking around, flaunting yourself, and getting some stranger excited.

"And I think they asked some questions, that, you felt they could be taken two ways, if you weren't led to explain what happened. And that bothered me, I just felt that they were trying to make more of me and him having this big romance—his lawyer was trying to read something more into this, than really was."

"Did you get any sense afterwards that people did make judgments about you? Any kind of negative judgements—were your fears at all justified, in that regard?" I asked.

"Right. Not at that point," she said. "I think I was sitting downstairs waiting to be called up to be on the stand, and one of them, an investigator for the prosecutor, or detective for the prosecutor, said, 'You know something, you shouldn't—you're too easygoing, you shouldn't talk to strangers.' "

I asked her if she remembered when she first saw Frank Miller.

"My first encounter with Frank Miller was—at the quarry," she said. "That particular day I didn't go down swimming. I didn't have any bathing suit, I was kind of, you know I'm a bulky type girl."

She laughed.

"So I didn't go down. I had laid down and was sunnin' myself. And this man came up and he asked if there was swimming allowed and how would you get down there.

"After that—he came around, there was a whole group of us. As a matter of fact it was the Hickson kids, from Raven Rock. And he kind of was talking about sex. The only thing I can remember, and I shouldn't say this, because I probably didn't even know that we had—he said something about a woman having three—holes, you know, one for her number one, number two, and her vagina. That was about it, that's all I can remember of this conversation, and it wasn't a long conversation. He wasn't preaching or anything like that.

"I went on home, and then, I guess it was a couple days, maybe a week had passed, and he—apparently at that point word was out that you had been attacked, and raped. The day that happened the Hickson kids walked all the way up to my house, and said, 'Well, don't go down because she'—they said, 'The police is all over, and you're not allowed to go swimmin' in the quarry anymore.' I said, 'Fine, what happened?'

They said that you had gotten raped. And we just couldn't believe, you know we were just sitting there talking, and I said, 'Gee, isn't it strange that this man said these things to us,' and we kind of half laughed, and then we just let it drop.

"I worked as a tray girl over at Hunterdon Medical Center, and a police officer came there, and he said, 'I want to talk to you.' I said, 'Fine,' and he said, 'Were you at the quarry?' and 'Do you know of this Martha Ramsey that got raped?' and I said, 'Yeah,' and he said, 'Can you tell me anything that happened? They said there was a man there talking to a few of you about sex,' and I said, 'It wasn't very much, and we kind of laughed it off.' But he said, 'Well, can we talk to you?' and I said, 'Fine.'

"He came home to my parents and asked if it was all right for me to testify at a trial. And my dad gave the okay.

"After that the prosecutor asked me in his office, and it was just me and him. He asked me, you know, 'Just talk to me as if I were your doctor, just tell me what this man said.' So I told him, and he left it go at that.

"After that then it was basically, the trial. Oh, no, you know what? Before that, your trial, I was in a car accident, I was hurt pretty bad, and I was in the hospital. The newspaper had said, 'Charlotte Tritt was injured in an automobile accident.' Apparently he [Miller] read it. My sister and my mother were in the room with me, and he came, he came walkin' around the corner real fast and then he stopped dead.

"And my mother struck up a conversation with him, and I'm laying there like, *Oh, God, please let this man leave this room,* and then when he—he did leave, he didn't stay long, I don't even think it was five minutes—I said, 'Mom. That was the guy who raped Martha—Ramsey.'

"Well, with that my sister bolted out of the room. And she said, 'Why didn't you say something?' and I said, 'Well, you kept talking and talking, and I didn't want to sound the alarm, here we are in the room all by ourselves, you don't know what he's capable of.'

"My sister came back and said, "The police know he's here, they're watching him, there's an officer down at the end of the hall.'

"I said, 'Fine.'

"I think it was [State Trooper] Russo's wife that had seen him get on the elevator, and had called the police, and they come up right away. He left, apparently, not knowing that there were police there or whatever.

"My next encounter was—a police officer picked me up at the house and brought me back, and, I don't know if it was a lineup—? I said, 'Yes, this is the man,' and he had shaved at that point and was very cleaned up, looked almost like a business-type person, in a suit, and he had on a tie, and whatnot."

For Charlotte, like me, there had been a great difference between Miller indoors in a suit and Miller in his T-shirt in the sun and heat on Quarry Road.

"But then after that I was home, and *he came to the house.* My sister was home with a small child, and pregnant with her second or her third. He came up to the door and knocked on the door, and I said, 'Frank Miller's here. Get one of the guns out.' My father had a gun cabinet.

"I said, 'Get a gun.'

"And she knew how to shoot and whatnot. So she got one, and left it in the dining room with me. I had a cot in there because I couldn't go up and down steps yet and was very weak. And her and Mom went to the door. And I heard him talking to my mom. I think he was upset and confused, a little bit, and he said, I heard him say, 'Mrs. Tritt, my lawyer wants to talk to Charlotte.' He said, 'Can I pick her up and take her to so-and-so's office?' He said, 'My lawyer wants to talk to her about all this, this accusations and whatnot, and get some information from her.' He said, 'I'll take her over.'

"And my sister said, 'You're not taking her anywhere. Get off the property and get out.'

"And he did, he kind of went off, I didn't hear a truck door slam or anything, he just left. Then my sister called the lawyer's office, and she read 'em the riot act, like 'Who the hell do you think you are sending this man over here who just raped somebody to pick my sister up and take her over and have her, you know, talk to her.' I think it was the lawyer, because he said, 'I didn't send him over to talk to you, to pick her up to come and talk to me.' With that she just ripped him out, and then slammed the phone down. And then we turned called the police, told them what happened.

"After the trial the police, or the prosecutor, said that Frank Miller had told him that he had me timed, from the time I got up in the morning, the time I left the house to go to work, the time I got to work, the time I left from work and got home, how long it took me, because I was on a schedule. I would always come home, change my clothes, and go down swimming, either in the river or in the quarry, depending on where the crowd was or my friends were. I had gotten myself into such a routine that it was very easy to know where I was at any given time. This is what they had told me. And that the day that I was late was the day that you came riding on your bicycle. He said he was waiting there for me to come by, that was the night he had planned to quote unquote rape me, and I didn't show up. And you had come by on your bicycle.

"It's spooky, to have someone know you that—I know when he got out, there was a rage—and I was a little fearful then. You know what I mean, it was like, if he came back for revenge. That only comes from TV. You see all these revenge shows, you think a little bit about it.

"The only thing that bothers me is, you don't know who's who. Especially to listen to him talk, no different from any other common man when he's in a crowd talking. And that's probably from being naive, you don't pick up on these things, and then somebody points 'em out to you and you think, *Oh, wow.*"

"So you didn't really think anything of the stuff he was saying to you at the quarry," I said. This was one of my main questions of Charlotte. I did not understand how a young woman of twenty would not have sensed, from the kinds of things he was talking about, that this man was, if not dangerous, at least very creepy.

"No. It was something that just sort of—it wasn't a long conversation with the group of kids there, whatever, and, it was more boys than it was girls, I had to get back home anyway. So I only picked up a little bit of what he said, and it really wasn't much, but it was enough to—"

"So when you first saw Miller, you really had no sense that anything was wrong, you had no cause to be suspicious, at all," I repeated.

"No! That was the other thing. You were brought up not to discriminate. You didn't put people down because of their clothes—of course, we weren't ones to talk, our clothes weren't that great, so you weren't putting people down because of the way they were dressed, because if you did you were putting yourself down, real quick.

"And we had, at that point in time, religion, we were Catholics at that time, and my mother always said you know you treat people the way you want to be treated, and what goes around comes around, if you're going to be nasty they're going to be nasty back to you. Up to that point everybody was nice to me. You'd walk down the road, or even like over in Lumberville, Carversville, I mean we'd talk to everybody, even strangers, and never were afraid of anyone."

I had ridden my bike through those villages on my way to and from Betsy Retivov's house the day of the rape.

She paused.

"It left me, it leaves me apprehensive from now on, and my husband knows, I've had a couple of calls after Frank Miller, and he knows what it's like, I've come home through the house, not crying but very, very upset, and he's called the police, we've made the charges, or, that kind of thing. No, it leaves me very apprehensive. I used to walk a lot, and there's days I wouldn't walk because I would think, not so much about what happened to you, as you see rape on the TV, you think, *Well, I don't have to really walk today.*

"You know how to live with it, you've come to the point where you, you function, you live with it. You don't forget it but you live with it."

"It's been like that for you as well," I said, though I wasn't sure that was how it was for me.

"Mm-hmm. It does change your life, because you've trusted people, they kind of let you down. But I guess in a way we were kind of sheltered from all—you know, people just in general. With the rape they kind of let you down there, you figured all grown-ups were, they're just authorative figures, they're not gonna do anything to hurt you, they'll do something to help you along or whatever, they're not gonna—abuse you—but they do. So. It was a rude awakening to what was really out there."

She paused.

"I have a sense of what you've been through, only because my father—I was working down by his workshop. He came up to me, and he grabbed me, and started kissing me. And just that look on his face, I knew something was definitely wrong."

"How old were you?" I asked.

"I was only about—fourteen. And then I got away from him. There was no harm, you know what I'm saying? And at that same point my mother called. And I went into the house and told my mother. I said, 'If he ever touches me again, I'll see the both of you in jail.' I said, 'I'll call the cops and, that's it, he's gone.'

"But as you say you learn how to deal with it, and you never forget it.

"And you can't get away from it. You look at the papers, the news is on, they always bring something up about someone getting raped or beaten, so that always leaves a fear inside of you. In my case it's probably good in a way because I am a kind of a—stupid person? You have to get burnt in the fire before you really stop trying to be—My husband, when he first met me, he said 'You're nothing but an introvert.' Because I wasn't outward going towards anybody. It was like I'd built this wall up and nobody was gonna get to me. That was the other thing, I think that stems from being —I don't know, I can't say it was sexual abuse from my father, because it never went that far.

"But it was starting to happen, and I guess I was lucky enough—brave enough—to go in and say this is the way it's gonna be. And I think I scared my father because I said, 'If you don't stop, Daddy,' I said, 'one of us isn't gonna walk away from here.' "

"Do you have any memory of, when Frank Miller was talking to you, about sex, that you were in any way sort of curious, or interested in what he was telling you?" I asked.

"No. We were brought up, my mom always would say, 'You don't let anybody touch you, that's dirty.' And I thought he was being—a little out of place. Because you just didn't, you weren't supposed to talk about this stuff. No one ever talked sex in our family, I mean we weren't even told how to have babies!"

"But it's interesting, I mean you were so aware that your father was crossing lines, but with Miller—it sounds like you weren't really worried by him," I said.

"No, there was no evidence, or anything that would make me feel that I was in danger at any time, or threatened, nothing. I mean it was just like sitting here talking to you."

"He had done it," I said, "it had happened, well, within minutes, of your—"

"Me coming up there."

"Yeah. If you had come down the road a few minutes earlier you probably would have passed me—"

"On your bicycle—"

"Coming home, after being raped. There were just a few minutes in between there. And meanwhile he had driven his truck back up Quarry Road, and up past your house, and then down to the quarry again."

"Probably at that point he was checking on me to see where I was, if I was home."

"Yeah; he drove by your house, and then you followed him down the road. He was in front of you as you drove down to the quarry."

"Now that—I remember him going past the house, but not thinking of it as—"

"That you were going to go out and follow him, that you wanted to see him—"

"No, it wasn't that at all. It never dawned on me that he was there—for me. It never dawned on me until I was told that this was what had happened, what was going on through his mind. I wouldn't have known that if somebody hadn't told me."

"That's what's so amazing to me," I said. "That within minutes of having committed this act, that he was there talking to you. As if everything was—"

"Just fine. I think it has to be—it's almost like a double life."

"It just seems so strange," I persisted. "I mean there you are, sitting there in the car, you're twenty years old and this guy is sitting in the car with you, and he's saying 'Well, I guess I won't have to rape you,' like, oh, this is normal."

"Yeah. You know I didn't—it wasn't that I was apprehensive. I was uncomfortable with what he was talking about, because we just didn't talk about that."

"But it's almost like you were so innocent that you didn't realize that it was inappropriate," I repeated, to make sure I understood.

"Yeah. That's right.

"And I guess this is the way this is, I mean I was very naive. I had been kept in, you know, and now I had a car. And then I could get down off the hill, I could go to Flemington. And that was a time of my life for—hey, I was what, eighteen, twenty, you're sexually aroused then too. When you get down to it. You know what I'm saying? I liked boys. I met a few too, being introduced and stuff like that, but then again, if you're introduced to somebody you think the person that's introducing you has enough—you feel that this person they're introducing you to is harmless. Even though they might not be. They might be very harmless to you, like this man was to his wife. It seemed like he was very harmless to her, and yet he was going out and doing everything to everybody else's daughter."

"When you heard that Miller himself said that he was tracking your movements," I said, "was that when it really dawned on you that you might have been his victim?"

"Yeah, at that point it dawned on me."

"And what was that like?"

"Well—don't take me the wrong way," she answered. "I was glad it was you and not me. For one reason. I probably would have been killed, where you were—a little girl, there wasn't anything mus—"

She broke off in the middle of the word "muscular."

"As I said I was a big girl, I was very much in shape, so I—I knew I was frightened anyway, of sex, because of everything my mom was always saying. I knew that if anybody had ever touched me I probably would have fought them. Where you, I don't know whether, what he did to you, but I don't think you fought, or could fight—"

"I didn't fight at all," I said.

"Yeah. That's why I was saying, I'm sorry it happened to you, but I'm glad it happened—not to me."

"Did that whole experience with Miller have a deep effect on you?" I asked. "I mean you already had the experience with your father, that was probably really scary."

"I think with Miller, it probably—I won't say ruined my life, but—it makes you—when I go for walks, or when I see people—let me tell you an experience I had. It was walking in the hospital. I don't know if it was too long after your trial, or if it was after Frank Miller had raped this girl and killed her. I was going to a psychiatrist at the time. Because it bothers me about rape, even though it really hasn't happened to me, and I can go along a whole lot better than, I'm sure you can, in your life, but I'm not one of these Danielle Steele heroines, they have ninety-nine things happen to them, and they come up like a rose, you know?"

We laughed.

"I was walking in to work one day. It was on the first floor of the new wing and the lights weren't on that day, and they had these sliding glass doors that opened. I caught a reflection of a guy walking toward these doors. This is how your mind—my imagination—ran away with you. Next thing you know I looked up, I was watching him and he seemed to stare at me. All of a sudden he started walking really fast.

"It was just like your legs were being paralyzed, my heart started pounding, and you can hear everything."

I remembered how I had reacted when our neighbor had emerged from the woods and I thought she was the rapist.

"It was pitch dark in this hallway, no one put the lights on. I couldn't even turn around and face this person that was coming. I was waiting for the blow or whatever to come upon me, and this guy whizzed right past me, right down the hall. It was like this relief, I had to stand there a couple minutes and just let myself settle down. I walked down the hall. He had run—this poor man, his wife was having a baby, he wanted to know where labor and delivery was. It goes right through you, you know how you get that fear?"

"At the time of the rape and the trial, was there anybody that you talked to intimately about what was happening?" I asked.

"No. There wasn't. If my sister was home, I think I would've, but she was away at college. We were very close. She was the one I would have confided in. Because I don't think my home life was that great that I could just talk to my parents. You felt like they wouldn't understand."

"Right," I said. "Especially if there was a real rule against talking about anything that related to sex in your family, so if you had brought it up it would have been—a nonsubject."

"Yeah."

"That's really—sad, I mean—"

"Yeah. It is. In a way you can't talk to anybody."

"I can really identify with a lot of what you went through," I volunteered. "You were older and in some ways probably stronger, but at the same time, the loneliness—"

"Yeah. Mm-hmm."

"A lot of your feelings were similar to mine," I continued. "Especially the fear, of going to the courthouse to testify, and to get up in front of—"

"Everybody. Like I said, sometimes, they felt like 'You were the one that brought all this on,' and other times they were trying to be very nice and understanding, but the way they're going—they're men, and I don't think they—"

She paused.

"You know the thing of it is, Martha, I don't think anybody knows how to console anybody who is either involved in a rape or has been raped. If I had to say something to you right now I wouldn't know what to say. I think people have the fear of not saying the right thing and saying the wrong thing."

"And even if you've been through it," I said, "You still don't quite know—"

"What you would say to somebody else that's been through it. I don't know. I think the best thing is probably just give them the moral support, and the comfort, and see where you would go from that, to talk, or whatever. I guess the support would be the big thing. And the understanding.

"And there's a lot of people out there who are not understanding. A girl at work says, 'Well, I can't still be bothered, it happened so many years ago, is it still bothering you?' That kind of thing."

While Charlotte talked I kept remembering the Tritts' lovely old pink stucco farmhouse less than a mile up the hill from ours. It was strange to think of her growing up there and suffering, struggling with an abusive father. I had walked by there many times, with and without my bicycle. I had often imagined it would be wonderful to live in that neat square house with its broad lawn and great old trees; I had not known anything of the life that went on within.

She had lived near me but had been so much older that we had never talked. Yet like me she had been a child growing up in the country and not knowing much about the ways of the world. She had a car, I had a bicycle. We had the same need to get out of the house and ride down the quiet roads. We knew some of the same places in the same way. She too was experiencing some stirrings of sexuality, private and personal, not yet a sharing. We were very different, yet in our vulnerability and our relationship with the country around us we were the same.

Even though she had been twenty and might have been more grown-up and able to take care of herself, she had been no more able to comprehend or fend off Miller than I had.

Toward me she expressed only sympathy, concern, and friendliness, and as she poured out her story to me she seemed completely unguarded.

I left her house feeling grateful for her open goodwill and haunted and angered by what had been done to her.

Later I imagined freshly how it was for him.

I wrote:

> He tried not to do it. When he saw me walk by, something in him wanted to do it. Then he thought quickly and discovered he knew just how. He would have to put on a stocking mask. When he put on the mask that would mean that he was going to do it. In the end the idea was too exciting not to leap into it. The excitement was not so much anticipating orgasm but in the exploit, the daring, the fast planning, the quick action and then being done.
>
> He said to me, "I'm not going to hurt you."

I knew that he told himself that it was not so terrible.

I knew these things. It was in my memory of when he came near, his sweatiness, the energy in him.

I remembered that some part of me was unsurprised, when I turned around and saw him, and when he took me back into the woods. I met him as one would meet a vaguely foreknown destiny; without complaint, with the resignation of children. Understanding that I could do nothing against him, I did as he told me with a kind of rueful sadness.

That he wanted to hurt me was no surprise. That I knew it was wrong, while he did not know, or could not stop himself, saddened me.

If an animal mauled me, would I blame the animal? If a man hurt me—wasn't a man also an animal? I was angry at him, saddened by him, as if I would have wanted even him to be my friend. My fellow human being.

Heading back to Boston, I passed again the old iron bridge over the Lockitong. I decided to stop and walk again the old lane that ran back into the woods along the creek.

In the woods I came to a rocky slope I remembered where there was a tiny recess under some tree roots that we had called a "cave." I climbed up to see it again. The rocks were shiftier and the hill both smaller and steeper than I remembered; I felt the danger of falling more than I ever had then. The cave was no more than a slight crevice underneath the roots of a tree clinging high on the hillside. I could not imagine being small enough to fit into it.

The old lane ran parallel to the creek but was separated from it by a screen of trees and an old stone fencerow. In our first explorations Alida and I had stayed close to the creek and played in its stony bed, creeping upstream along the margins of mud, crawling over roots barely wide enough for two bare feet.

Loch had known much more than Alida and me about things that were out in the woods, and he had told us how to find this place.

It had always been an adventure, not something we did often. It was a long walk back to the abandoned farm at the end of the lane, and you had to be in the mood to be among ruins. We were a little scared of the place. We knew nothing of who had lived there or what had happened to them. Whoever they were, their little farm by the creek had not worked out, and that made us feel obscurely sad, because it was a beautiful spot, and we would have liked to live near the water in the narrow field below the steep, wooded hill. One June day Alida and I found many old-fashioned irises blooming there. A stone path led from the front door of the house to an opening in the old stone fencerow where a wooden gate might have hung, we decided.

The house itself was small and square and sided with asbestos shingles. Inside you could see what had been one front room and two tiny back ones. We stood on the doorstep, a big block of stone, and peered in past the peeling door that still hung ajar, wondering about the children who might have slept upstairs. Maybe if things had been different we would have known them. They were in our neighborhood and would have been our friends.

I turned and began to walk back toward the road, and I found I was sobbing.

I wanted to put my arms around a tree, as I had often done when alone on my walks. I wanted simply to sit down on the ground, in this familiar strange pale grass that I had forgotten about.

I felt that she was here, with me—the girl who had come here sometimes alone, braving the sense of ghosts and mystery; the girl who had wandered so many hours in the woods on the hill above, and along the roads with her bicycle, alone.

"What do you want?" I said.

I was answered by a wave of great loneliness, or longing. I found I could not bear the thought of walking away and leaving her there. I felt I must leave this place behind, I must bring her with me back into the world. Crying, I walked on through the woods back along the old lane, drawing her on. She was with me now.

It's in my nature, full of fantasies and a stubborn belief in happy endings, to want to make and see a happy ending. That's what I did for so long, though, saying I survived and was fine. Now it's important that I say instead: the story does not ever really end. There is no "fine."

I now knew that I was someone who was raped. This was my particular experience of the human condition, and it conditioned me. In my youth I had had an experience of everything coming apart, taking me with it—my body, the fabric of my connection with everyone, the earth under me, the sunlight, time. I had feared that I could not be put together again. In that fear I had insisted a little too hard that I had been, while anxiously wondering about my glued cracks.

The cracks had to come unglued. My long remembering, my reading of the trial, my confrontation in New Jersey with the real people and facts of the case all opened a kind of gulf inside me. Deep down it felt right and necessary. On the surface for a while there was trouble. I did not know how to attend to the hurt girl within me whom I had awakened. A long passage remained.

I was thrown off-balance. Sometimes I felt as if I were drowning in the inner gulf, with no one seeing that I was in trouble. At times I was convinced that Eric, whose love and support had been so sustaining for so long, and my friends, who had followed my progress with concern, simply could not grasp the nature of what was going on. There were in fact limits to what he or anyone could do. There were times when I felt I desperately needed him and he had to attend to his own self, and I felt like I couldn't stand it. Our marriage suffered, and my closest friendships for a time yielded me little solace.

Help came in a relationship with a gay male therapist who was able to convince me, over the course of many months, of his caring for me, mainly through his touch, the look in his eyes, and the sound of his voice. I lay quietly in his lap, greatly depleted, sometimes too exhausted even to move. In that realm of calm and peace it felt as though at last had come the nurse, the compassionate one who could sing out the splinter. This relationship sparked a connection with an inner spiritual source. My connections with Eric, and with those others I loved, began to recover firm ground—a place that felt newly fresh and alive—as I began the work of self-repair.

I no longer have a strong need or desire to forget what happened to me. The memory surfaces at odd times—in the dentist's chair, at the garage with the men who fix my car—and at the obvious time, in bed with my husband. Out in the world these rough spots don't get talked about, but he and I make sure not to ride hard over them.

Often now when I see and am myself again on Quarry Road, girl slender and raw in my new red dress, my feet stirring up the dust, a singing resounds in my inward ear. I reach out and lay out under her a great fluid blanket of my caring, and a spring rises and flows from within so that more of her injury is dissolved.

In each year of my life I can look forward to shedding more. Each time I stumble—at the dentist's, at the garage, or with Eric—the memory grows easier, for I find I can also hold the others—all the men, the witnesses, mother and father, everyone who did not know how to help me—in that river of my awakened heart. The love of her, the child, and her reawakened joy, somehow are wide enough to encompass all of us.

I am no longer ashamed of my longing to be loved and held. I can talk to her about it whenever she wants to. What grew in the grass and trees around her, what resided in the presence of the detective, what made her sister angry, what brought her the words with which she found herself was love, and this is real.

ABOUT THE AUTHOR

Martha Ramsey is the author of a book of poems, *Blood Stories,* published by the Cleveland State University Poetry Center. She lives in Vermont.